Effective Assessment of Students

DETERMINING RESPONSIVENESS TO INSTRUCTION

Shireen Pavri
California State University, Long Beach

Boston   Columbus   Indianapolis   New York   San Francisco   Upper Saddle River
Amsterdam   Cape Town   Dubai   London   Madrid   Milan   Munich   Paris   Montreal   Toronto
Delhi   Mexico City   Sao Paulo   Sydney   Hong Kong   Seoul   Singapore   Taipei   Tokyo

Vice President and Editor in Chief: Jeffery W. Johnston
Executive Editor: Ann Castel Davis
Editorial Assistant: Penny Burleson
Vice President, Director of Marketing: Margaret Waples
Senior Managing Editor: Pamela D. Bennett
Senior Production Editor: Sheryl Glicker Langner
Project Manager: Susan Hannahs
Senior Art Director: Jayne Conte
Cover Designer: Bruce Kenselaar
Cover Art: Shutterstock
Project Management: Jogender Taneja/Aptara®, Inc.
Composition: Aptara®, Inc.
Text and Cover Printer/Bindery: Courier/Stoughton
Text Font: 10/12 Palatino

Credits and acknowledgments of material borrowed from other sources and reproduced, with permission, in this textbook appear on the appropriate page within the text.

Every effort has been made to provide accurate and current Internet information in this book. However, the Internet and information posted on it are constantly changing, so it is inevitable that some of the Internet addresses listed in this textbook will change.

Library of Congress Cataloging-in-Publication Data
Pavri, Shireen.
   Effective assessment of students : determining responsiveness to
instruction / Shireen Pavri.
      p. cm.
   ISBN-13: 978-0-13-714780-9
   ISBN-10: 0-13-714780-5
   1. Learning disabled children—Education.   2. Learning disabled
children—Identification.   3. Response to intervention (Learning disabled
children)   4. Learning disabilities—Diagnosis.   I. Title.
   LC4704.P39 2012
   371.9'043—dc22

                                                          2010047616

10 9 8 7 6 5 4 3 2 1

www.pearsonhighered.com

ISBN 10:   0-13-714780-5
ISBN 13: 978-0-13-714780-9

PREFACE

The field of education faces a multitude of pressures due to reduced budgets, increased accountability, and changing social demographics. Consequently, we see academic achievement gaps between students from different ethnic and socioeconomic groups; greater numbers of students with mental health, emotional, and behavioral difficulties than ever before; and a continuing trend to serve struggling students through special education programming. Effective educational policy involves a cradle-to-college-and-career approach that provides a continuum of comprehensive solutions for students at different ages and developmental levels. Services to support student success are offered both within the school and through community-based resources.

A promising approach to tackling these educational challenges involves the development of an effective system of early screening and identification of children and youth who display learning and behavioral difficulties. These students are provided with increasingly intensive and comprehensive interventions in response to their identified needs. A critical component of such a preventative approach is the effective assessment of the students' learning and behavior. Appropriate assessment strategies must be used for universal screening and early identification and diagnosis of learning and behavioral difficulties, to tailor instruction to student strengths and needs, and to monitor student progress continuously in response to such interventions.

School professionals need a repertoire of assessment strategies in order to make data-based instructional decisions that lead to improved educational outcomes for students. Inspired by this author's work with practicing teachers, special educators, administrators, and school psychologists, this textbook is written to assist school professionals to build their assessment competencies.

This book is intended to provide educators with a clear understanding, enhanced application, and increased proficiency in the use of research-validated assessment strategies across different content domains. Effective assessment strategies are presented from a Response to Intervention (RTI) framework. Beginning with an overview of the history, context, rationale, models, benefits and challenges of RTI, the book goes on to explain the traditional special education assessment process and introduce various types of assessment techniques for use with typically developing students and students with disabilities. The legal and ethical foundations of RTI are explained, followed by a comprehensive overview of the selection, administration, scoring, interpretation, and dissemination of data obtained using norm-referenced tests. Alternative assessment techniques, including curriculum-based measurement, portfolios, and ecological assessments are discussed next. Principles and applications of universal design, alternate assessments, and assessment accommodations are introduced. Later, the book will describe specific assessment approaches across the content domains of cognition, behavior and social-emotional functioning, oral language, career and vocation, reading, written language and spelling, and mathematics, focusing on assessment strategies that are aligned with an RTI framework. The concluding chapter in the book raises key issues, applications, future directions, and unanswered questions associated with assessment in an RTI framework.

It is my hope that this book serves as a valuable resource for both beginning and experienced teachers and other school professionals in assessing students' learning needs and monitoring student progress in response to instruction and interventions.

Shireen Pavri
June 2010, Long Beach, CA

ACKNOWLEDGMENTS

I would like to thank my credential and graduate students in the College of Education at California State University, Long Beach, who were the inspiration and driving force behind this book. Their questions, quandaries, dilemmas, successes, and insights shaped my conceptualization and coverage of topics in this book. Thanks as well to the teachers, administrators, and other school personnel and colleagues with whom I have worked over the years who had the vision, dedication, creativity, and persistence to establish and systematize an RTI model to ensure improved outcomes for all the students at their schools. I have learned so much from my work with you.

Thank you to the Pearson family for your encouragement and support. I am particularly grateful to Ann Davis, Executive Editor; Penny Burleson, Editorial Assistant; and Sheryl Langner, Production Manager, who were always available and ready to provide assistance. I also thank my peer review team, whose suggestions and critical comments were invaluable in shaping and improving the book: Marcia Burrell, State University of New York-Oswego; Lynne Chalmers, University of North Dakota; Moon K. Chang, Alabama State University; Rebecca Fogarty, Eastern Illinois University; Dorothy Fulton, Fort Hays State University; Ann N. Garfinkle, University of Montana-Missoula; Jamey Nystrom, Frostburg State University; Marietta Esposito Peskin, Seton Hall University; Sharon Piety-Nowell, Bethune-Cookman University; Kaye Ragland, Pacific Oaks College and Antioch University-Los Angeles; Julia Shaftel, University of Kansas; and Carolyn H. Wilson, Virginia State University.

To my colleagues, friends, and family, I owe a debt of gratitude for your ongoing encouragement and belief that I could get this book done! I would like to express my special thanks to my parents, parents-in-law, and wonderful husband and children for their steadfast support.

BRIEF CONTENTS

CONTENTS

Introduction to the Response to Intervention Framework for Assessment

Ms. Boyd, a second-grade teacher, is frustrated about the lack of progress that two of her students have shown in reading and writing. Miguel and Roberto have attended Lincoln Elementary since kindergarten, but they struggled in both kindergarten and first grade. Given that Lincoln Elementary is an urban school with many English language learners and students from lower socioeconomic backgrounds, Ms. Boyd is accustomed to her students needing extra support to meet second-grade standards. Yet Miguel and Roberto have proved to be more challenging than most of her students. They started in Ms. Boyd's second-grade class barely reading simple consonant–vowel–consonant words and comprehending little of what they read. Miguel is extremely hardworking and does whatever he can to please the teacher. Roberto is easily frustrated and has started acting out in class and being defiant. He is unmotivated to read and write. Both students were referred to the student study team early in the school year and assessed for a possible learning disability, but neither student demonstrated a large enough discrepancy between ability and achievement to qualify for special education. Ms. Boyd has met with the boys' parents several times to emphasize the importance of reading to them at home and has tried to provide them with extra help before and after school. Ms. Boyd is concerned about a few other students in her class as well, but she is not quite sure how to provide these students with the assistance that they need. She recently attended a state reading conference and heard about a school that used a Response to Intervention approach to raise reading scores. Ms. Boyd decided to speak to her school psychologist and principal to find out more about that approach.

Reflections on the Scenario

1. What are some ways in which Ms. Boyd might be able to assist Roberto, Miguel, and the other struggling students in her class?
2. How could she get more support from other school personnel to meet the needs of her students?

3. What are some assessments that Ms. Boyd might be able to use early in the year to identify the instructional levels of her students?
4. What do you know about the Response to Intervention approach?

WHAT IS RESPONSE TO INTERVENTION?

Response to Intervention (RTI) is an approach whose time has come. RTI is based on the simple premise of early intervention and ongoing monitoring of progress, or *progress monitoring*, and epitomizes the data-based decision-making model. In this model, instructional decisions are made on the basis of constant and ongoing monitoring of students' responses to the instruction they receive. For instance, when second-grader Laura completes only three subtraction problems correctly in a minute, her teacher knows that she should shift the focus from multiplication concepts to teaching her basic math facts in order to increase her subtraction fluency, and when eighth-grader Benjamin provides correct responses to only 4 out of 10 comprehension questions on a science quiz, his teacher decides to tailor his instruction to building Benjamin's science vocabulary.

Schools adopting the RTI model have systems in place that allow for the early detection of academic and/or behavior problems in youngsters and the use of empirically sound intervention techniques or programs that address these problems as soon as they appear (D. Fuchs & L. Fuchs, 2006; Fuchs, Mock, Morgan, & Young, 2003; Vaughn & Fuchs, 2003). In order to ensure that interventions are indeed improving academic and/or behavioral outcomes for students, teachers conduct ongoing progress monitoring. The intensity and duration of interventions and the frequency of progress monitoring increases with increased severity of the academic and/or behavioral difficulty (L. S. Fuchs & D. Fuchs, 2007).

Ed Kame'enui, the Commissioner for Special Education Research at the U.S. Department of Education's Institute of Education Sciences, asserts that RTI dovetails nicely with the special education model of practice that requires a diagnosis of the child's needs, followed by the development and implementation of individualized interventions and consequent evaluation of student progress. RTI reinforces this approach to educating youngsters and raises the bar by requiring the use of scientifically validated interventions, implementing these interventions consistently and with fidelity, and using technically sound progress-monitoring tools to measure the students' response to the interventions (Kame'enui, 2007).

Definitions of RTI:

Response to intervention is a systematic and data-based method for identifying, defining, and resolving students' academic and/or behavioral difficulties.

Brown-Chidsey & Steege (2005, p. 2)

RTI uses data based decision making as a basis for modifying, titrating, or changing the nature of interventions.

Gresham (2005, p. 331)

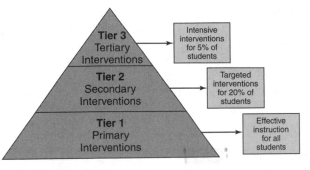

FIGURE 1.1 The RTI Pyramid

THE RTI PYRAMID

RTI uses a tiered system of supports for struggling learners. The intensity of the interventions and progress monitoring are increased with the increasing needs of the student. Several different perspectives are evolving in the field with regard to the optimal number of tiers in an RTI model. The simplest model, which has been studied extensively by Lynn and Doug Fuchs and their colleagues at Vanderbilt University in Tennessee and Sharon Vaughn and her colleagues in Texas, is composed of three tiers as described in Figure 1.1.

Primary Interventions (Tier 1)

At Tier 1 there is an underlying assumption that all students receive high-quality, empirically based curriculum and instructional techniques and behavior supports that facilitate their learning and allow them to make steady progress. Proactive techniques are adopted in the general education classroom to prevent learning and behavioral difficulties (Foorman, 2007; Reschly, 2005). Several state departments of education have identified core curricula that have been validated and proven effective in achieving student outcomes and thus have been approved for use within the state. For example, the California Department of Education (http://www.cde.ca.gov/ci/) provides curriculum frameworks and core reading programs (e.g., Open Court, Reading: A Legacy of Literacy) to guide districts and schools in selecting their state-approved instructional materials. In order to assist schools in selecting empirically validated curricula and instructional strategies, the U.S. Department of Education lists research on the effects of different curricula on student learning outcomes on its What Works Clearinghouse website (http://ies.ed.gov/ncee/wwc/).

Universal Screening Systems

Universal screening occurs either prior to or within the Tier 1 structure in order to identify students who are struggling academically or behaviorally (Stecker, 2007; Vaughn, Wanzek, Woodruff, & Linan-Thompson, 2007). Screening allows teachers to identify at-risk students early and improves the likelihood of these students catching up with their grade-level peers when they receive effective instruction that is based on their needs. There are two ways to conduct universal screening. It may be done once at the beginning of the year by administering a brief screening measure (e.g., a standardized test or a curriculum-based measure) to all the students in the school. Students who fall behind predetermined cutoff scores qualify for preventive intervention programs. Ideally, this one-time universal screening would be followed up by a few weeks of ongoing progress monitoring to verify that the students who were identified truly are struggling. Doing so would prevent the misidentification of students for Tier 2 (Fuchs & Deshler, 2007; L. S. Fuchs & D. Fuchs, 2007). Alternatively, schools might use a combination of measures, including low scores on the universal screening tool and ongoing data from other sources, such as district reading and math benchmark assessments, trimester tests, standardized achievement tests, teacher-made tests, curriculum-based measurement, and classroom observation data, to determine whether a student needs intervention.

Secondary Interventions (Tier 2)

Tier 2 is the safety net for those students, usually about 20% of the students in a class, who are not demonstrating learning outcomes at the same rate and level as their grade peers (Reschly, 2005; Vaughn & Roberts, 2007; Vaughn et al., 2007). These students receive additional support in their areas of academic and/or behavioral need through scientifically based intervention strategies over a certain time, usually 10 to 20 weeks. A certified teacher, reading specialist, or trained paraprofessional generally provides this support in 20–30-minute sessions three to five times a week, although parent volunteers or other support staff also could be trained to implement these interventions (Vaughn & Roberts). Small, homogeneous groups of three to no more than six students are ideal for implementing such secondary interventions. The progress made by these students is evaluated at least biweekly with measures that directly assess the target behavior or academic skill and that are sensitive to student growth. Students who catch up with their grade peers exit Tier 2 and return to Tier 1 instruction. Students who make gains but do not reach their target objectives in Tier 2 may receive additional Tier 2 interventions. A majority of students catch up with their grade peers. Students who continue to struggle, usually about 5% of the class, may benefit from more intensive Tier 3 interventions and frequent assessment of the areas targeted for intervention to determine their progress (Stecker, 2007; Vaughn & Roberts; Vaughn et al.).

Tertiary Interventions (Tier 3)

Tier 3 includes specialized and intensive interventions that are usually specifically tailored to the students' needs. At Tier 3, interventions are often provided one-on-one or in very small, homogeneous groups by a special education or reading teacher or therapist who has expertise in implementing interventions (Stecker, 2007; Vaughn & Roberts, 2007). The intensity, frequency, and duration of interventions is greater than in Tier 2, and it is not unusual for a student to receive specialized assistance for up to 90 minutes daily, at times in place of the regular classroom instruction. Progress monitoring occurs more frequently as well, usually weekly. Students in Tier 3 have not responded adequately to general education instruction or to the small-group support they received in Tier 2, and they need individualized and prolonged interventions that are tailored to their unique learning difficulties.

Typically, this level of individualized instruction is not possible in general education settings, and often school districts require a referral to special education in order for students to participate in Tier 3 intervention. Special education supports allow for continued individualized interventions to meet the student's academic or behavioral needs, and instruction is developed to meet measurable annual goals (Stecker, 2007). RTI is also based on the premise that students exit a particular tier of intervention after they make adequate progress. Consequently, it is not presumed that a student will require continued special education services throughout his or her school career.

Figure 1.2 depicts a flowchart of the RTI decision-making model, which describes the key decisions that are made at each of the three tiers.

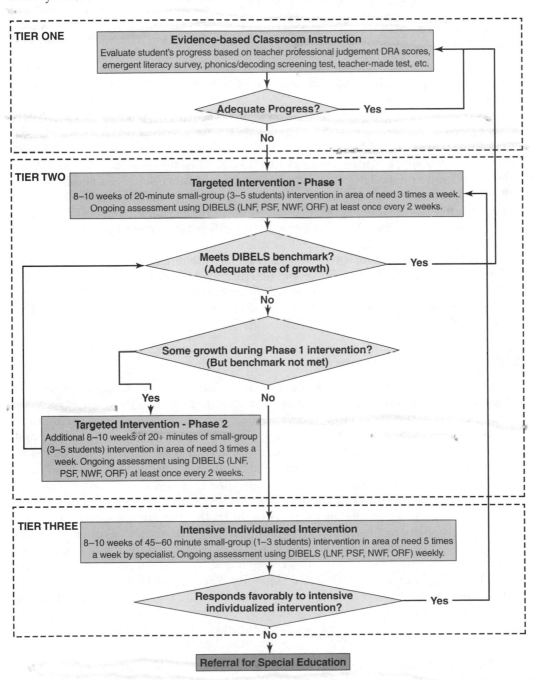

FIGURE 1.2 RTI Flowchart

HISTORY AND CONTEXT FOR RESPONSE TO INTERVENTION

There has been much criticism about the way that we have served failing students in our schools (Bradley, Danielson, & Doolittle, 2007; Patton, 1998; President's Commission on Excellence in Special Education, 2002). Traditionally, there has been no safety net for students who struggle academically or behaviorally, and often they have been allowed to continue to fail, ultimately scoring low enough on achievement tests to qualify for special education services. Poor school performance, in turn, reduces these students' school satisfaction and motivation to succeed and increases the likelihood that they will become alienated and drop out of school, affecting their future life outcomes (Seidel & Vaughn, 1991).

Special education in and of itself has not been the panacea for these students' learning and behavior difficulties, and in many cases it has been a one-way street from which there is no turning back (Patton, 1998). Students with low achievement levels have continually slipped "through the cracks" of our education system and have not received needed accommodations and modifications to achieve success. In addition, the flawed process that is used to identify students who have disabilities has resulted in an overrepresentation of students from culturally and linguistically diverse backgrounds in special education. Often, these students are misidentified as needing special services (Harry, Klingner, Sturges, & Moore, 2002; Patton).

Some of the direct criticism of how students are identified as having learning disabilities has spearheaded a legislative and practical push toward RTI. There is growing criticism as well of the way that we identify students as having emotional disturbances, and some leaders in that field (e.g., Gresham, 2005) also have advocated the use of RTI in the social–emotional and behavioral domains.

IQ–Achievement Discrepancy Model

The IQ–achievement discrepancy model has been used since 1977 to identify students as having learning disabilities. It requires a student to demonstrate a significant discrepancy (usually 1–2 standard deviations) between his or her obtained score on a measure of cognitive ability and a measure of academic achievement in the areas of oral expression, written language, reading, and/or math (Rutter & Yule, 1975). Children in the early elementary grades do not readily exhibit this large achievement gap, so there often is a delay before a child receives much-needed services. Furthermore, state departments were given leeway in the specific formula that they chose to determine how a student would be found eligible for services under the category of learning disabilities. There are many inconsistencies in identification practices across different states. Consequently, a student may be identified as having a learning disability in one state but may miraculously be "cured" and cease to qualify for services when he or she moves to a different state with different eligibility criteria. In addition, local education agencies sometimes place a child in the learning disability (LD) category to allow the child to receive special education support, even though the student did not technically qualify for special education on the basis of state and district guidelines.

Some of the criticisms of the discrepancy model are as follows:

1. *Inaccurate categorization of students*—The model has been criticized for failing to distinguish between students who are low achieving and those who have learning

disabilities. Many students who have incorrectly been identified as having a learning disability by this formula could actually remedy their "learning disability" if they received appropriate instruction in phonological processing skills (Torgesen, Morgan, & Davis, 1992; Vellutino et al., 1996).

2. *Wait-to-fail approach*—The discrepancy model expects a severe discrepancy between ability and achievement that typically is not evidenced until a student reaches the second or third grade, when the academic content is sufficiently challenging for their skill deficits to show up. Thus, students with learning difficulties have to wait to receive much-needed support and services.

3. *Disproportionality and bias issues*—Yet another criticism of this model of identification of students with LD relates to which students get referred for a multidisciplinary evaluation. Teacher referral is essentially a subjective process that is influenced by the teacher's understanding of, and explanations for, the students' poor performance. Teacher bias often has been cited as a reason that males and students from underrepresented and low-income backgrounds get referred to special education (Donovan & Cross, 2002; Harry et al., 2002). Adopting an RTI approach is expected to reduce some of this inherent bias and subjectivity, as the approach requires more objective and data-based criteria related to student responsiveness to interventions in order to make a referral (Klingner & Edwards, 2006; Vaughn & Fuchs, 2003).

4. *High cost of special education*—Because of the skyrocketing increase in the number of students identified as having a learning disability in the past 20 years, administrators and politicians alike are examining more closely which students get placed in special education and whether these labels are truly warranted (Fuchs et al., 2003). Hence, there is a need for greater scrutiny to prevent the misclassification of students with learning difficulties as having learning disabilities.

Alternative Approaches to Identifying Students with Learning Disabilities

There is growing frustration with the "wait-to-fail" IQ–achievement discrepancy model of eligibility for a learning disability. RTI has been viewed as a promising alternative (Bradley et al., 2007; Fuchs et al., 2003, Vaughn & Klingner, 2007). RTI also has been hailed as a way to make schools more effective for all students. Three broad initiatives have paved the way for further research and investigation on the effectiveness of RTI (Vaughn & Klingner): the President's Commission on Excellence in Special Education (2002), the Learning Disabilities Initiative sponsored by the Office of Special Education Programs at the U.S. Department of Education (Bradley et al., 2007), and the National Research Council Report on minority students in special education (Donovan & Cross, 2002).

When he assumed office in 2001, President George W. Bush instituted a commission to investigate the status of special education and make recommendations for improving educational outcomes for individuals with disabilities. This commission, the President's Commission on Excellence in Special Education (PCESE), gathered data from across the country through town hall meetings and open forums. The commission's 2002 report included three broad recommendations: (1) Reduce the excessive paperwork burden that serves as an obstacle to effective and strong instruction and interventions for students; (2) move away from the "wait-to-fail" model and toward a model of prevention and early intervention for learning and behavior problems; and

(3) achieve greater unification of the general and special education systems, both of which share responsibility for children with disabilities. As is evident in the second recommendation of the PCESE, there were flaws in the prevailing IQ–achievement discrepancy model. The PCESE report includes the following quote from Commissioner Wade Horn that captures some of the frustration about this approach:

> I would like to encourage this Commission to drive a stake through the heart of this overreliance on the discrepancy model for determining the kinds of children that need services. It doesn't make any sense to me. I've wondered for 25 years why it is that we continue to use it and overrely on it as a way of determining what children are eligible for services in special education. (PCESE, 2002, p. 25)

A second catalyst for RTI was the Learning Disabilities Initiative sponsored by the Office of Special Education Programs (OSEP), which brought together researchers, professional organizations, parents, advocates, and practitioners in the field to discuss ways to improve procedures for identifying individuals with learning disabilities (Bradley et al., 2007). As part of this initiative, a Learning Disabilities Summit was held in August 2001. RTI emerged as the most promising alternative in the appropriate identification of students with LD (Vaughn & Klingner, 2007). In addition, RTI was seen as having the potential to bridge the gap between identification and intervention. In 2001, acknowledging the need for increased research on RTI, OSEP funded the National Research Center on Learning Disabilities (NRCLD), which is housed jointly at Vanderbilt University and the University of Kansas. The NRCLD has been charged with investigating various LD identification methods, including RTI, and with providing technical assistance on RTI to states and districts. For additional resources on RTI from the NRCLD, visit http://www.nrcld.org/.

A third push for RTI stemmed from the report on minority students in special and gifted education that was published by Donovan and Cross (2002) of the National Research Council, which addressed the disproportionality in special education. They recommended developing early identification and intervention programs that could be implemented schoolwide to prevent reading and behavior problems in youngsters. The report also pushed for increased collaborative efforts between general and special education to better serve struggling students and recommended that students exhibiting learning and behavior problems not be referred for special education unless they had failed to respond to high-quality interventions implemented at the school in their areas of need. The underlying message behind the National Research Council report echoed the findings of the other two commissions, emphasizing the importance of early and prereferral interventions aligned with the student's learning and behavior difficulties.

Growing Criticism of the Process to Identify Emotional Disturbance

RTI is front and center in the field of learning disabilities, and it is increasingly being considered as an alternative way of identifying students with emotional disturbance as well (Barnett et al., 2006; Fairbanks, Sugai, Guardino, & Lathrop, 2007; Gresham, 2005; Harris-Murri, King, & Rostenberg, 2006). Practitioners have long been discontented with the subjective criteria that are used to diagnose students as having emotional disturbances (ED), particularly because there are no objective and uniform standards for what constitutes a "marked degree" or "prolonged duration," terms that are used to describe the severity and duration of emotional or behavior problems. In addition, the social maladjustment exclusion clause in the definition of ED increases ambiguity in practice by prohibiting the identification of students as having ED if they also are socially maladjusted. Given the systematic and data-based nature of RTI, as well as its compatibility with the tiers of prevention in a schoolwide positive behavior support model, RTI is considered a potentially viable alternative for the ED diagnosis as well (Gresham, 2005). Furthermore, the overrepresentation of students from minority backgrounds who qualify for ED services has been a cause for concern, and RTI has the potential to decrease this disproportionality (Harris-Murri et al., 2006). Additional research is needed to better study how RTI can be used as part of the eligibility determination for those with emotional disturbances.

LEGAL MANDATES FOR RTI

Recent legislation has opened the doors for the widespread implementation of the RTI model. The 2004 reauthorization of the Individuals with Disabilities Education Improvement Act (IDEA), as clarified in its regulations released in 2006, allows states and local education agencies to use an alternative approach to the IQ–achievement discrepancy model for finding students eligible for special education under the category of a learning disability. The definition of a learning disability remains unchanged, but Section 614 (b) (6) (B) of IDEA (2004) states, "In determining whether a child has a specific learning disability, a local educational agency may use a process that determines if the child responds to scientific, research-based intervention as a part of the evaluation procedures." Specifically, "a local education agency shall not be required to take into consideration whether a child has a severe discrepancy between achievement and intellectual ability in oral expression, listening comprehension, written expression, basic reading skill, reading comprehension, mathematical calculation, or mathematical reasoning." Alternative approaches that are research-based procedures for determining whether a child has a learning disability are sanctioned, and as seen in the preceding sections, RTI is considered the most promising alternative.

There is still some controversy regarding the precise nature of the special education eligibility determination that, by law, needs to be conducted in order to use an RTI approach for special education placement. The 2004 IDEA and its 2006 regulations make it clear that a comprehensive evaluation must be conducted in order to identify an individual as having a disability and that no one measure can be used as the sole criterion for an eligibility decision. The RTI process does not replace the comprehensive nondiscriminatory assessment, including aptitude and achievement tests, that is required by IDEA in order to find a student eligible for special education. Whereas the conservative approach is to conduct a comprehensive multidisciplinary evaluation after a student has participated in a multitiered intervention process, some leading researchers in the field recommend conducting only instructionally meaningful assessments that assist in both guiding instruction and distinguishing between learning disabilities and other high-incidence disability conditions (L. S. Fuchs & D. Fuchs, 2007). In the latter approach, assessments of adaptive behavior and cognitive functioning are required to determine whether a student has mental retardation, and language assessments are required to identify a student as having speech and language impairments. IDEA regulations require that children be observed in their natural learning environment to document their academic performance and behavior in the targeted areas of need. Teacher rating scales, classroom observations, and parent interviews are always recommended to get a holistic picture of the students' strengths and needs (L. S. Fuchs & D. Fuchs).

MODELS OF RTI

Two common models have been used to implement RTI in schools: the problem-solving model and the standard-protocol model (Fuchs et al., 2003). Most schools select just one of these approaches to implement RTI at a particular tier, but it is possible to blend the two models, particularly by using a standard-protocol approach in Tier 2 and then a more individualized problem-solving approach in Tier 3.

The Problem-Solving Model

The problem-solving model of RTI is rooted in behavioral consultation. It follows a four-step process in dealing with student learning and behavior problems: problem identification, problem analysis, plan implementation, and problem evaluation (Brown-Chidsey & Steege, 2005; Fuchs et al., 2003). In the first phase, the team attempts to understand what the problem looks like, how often it occurs, and how long it lasts. The teacher making the referral and/or the parent may be a primary informant at this stage. It is helpful to determine the student's strengths and talents at this stage, too, to assist in intervention planning (Wright, 2007). Second, the team operationally defines the problem by reviewing the data on the student's present performance. During the third step, intervention plans are tailored to the problem that has been evidenced. The team prioritizes concerns, establishes academic or behavioral goals, and develops a plan for monitoring progress. Feasible scientifically based interventions are identified to achieve the stated goals. Step four consists of plan implementation and requires a systematic implementation of the plan with fidelity. Finally, the problem-evaluation step consists of evaluating the effectiveness of the intervention, monitoring the plan, and developing ideas to improve the intervention's effect on the targeted outcomes.

There is some evidence of the effectiveness of the problem-solving model of RTI. For example, the Ohio State Department of Education adopted the Intervention Based Assessment model, which permitted schools to apply for a waiver to use the problem-solving model with students who were at risk and also to substitute for the traditional IQ–achievement discrepancy model that was used by the multidisciplinary evaluation team. Similarly, Pennsylvania adopted the Instructional Support Team model of collaborative problem solving as part of its prereferral intervention process. Both these models met with mixed success (Conway & Kovaleski, 1998; Fuchs et al., 2003; Telzrow, McNamara, & Hollinger, 2000). The Heartland Area Education Agency in Iowa has been acclaimed a leader in using a problem-solving approach to prereferral interventions and eligibility determination since the mid-1980s (Grimes, Kurns, & Tilly, 2006).

Experts recommend that a structured problem-solving team approach be adopted by an RTI team representing respected colleagues from various disciplinary backgrounds who work closely with parents in determining research-based interventions to assist the student (Wright, 2007). A problem-solving approach to RTI is versatile and can be used for academic or behavior problems, but it is highly individualized and hence is both time and personnel intensive. Consequently, some researchers have recommended that this approach be used primarily for students demonstrating behavioral problems that require more individualized intervention (L. S. Fuchs & D. Fuchs, 2007).

The Problem-Solving Approach to RTI:

Marcelo is a kindergartener who moved to Hudson Elementary in the middle of the year. He uses minimal oral language and communicates mostly through gestures and a few short words and phrases. He has been receiving speech and language therapy and academic interventions from a tutor. Over the past month, Marcelo has been physically aggressive to his peers, biting and spitting on them when they try to play with the toys he is playing with. The school RTI team decided to meet to discuss ways to assist Marcelo. Permanent members of the RTI team include the school psychologist and two veteran teachers at the school. Invited members include Marcelo, his parents, and his teacher.

Problem-Solving Steps

I. Problem identification
   (i) *Understanding the problem*—Using functional behavior assessment (FBA), a member of the support team observed Marcelo interact with peers in class and on the playground, and another team member interviewed his parents and teacher to learn more about his behaviors and adjustment at home and school. The team determined that Marcelo is frustrated by his limited expressive communication skills. He finds it difficult to take turns and share with peers. He has difficulty building friendships. He does not have the skills he needs to express himself appropriately, and he engages in spitting and biting when he feels that someone will prevent him from continuing to play with a desired object. The peer usually leaves the scene as a result of Marcelo's aggressive behavior.
   (ii) *Identifying student strengths*—The RTI team member who observed him determined that Marcelo is quick with numbers, can recognize basic shapes and numbers from 1 to 20, and can identify simple patterns. He follows simple directions and seems to enjoy physical activities and sports. His mother reports that he is very fond of animals.

II. Problem analysis
   (i) *Reviewing the data*—FBA and interview data indicated that the physical outbursts are triggered when Marcelo is engaged in solitary play with an object and a peer approaches him to play with the same object.
   (ii) *Defining the problem*—The team defined the problem as "Spitting and biting peers when they approach him while he is playing with an object either outdoors in the play yard or indoors in the activity areas."
   (iii) *Prioritizing concerns*—The team agreed that ongoing therapy is needed to build Marcelo's communication strategies and skills, but the top concern is to help him find appropriate ways to communicate with peers.
   (iv) *Establishing goals*—Two goals were developed: (1) Marcelo will take turns and share toys with peers, and (2) Marcelo will say, "I will give when done" when a peer approaches him as he plays with an object.
   (v) *Planning the intervention*—The goal was for Marcelo to replace his aggressive behaviors with a socially appropriate verbal response. Marcelo will review his behavior at the end of the day with his teacher and earn a sticker on his behavior chart if he behaves well . He will get 15 minutes of free time to play with stuffed animals (a preferred activity) each time he earns six stickers.

(continued)

(vi) *Establishing a plan for monitoring progress*—An observation protocol was developed to record data about taking turns and sharing, using the target phrase, and spitting and biting. Marcelo will be observed for 10 minutes during outdoor play time and 10 minutes during indoor free-play activities at the same day and time every week. Data from the observation will be graphed to demonstrate student progress.

III. **Plan implementation**
   (i) *Systematically thinking through the intervention steps*—Steps that need to be followed in implementing the intervention are laid out.
   (ii) *Ensuring fidelity in the intervention*—A fidelity checklist is developed around these steps to ensure that the teacher is following the steps of the intervention as intended on a regular basis.

IV. **Problem evaluation**
   (i) *Reviewing the data*—Graphs based on the ongoing observation are reviewed to determine Marcelo's growth in decision making. The team will decide whether to continue the intervention; design a new, more intensive intervention; or cease implementation on the basis of Marcelo's progress.
   (ii) *Follow-up*—A time and date are set for follow-up meetings.

The Standard-Protocol Model

In contrast with the individualized problem-solving approach, the standard-protocol approach to RTI adopts a series of prescriptive, evidence-based interventions to help a group of students meet target skills that have been identified as lacking. First, student skill deficits are identified. Then a packaged intervention that has been validated in previous research is implemented in a uniform manner with the group of struggling students (Fuchs et al., 2003; Vellutino et al., 1996). Figure 1.3 depicts a sample weekly lesson planning template that is based on a scientifically validated intervention routine. A sample weekly lesson plan is illustrated in Figure 1.4. Because the standard-protocol approach is easier and more cost effective to implement with groups of students, it has gained favor over the past few years.

Researchers tend to prefer the standard-protocol approach to RTI for dealing with academic problems because there is a growing body of evidence suggesting that it is effective with increasing academic achievement (L. S. Fuchs & D. Fuchs, 2007). In addition, given that most students demonstrate early problems in the area of literacy, and given that systematic literacy interventions address most early literacy skills, it is possible to intervene more cost effectively by using standard treatments that have been proven effective in previous research, particularly at Tier 2.

HOW DOES RTI AFFECT GENERAL AND SPECIAL EDUCATION?

RTI and General Education

RTI essentially is a general education initiative. A high-quality general education system serves as the foundation of the RTI model. Although a majority of students respond to the extra support they receive in general education, those students who continue to be nonresponsive to prolonged, intensive, and individualized interventions qualify for special education services. Early screening allows students' learning and behavior

Biweekly Lesson Planning Template				
Objective 1:				
Objective 2:				
Day				**Notes**
Monday *Target Skill:*				
Wednesday *Target Skill:*				
Friday *Target Skill:*				
Monday *Target Skill:*				
Wednesday *Target Skill:*				
Friday **ASSESS!!!!**	**Notes for next sessions:**			

FIGURE 1.3   Weekly Lesson Planning Template Using Standard Protocol for RTI in Reading
Reprinted with permission from Richards, C., & Leafstedt, J. M. (2010). *Early reading intervention:
Strategies and methods for teaching struggling readers.* Boston: Allyn & Bacon.

problems to be identified early, and the students benefit from targeted interventions
aimed at developing key learning skills that enhance their later academic and life outcomes (Brown-Chidsey & Steege, 2005).

RTI enhances the collaboration between general and special education. It is based
on the premise that different school personnel need to work jointly to enhance student
learning outcomes. This collaboration has implications for the skills and preparation of
all school personnel who need to be proficient with RTI techniques in the areas of early
identification, empirically validated intervention, and sound progress monitoring. As
the most crucial players in the RTI process, general education teachers often need professional development in the relevant skill areas. Administrator support and leadership
allow the school staff to study their own needs and strengths, develop a vision, and
plan strategically for RTI. Resources such as time, data management systems, and assistance from other teachers, paraeducators, and volunteers also are key to the successful
implementation of RTI.

When	Objective	Interventions			Notes
Week of: January 18, 2010		Phonological Awareness (5 minutes)	Decoding (5 minutes)	Fluency (10 minutes)	
Monday	Practice spelling and reading words with *cvc, ccvc,* and *ccvvc* patterns	Manipulate words to make words that rhyme with the following word families: *Ay, oy*	Make words using magnetic letters— write each letter as you hear it, blend to read the word	Echo reading— introduce the story, model read, have students read chorally	Mindy and Sam got 100% correct Darius was absent
Wednesday	Practice spelling and reading words with *cvc, ccvc,* and *ccvvc* patterns	Manipulate words to make words that rhyme with the following word families: *Ay, oy*	Make words using magnetic letters— write each letter as you hear it, blend to read the word	Read word list with these sounds, read passage with these word families	Juan mastered *ay,* 80% on *oy*
Friday	Assess progress				

FIGURE 1.4   Sample Weekly Lesson Plan for Reading Interventions Using Standard Protocol Template

Above all, though, in order for RTI to take hold at a school and drive instruction, it must be perceived as an integral and meaningful part of sound teaching practice with interventions tied to the core curriculum, rather than as an additional task that a teacher needs to complete in an already extremely busy day. It is this attitudinal change in how a teacher conducts his or her practice that is often the biggest and most critical challenge in the implementation of RTI.

RTI and Special Education

There is evidence that, by providing early and effective interventions informed by on-going progress monitoring, RTI improves academic and behavioral outcomes for struggling students and reduces the number of referrals for special education evaluations and placement (Fuchs et al., 2003; O'Connor, 2007). RTI also reduces the inappropriate referrals of students from minority cultural and language backgrounds to special education. General education teachers who are prepared in the RTI model are better equipped to serve struggling students in the classroom and do not feel pressured to refer them right away to outside services in order to get them assistance (Fuchs et al., 2003).

The role of a special educator is significantly expanded in an RTI model. Special educators provide direct support to a larger group of struggling learners, as well as intensive and individualized support to students who are identified as having a disability. IDEA (2004) allows up to 15% of special education resources to be expended for prereferral support and interventions to at-risk students. Consequently, several special education teachers are permitted to work with such students in general education settings, providing them with required interventions and giving them a much-needed boost. Those students who are ultimately referred and evaluated for special education in an RTI model indeed demonstrate more intense learning needs because they have not been responsive to high-quality Tier 2 and 3 interventions. Thus, special education teachers are called on to have greater expertise and skill in working with these chronically nonresponsive students.

As a side benefit of RTI, it is likely that schools will become more inclusive. RTI promotes collaborative models of service delivery and allows special education teachers to coteach and support a wide range of students in a general education setting. When general educators are better prepared and receive the supports they need to work with at-risk students, it is possible that they will differentiate instruction for all learners in their classroom.

THE STRENGTHS AND CHALLENGES OF RTI

As discussed in earlier sections, RTI has great promise in revamping how we provide services to children in schools. It is a commonsense approach to early intervention that targets learning and behavior problems as soon as they are observed so that they are not allowed to escalate into chronic conditions. Ed Kame'enui (2007) appropriately characterized RTI as an approach that is both timely and premature at the same time. Although large strides have been made in the past few years in building a solid knowledge base on RTI principles, models, and techniques, many unanswered questions remain. The next section briefly reviews the benefits and challenges of RTI.

Strengths of RTI

An important benefit of RTI is early identification, which, to a large extent, prevents the need for later remediation of school problems (Vaughn & Fuchs, 2003). RTI uses objective and authentic outcome measures to identify students who are at risk for school failure. Such an approach minimizes teacher bias and reduces the number of inappropriate referrals to special education (Fuchs et al., 2003; Vaughn & Fuchs). Of particular note is the fact that RTI requires the ongoing collection of instructionally meaningful assessment data that inform instructional planning and decision making (Vaughn & Fuchs). These data allow for student goal setting and, because they are sensitive to progress, inform the teacher when instruction needs to be modified.

RTI also promotes a cohesive and collaborative school system in which general education, special education, and related school services work together to improve student outcomes. RTI has a revolving-door policy that allows students to receive special services, including special education, as needed. Students often exit a particular tier of support when their performance indicates that they have responded to the intervention.

Challenges of RTI

Despite all its promise, there are still many unknowns regarding RTI. There is little research on the effectiveness and use of RTI in content areas other than reading (Fuchs & Deshler, 2007; D. Fuchs & L. Fuchs, 2006). For instance, only a few studies have applied RTI principles to the social–emotional–behavioral domain (Barnett et al., 2006; Fairbanks et al., 2007; Gresham, 2005). Similarly, much of the research on RTI has been limited to working with elementary school–aged students who are at risk for or demonstrate reading difficulties, with only a few recent studies investigating the use of RTI with middle and high school students. Although the essential principles of RTI have widespread relevance for all learners in schools, the utility of an RTI approach for students with moderate to severe disabilities may be questionable because students with more severe disabilities are usually identified earlier in their lives.

Each school needs to develop an RTI model that works for it, and orchestrating all the components of RTI into a finely tuned symphony is difficult work. As with any type of organizational change, the right mix of ingredients is necessary for the model to be effective (e.g., district and school leadership and support, enthusiastic staff who have the prerequisite skills, adequate support staff, required professional development).

ESSENTIAL ELEMENTS OF THE RTI APPROACH USED IN THIS TEXT

This text approaches the assessment of learners with learning and behavior problems through an RTI approach. The chapters in the text focus on three stages of assessment that are integral to RTI:

1. Early screening, identification, and diagnoses of learning and behavior difficulties;
2. Assessment for eligibility determination; and
3. Ongoing progress monitoring to assist with planning and instruction.

The text adopts the following core elements of the RTI approach in reviewing current assessment theory, principles, and practice across multiple domains with a wide range of learners who have special learning and behavior needs:

1. *Focus on student outcomes*—The element of interest in such an approach is the improved academic, social, emotional, and behavioral outcomes of the students, rather than the process of teaching and learning.
2. *Use systematic and data-based decision making*—Educators should use empirically validated and meaningful assessment techniques to inform and guide instruction at all levels.
3. *Take a team approach*—Clearly, RTI requires a collaborative team approach by a group of professionals working together to ensure that students who are falling behind their grade peers are quickly identified and receive the supports and services they need to provide them with opportunities to succeed.

End-of-Chapter Questions

1. What is your understanding of the RTI model?
2. Explain the different tiers of RTI to a friend. What elements characterize each tier?
3. What are the two models of RTI? Under what circumstances might a school decide to use one model over the other?
4. What are some of the criticisms leveled against the IQ–achievement discrepancy model that has been in use since the 1970s to identify a student as having a learning disability?
5. How does RTI overcome some of these criticisms?

6. How do you anticipate that moving to an RTI model will change the roles of the following school personnel?
   (a) General education teachers
   (b) Special education teachers
   (c) Related service providers
   (d) Paraeducators
   (e) Administrators

7. What are some reasons that a school might consider in adopting an RTI approach? What are some challenges that the school might face along the way?

8. Assume that you are part of a school team charged with setting up an RTI model. What are some factors you will consider in developing an RTI plan that will work for your school?

References

Barnett, D. W., Elliott, N., Wolsing, L., Bunger, C. E., Haski, H., McKissick, C., et al. (2006). Response to intervention for young children with extremely challenging behaviors: What might it look like? *School Psychology Review, 35*(4), 568–582.

Bradley, R., Danielson, L., & Doolittle, J. (2007). Responsiveness to intervention: 1997 to 2007. *Teaching Exceptional Children, 39,* 8–13.

Brown-Chidsey, R., & Steege, M. (2005). *Response to intervention: Principles and strategies for effective practice.* New York: Guilford Press.

Conway, S. J., & Kovaleski, J. F. (1998). A model for statewide special education reform: Pennsylvania's Instructional Support Teams. *International Journal of Educational Reform, 7,* 345–351.

Donovan, M. S., & Cross, C. T. (2002). *Minority students in special and gifted education.* National Research Council Committee on Minority Representation in Special Education. Division of Behavioral and Social Sciences and Education. Washington, DC: National Academies Press.

Fairbanks, S., Sugai, G., Guardino, D., & Lathrop, M. (2007). Response to intervention: Examining classroom behavior support in second grade. *Exceptional Children, 73,* 288–310.

Foorman, B. (2007). Primary prevention in classroom reading instruction. *Teaching Exceptional Children, 39,* 24–30.

Fuchs, D., & Deshler, D. (2007). What we need to know about responsiveness to intervention (and shouldn't be afraid to ask). *Learning Disabilities Research and Practice, 22,* 129–136.

Fuchs, D., & Fuchs, L. (2006). Introduction to response to intervention: What, why, and how valid is it? *Reading Research Quarterly, 41,* 93–98.

Fuchs, D., Mock, D., Morgan, P. L., & Young, C. L. (2003). Responsiveness-to-intervention: Definitions, evidence, and implications for the learning disabilities construct. *Learning Disabilities Research & Practice, 18,* 157–171.

Fuchs, L. S., & Fuchs, D. (2007). A model for implementing responsiveness to intervention. *Teaching Exceptional Children, 39,* 14–23.

Gresham, F. (2005). Response to intervention: An alternative means of identifying students as emotionally disturbed. *Education and Treatment of Children, 28,* 328–344.

Grimes, J., Kurns, S., & Tilly, D. W. (2006). Sustainability: An enduring commitment to success. *School Psychology Review, 35,* 224–244.

Harris-Murri, N., King, K., & Rostenberg, D. (2006). Reducing disproportionate minority representation in special education programs for students with emotional disturbances: Toward a culturally responsive response to intervention model. *Education and Treatment of Children, 29*(4), 779–799.

Harry, B., Klingner, J., Sturges, K., & Moore, R. (2002). Of rocks and soft places: Using qualitative methods to investigate disproportionality. In D. Losen & G. Orfield (Eds.), *Racial inequity in special education* (pp. 71–92). Cambridge, MA: Harvard Education Press.

Kame'enui, E. (2007). A New Paradigm: Responsiveness to intervention. *Teaching Exceptional Children, 39,* 6–8.

Klingner, J., & Edwards, P. (2006). Cultural considerations with response to intervention models. *Reading Research Quarterly, 41,* 108–117.

O'Connor, R. E. (2007). Layers of intervention that affect outcomes in reading. In D. Haager, J. Klingner, & S. Vaughn (Eds.), *Evidence-based reading practices for response to intervention* (pp. 139–159). Baltimore, MD: Paul H. Brookes Publishing.

Patton, J. (1998). The disproportionate representation of African Americans in special education: Looking behind the curtain for understanding and solutions. *The Journal of Special Education, 32,* 25–31.

President's Commission on Excellence in Special Education. (2002). *A new era: Revitalizing special education for children and their families.* Washington, DC: U.S. Department of Education.

Reschly, D. (2005). Learning disabilities: Primary interventions, secondary intervention, and then what? *Journal of Learning Disabilities, 38*(6), 510–515.

Rutter, M., & Yule, W. (1975). The concept of specific reading retardation. *Journal of Child Psychology and Psychiatry, 16,* 181–197.

Seidel, J. F., & Vaughn, S. (1991). Social alienation and the learning disabled school dropout. *Learning Disabilities Research and Practice, 6,* 152–157.

Stecker, P. (2007). Tertiary intervention: Using progress monitoring with intensive services. *Teaching Exceptional Children, 39,* 50–57.

Telzrow, C. F., McNamara, K., & Hollinger, C. L. (2000). Fidelity of problem-solving implementation and relationship to student performance. *School Psychology Review, 29*(3), 443–461.

Torgesen, J. K., Morgan, S. T., & Davis, C. (1992). Effects of two types of phonological awareness training on word learning in kindergarten children. *Journal of Educational Psychology, 84,* 364–370.

Vaughn, S., & Fuchs, L. (2003). Redefining learning disabilities as inadequate response to instruction: The promise and potential problems. *Learning Disabilities Research and Practice, 18,* 137–146.

Vaughn, S., & Klingner, J. (2007). Overview of the three-tier model of reading intervention. In D. Haager, J. Klingner, & S. Vaughn (Eds.), *Evidence-based reading practices for response to intervention* (pp. 3–9). Baltimore, MD: Paul H. Brookes Publishing.

Vaughn, S., & Roberts, G. (2007). Secondary interventions in reading: Providing additional instruction for students at risk. *Teaching Exceptional Children, 39,* 40–46.

Vaughn, S., Wanzek, J., Woodruff, A., & Linan-Thompson, S. (2007). Prevention and early identification of students with reading disabilities. In D. Haager, J. Klingner, & S. Vaughn (Eds.), *Evidence-based reading practices for response to intervention* (pp. 11–27). Baltimore, MD: Paul H. Brookes Publishing.

Vellutino, F. R., Scanlon, D. M., Sipay, E. R., Small, S. G., Pratt, S., Chen, R., et al. (1996). Cognitive profiles of difficult-to-remediate and readily remediated poor readers: Early intervention as a vehicle for distinguishing between cognitive and experiential deficits as basic causes of specific reading disability. *Journal of Educational Psychology, 88*(4), 601–638.

Wright, J. (2007). *RTI Toolkit: A practical guide for schools.* Port Chester, NY: Dude Publishing.

CHAPTER 2

Assessment in Special Education

Tre Vasquez is a first-year teacher in an inner city elementary school in a large urban district. He teaches third grade and has 26 students in his room. Tre feels very supported by his principal and grade-level team. Currently three students in his class have learning disabilities and are doing well with the modifications and accommodations that were suggested by the special education teacher. He is concerned about two other students in his class whose academic achievement is a lot lower than that of his students with identified disabilities. Phillip is highly distractible and finds it very difficult to sit still. Consequently, he is almost always out of his seat, talking out of turn, not following classroom directions, bothering his peers, and missing out on academic learning. Missy, on the other hand, has received speech and language support from a private therapist in the past but has not been identified as having a disability. She reads at a beginning second-grade level but comprehends little of what she reads, even though English is the only language spoken in her home. She has only recently begun to master basic addition and subtraction facts. Missy prefers to socially isolate herself from peers and gets very upset when there are any changes in the classroom routine. Tre thinks that Phillip and Missy are good candidates for special education and wants to call a meeting with his principal and school team to discuss next steps for these two students.

Reflections on the Scenario

1. Under the Individuals with Disabilities Education Act (IDEA), what steps must Tre take prior to referring Phillip and Missy for special education?
2. What role does the prereferral assistance team play in assisting Tre?
3. Who are the members of the multidisciplinary team and what role does each person play in the special education process?
4. What are the different types of assessments that a multidisciplinary team uses to make eligibility decisions about a student?
5. What are some reasons why Tre will need to document the ongoing progress of Phillip and Missy over the course of the school year?
6. How does the federal government determine whether all students in public schools are making adequate progress toward state-level content standards?

COUNCIL FOR EXCEPTIONAL CHILDREN (CEC) STANDARDS

This chapter addresses the following CEC standards:

ICC8K1—Basic terminology used in assessment.

ICC8K3—Screening, prereferral, referral, and classification procedures.

GC8K1—Specialized terminology used in the assessment of individuals with disabilities.

GC8K2—Laws and policies regarding referral and placement procedures for individuals with disabilities.

GC8K3—Types and importance of information concerning individuals with disabilities available from families and public agencies.

GC8K4—Procedures for early identification of young children who may be at risk for disabilities.

ICC8S6—Use assessment information in making eligibility, program, and placement decisions for individuals with exceptional learning needs, including those from culturally and/or linguistically diverse backgrounds.

Assessment has been defined as the systematic process of collecting data in order to make educational decisions (Salvia, Ysseldyke, & Bolt, 2007). A skilled educator is constantly assessing his or her students and using that information to guide instruction. For instance, when 12 of the 30 students in an eighth-grade classroom do poorly on the math test, their teacher knows that it is necessary to go back and reteach certain skills. When Rita demonstrates that she can read 1-minute passages at grade level with 100% accuracy on repeated trials, Ms. Smith knows that she can now introduce more difficult reading materials.

Traditionally, assessment has served a gatekeeper function in education. Assessment results have been the cornerstone in eligibility decisions regarding whether a student qualifies for special services. A rigorous assessment system needs to be in place so that students who are diagnosed as having a disability are correctly identified and do not receive a special education label for inappropriate reasons, such as lack of access to schooling, poor teaching, English language learning status, or socioeconomic, ethnic or racial factors (Artiles, Rueda, Salazar, & Higareda, 2005; Klingner & Harry, 2006).

The 2006 regulations of IDEA widened the role of assessment in the special education process. IDEA mandates continuous monitoring of student progress in response to the use of scientific, research-based instruction. Teachers are required to systematically collect and analyze data on a student's performance on grade-level standards in reading and math and to tailor individualized instruction in response to a student's performance. Parents of children with disabilities are to be kept informed of their student's progress once every 9 weeks or at least as frequently as report cards are sent home for general education students. Teachers are also required to use student performance data to evaluate the effectiveness of instructional strategies used in the classroom and to modify instruction accordingly (Yell & Drasgow, 2007).

This chapter reviews the different steps that typically are part of the assessment process in both traditional special education models and the more recent Response to Intervention (RTI) model, with an explanation of the purpose and techniques used in each of these steps. Two pieces of recent legislation, IDEA (2004) and the No Child Left Behind Act (NCLB; 2001) require educators to pay increasing attention to implementing *prereferral interventions* for at-risk learners and calls for early screening and identification of students' learning difficulties. There is a need to document how these prereferral interventions are implemented and what impact they have on outcomes for the targeted students. Students who do not make adequate progress in response to pre-referral interventions typically are referred for a *multidisciplinary team evaluation* that provides information to determine whether the student qualifies for special education support and services. After eligibility is determined, the assessment data are used for *instructional planning*. Students need to be *assessed on an ongoing basis* to determine instructional gains and to tailor appropriate instructional interventions. Finally, under the NCLB reporting requirements, the teacher, school, district, and state are held *accountable* to the U.S. Department of Education for the adequate yearly progress made by all students.

THE SPECIAL EDUCATION ASSESSMENT PROCESS

I. Screening and Prereferral Activities

The *child find* provision of IDEA mandates that all states participate in activities that allow for the early assessment and identification of children who are at risk for learning and behavior problems. Children who are found to be at risk must be *tracked* to monitor their ongoing progress. Consequently, states have instituted public awareness and media campaigns and offered free health screenings in locations such as malls or grocery stores that are easily accessed within the community. IDEA requires that particular attention be devoted to early identification of children from traditionally underrepresented backgrounds, including children from diverse cultural and language backgrounds and those living in poverty in inner city or rural areas. Most youngsters with moderate to severe physical, sensory, and cognitive disabilities are identified early in their infancy, sometimes even prior to their birth. Early identification results in early intervention that allows young children to receive intensive supports to build proficiency in their areas of weakness. Many child-find activities occur in the community in conjunction with medical practitioners who have early interactions with parents and families, but school districts also play a role in the child-find process. Districts often conduct universal screenings of all incoming kindergarteners at the start of the school year. The objective for these screenings is to determine whether incoming students have delays in cognitive, motor, speech and language, social-emotional, and academic domains and to develop intervention plans to address any identified needs.

Often children exhibit academic or behavior difficulties after they start school and encounter new challenges. When a classroom teacher is concerned about the academic or behavioral progress of a student in his or her class, particularly if the student does not make progress despite the teacher's interventions, the teacher can request *prereferral assessment and intervention support*. Many schools have a Student Study Team or a Teacher Assistance Team composed of veteran teachers and possibly a special educator, an administrator, and the student's parents, as well as other specialists if necessary, such as the speech pathologist or school psychologist. This team is convened at the request of the teacher or parent. Team members meet to discuss the student's difficulties and generate intervention strategies to assist the student. The team then schedules a date to reconvene to follow up on progress made by the student in response to the interventions implemented. If minimal or no progress is seen, either more intensive interventions or a referral for a formal special education evaluation may be recommended.

The prereferral team may request that the child be *screened* using a measure such as a norm-referenced screening test, teacher-made screening tool, checklist, rating scale, observation, or interview. Screening provides a quick measure of how the student performs in the targeted academic or behavioral domain of interest. It might also involve a check of the student's medical history, hearing and vision tests, educational history, and attendance records to determine whether these factors had an adverse effect on the student's performance at school. Screening measures usually are brief and easy to administer and provide a rough index of the student's current performance levels. IDEA (2004) clarifies that screening for the purposes of designing appropriate instruction for a student is not part of the evaluation for determining eligibility for special education. Screening activities can be likened to taking the temperature of an individual who feels ill to determine whether he is indeed running a temperature. It does not tell the person who is taking the temperature the cause of the temperature or discomfort. Further testing is likely required to determine the cause of the learning difficulties.

Prereferral activities include all approaches and interventions designed to improve the functional capabilities of at-risk learners within the general education setting (Chalfant & Pysh, 1989). Some examples of prereferral interventions include intervention groups, one-on-one tutoring, behavioral contracts, proximity control, peer tutoring, increasing student choice, frequent teacher feedback and encouragement, after-school enrichment activities, and mental health support from counselors.

In the traditional model of prereferral intervention, a vast majority of youngsters referred to a Student Study Team go on to be referred for a multidisciplinary evaluation, and subsequently approximately 90% of students referred are found to qualify for special education (Algozzine, Christenson, & Ysseldyke, 1982). Such high identification rates may indicate a positive selection bias whereby students experiencing difficulties at school are inaccurately diagnosed as having a disability. To further exacerbate this problem of overrepresentation in special education, empirical trends over the years indicate that male students, students from minority ethnic and racial backgrounds, and English language learners are disproportionately referred to special education services and found eligible for these services (Artiles et al., 2005; Klingner & Harry, 2006; MacMillan & Reschly, 1998; Wehmeyer & Schwartz, 2001). This disproportionality is particularly noticeable in the disability categories of learning disabilities, mental retardation, and emotional disturbance because their eligibility criteria tend to be amenable to subjective interpretation.

The 2004 reauthorization of the IDEA allows up to 15% of Part B special education funds to be spent on prereferral activities for students in kindergarten through grade 12 who need extra support but who have not yet been identified as requiring special education (Yell & Drasgow, 2007). These funds can support activities including professional development for teachers on scientifically based interventions, early screening and intervention, and support for academic and behavioral instruction and interventions. Special education teachers are permitted to work with students who are at risk prior to the students being referred for special education eligibility determination, if that level of intensive support is deemed necessary. The academic and behavioral interventions adopted in an RTI model are generally considered to be prereferral activities, and data on students' responsiveness to these interventions are used in determining next steps for the students.

II. Assessment for Eligibility Determination

As depicted in Figure 2.1, if prereferral intervention strategies have been implemented and a student is still experiencing significant academic or behavioral problems, the teacher

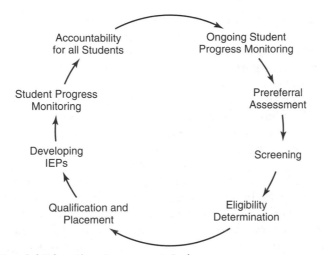

FIGURE 2.1 The Special Education Assessment Cycle

or the student's parents may make a referral to determine whether the student has a disability. The teacher or parent must complete a referral form and submit it to the school administrator. IDEA requires that a multidisciplinary conference (MDC) be convened to conduct this eligibility determination within 60 days of receiving the referral and that parents be informed of their rights and provide permission for their child to be assessed. IDEA also requires that a student be re-evaluated by the MDC team, usually once every 3 years, to verify whether he or she still meets the eligibility criteria for special education. Parents or teachers may request a reevaluation before the 3-year limit is up, or the individualized education program (IEP) team, which includes the parent, may decide to delay the 3-year reevaluation to an upcoming natural transition period in the student's life (e.g., entering middle school) if the team agrees that a reevaluation is not necessary at that time.

This MDC team generally includes an administrator, a school psychologist, a special education teacher, the student's general education teacher, the student's parent, and various therapists (e.g., physical, occupational, speech), depending on the student's needs. The MDC team uses an in-depth battery of multiple measures including diagnostic tests, interviews, and observations to gather data from the student, parents, teachers, and other professionals and determine whether the child has an identified disability that adversely affects his or her performance at school. A student is assessed in the broad areas of academic performance, cognitive and processing skills, social-emotional-behavioral functioning, vocational skills, and motor functioning and mobility. State departments of education develop guidelines for their state that clarify the evaluation criteria that the MDC team must follow in determining whether a student meets the characteristics of one or more of the 13 disability categories recognized by IDEA.

In its 2002 recommendations for enhancing the excellence of special education programs nationwide, the President's Commission on Excellence in Special Education (PCESE) recommended significant changes to the eligibility determination process. The Commission found troubling data regarding misidentification, disproportionate representation, and a "wait-to-fail" approach. Many children were casualties of poor instruction that caused low academic performance, and then the children were inaccurately construed as having a disability (PCESE, 2002). The Commission recommended implementing early identification processes that were based on an RTI approach. The IDEA (2004) legislation prohibits districts from requiring the use of an IQ–achievement discrepancy formula as the sole method for determining eligibility for special education, although districts may still allow this formula to be used as one approach. States must allow districts to use RTI models as part of their eligibility determination process for special education. Under the RTI model, students would be referred for special education eligibility determination only after multiple documented attempts at using scientifically validated interventions have proven unsuccessful. Students who have not had access to scientifically based instruction in a general education classroom from a qualified teacher in the areas of reading and math, or those who have limited English proficiency, are excluded from eligibility for special education (IDEA, 2004).

In the traditional model of determining eligibility (e.g., IQ–achievement discrepancy model for learning disabilities), the results of a multidisciplinary assessment battery provide much of the data for determining a student's eligibility for special education. In contrast, the RTI model allows for increased flexibility in the use of the multidisciplinary assessment data. Academic progress-monitoring data gathered during the intervention phases are used as evidence of a student's lack of responsiveness to intervention. Data from norm-referenced test batteries often are required to sort out the nature of the student's disability (i.e., whether the student has a learning disability, speech/language impairment, mental retardation, or emotional disturbance). Consequently, tests that may be included in the MDC evaluation include intelligence and cognitive measures and adaptive behavior scales to distinguish between learning disabilities and mental retardation, receptive and expressive language measures to verify speech and language disabilities, and teacher, parent, and student rating scales and observation data to make determinations regarding emotional and behavioral disabilities. A full-blown evaluation made up of a complete battery of cognitive, perceptual, achievement, and behavioral assessments may not be necessary in an RTI model in which the eligibility determination data are less important for determining whether the student has a disability, and more important for instructional design and grouping purposes (L. S. Fuchs & D. Fuchs, 2007).

III. Assessment for Instructional Planning

Assessment data gathered by the MDC team are used to develop the student's IEP. Assessment data are used to make decisions about the types of supports the student may need. For instance, if 14-year-old Max demonstrates difficulties with fine motor skills, the IEP team may identify assistive technologies such as the Alpha Smart that would assist Max with writing tasks.

The IEP is the mechanism that drives instruction for students with disabilities. It clearly identifies the student's present performance levels, from which annual goals and benchmarks are developed, and identifies the educational setting or placement where the student will best be served. The IEP also lists which school personnel are responsible for addressing these annual goals, how student progress toward the goals will be assessed, what services will be received in which settings, and an accompanying rationale if a student cannot be served in a general education setting. The accommodations and modifications needed by the student for assessment and instruction are also listed in the IEP. According to the IDEA (2004), when a student reaches his or her 16th birthday, he or she must have an individualized transition plan (ITP) as part of the IEP. The ITP is the document that contains plans for postschool transitions in the domains of postsecondary education, vocational skills and employment, community skills and independent living, and socialization, recreation, and leisure. Toddlers and preschoolers who are younger than 3 years are serviced under an individualized family support plan (IFSP) in lieu of the IEP. The IFSP is focused on the entire family unit and keeps in mind the context and needs of the child's family. It includes goals, supports, and services that the infant or toddler will receive.

IV. Ongoing Progress Monitoring

Ongoing assessment data are gathered to determine whether students are meeting their IEP objectives and state and district content standards and whether modifications need to be made to the instruction being provided. These data also guide the day-to-day teaching and learning decisions made by the teacher (e.g., type of instructional accommodation that would benefit the student, effectiveness of a positive behavior support strategy, usefulness and efficiency of a voice output device for a child with severe disabilities, which academic skills need to be retaught).

In an RTI model, benchmark goals are set for the student progress that is expected at the end of a given intervention period and data are collected systematically and frequently to determine whether students are making progress toward these goals. Generally data are graphed to ensure that the student's performance meets or exceeds the target goals set. If the rate of the student's progress appears to be flat or declining, a teacher can immediately note this trend and modify the curriculum and/or instruction accordingly.

V. Assessment for Accountability and Program Evaluation

We are living in an age of educational accountability, and strict requirements exist for reporting the effectiveness of educational programs for a particular child, classroom, school, district, or state. To meet the Adequate Yearly Progress (AYP) requirements of NCLB (2001), school districts and states must report annually to the federal government data on student performance on critical high-stakes tests in reading or language arts and math. These data must be disaggregated by critical subgroups on the basis of ethnic distribution, socio economic status, English learner status, special education status, and other factors and made available to the public. Schools are thereby held accountable for ensuring that each of these subgroups of students demonstrates adequate annual progress. Parents of children in low-performing schools that have not met their AYP are permitted to transfer their children to another school in the school district. Most students with disabilities are required to take the same district and state tests as their age peers, but 1% of school-aged students with the most significant cognitive disabilities are permitted to participate in alternate assessments that are based on alternate academic achievement standards for accountability purposes. An additional 2% of students with disabilities may participate in an alternate assessment that is based on modified academic achievement standards for accountability purposes.

Generally, the IEP team determines that a student requires modified assessments if the student is working toward the same performance standards and class activities as his or her general education peers, but at a slower pace or lower difficulty level. The student also may require modifications to the test format or mode (e.g., shorter reading

	State/District Assessments	Modified Assessment	Alternate Assessment
For whom	Required for all students under NCLB accountability mandates	Permissible for 2% of students with disabilities who are working on the same standards as their classmates but at a lower level or slower pace	Permissible for 1% of students with significant cognitive disabilities
Standards	Based on state and district standards	Based on modified academic achievement standards aligned to state standards	Based on alternate academic achievement standards aligned to state standards
Type of accommodations	Only standard accommodations are permissible	Accommodations per the student's IEP	Accommodations per the student's IEP
Decided by	State requirement for all students	IEP team	IEP team

FIGURE 2.2   Differences between Types of Assessments Used for Accountability

passages with pictures and graphics, marking answers in the test booklet rather than writing sentences) in order to perform optimally on the test. These modified standards may be less difficult than grade-level achievement standards but more challenging than the alternate achievement standards. Figure 2.2 explains the differences between these types of assessments.

TYPES OF EDUCATIONAL ASSESSMENTS

There is a wide variety of commercially available and teacher-made assessment measures and techniques, as displayed in Figure 2.3. It is important to know the purpose and uses of the various measures in order to select the tools that provide the most useful,

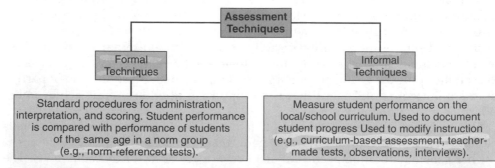

FIGURE 2.3   Types of Assessment Techniques

meaningful, and efficient information for making educational decisions regarding a particular student or group of students.

Norm-Referenced Tests (NRTs)

Also known as formal assessments or traditional assessments, NRTs consist of a set of items that have strict rules for how they can be administered, scored, and interpreted. Deviation from these guidelines could invalidate the test results. NRTs are normed on a sample of students using prescribed administration criteria and must be administered in exactly the same way in order for scores to be interpreted using normative data. As is apparent from their title, NRTs involve a comparison of the target student's perform-ance with that of other students in the norm sample of the test who share the same age, grade, or other critical variables. Whereas some NRTs must be administered individu-ally to a single student (e.g., the Wechsler Intelligence Scale for Children), other NRTs may be administered to a small or large group of students at the same time (e.g., the SAT Reasoning Test).

NRTs promote objective interpretations of a student's performance because the same items are presented to all the students who take the test and their responses are scored using clear predetermined scoring criteria. These measures also suggest how a student's performance compares with that of other students of the same age or grade in a large, representative, often national sample.

Alternative Assessments

Also known as informal measures, alternative assessments include a variety of measures that complement the data that are obtained through NRTs. These measures include criterion-referenced measures, curriculum-based assessments, curriculum-based measurement, portfolios, observations, interviews, rating scales, and ecological inventories amongst a long list of tools, many of which are described in greater detail in Chapter 5 of this book. Generally, alternative assessments pro-vide information on a student's performance as it relates to the local school curricu-lum, and they are more directly applicable to making instructional change. For the most part, alternative assessments are also more sensitive to student growth and provide a more accurate index of the content and skills that a student has or has not mastered.

SELECTING THE RIGHT TOOL FOR DETERMINING RESPONSIVENESS TO INSTRUCTION

Given that ongoing progress monitoring is a key component of any RTI model and that there is a wide array of assessments available, selecting the right progress moni-toring tool requires weighing variables such as instructional utility, administration time, cost effectiveness, and training needs. Riley-Tillman, Kalberer, and Chafouleas (2005) recommend that six criteria be used to select appropriate measures for moni-toring academic and behavioral progress in students. The criteria include 1) goodness of fit of the assessment tool with the target behavior; 2) directness of the measure;

3) generalizability of the obtained data to everyday performance; 4) feasibility of use of the measure; 5) minimal need for training; and 6) minimal intrusiveness. Each of these six criteria is described in the following section.

1. *Goodness of fit*—The tool selected should match the academic skill or behavior of interest in terms of the purpose for assessment, adaptability of the tool for the stated purpose, and instructional utility of the tool. For instance, curriculum-based measurement would be an appropriate choice to measure ongoing progress in reading given its instructional utility, sensitivity to growth, and ease of administration, whereas an NRT would not be a good choice because it is not sensitive to student growth and is costly in terms of administration time and personnel.

2. *Directness*—The assessment selected should directly monitor progress on the behavior or academic skill of interest. If the variable of interest is the number of words read correctly per minute, the progress-monitoring tool selected should involve collecting authentic data of the student reading aloud for a minute from an instructional-level text. If the target behavior of interest is the number of times that the student was physically aggressive at recess, a frequency tally sheet recording each instance of aggressive behavior would be a more accurate measure than an interview with the recess supervisor.

3. *Generalization*—In certain instances, the assessment activity is conducted in order to make general summary statements about a student's behavior or academic skills rather than to provide detailed and direct descriptions of performance on specific skills or target behaviors. In such an instance, tools like behavior-rating scales or academic achievement tests that look at a broad range of skills would be an appropriate choice of tools.

4. *Feasibility*—In addition to reviewing the technical qualities of the assessment measure, such as its reliability and validity, other variables such as ease of use, time taken to administer the tool, need for skilled outside observers, and cost of the tool are serious considerations in selecting a measure that can be used on an ongoing basis.

5. *Need for training*—Whereas most measures require some level of orientation and training, some progress-monitoring tools are more resource intensive and require many hours of supervised training in order for an educator to become qualified to administer them.

6. *Intrusiveness*—The impact of the progress-monitoring measure on the teaching/learning environment is a key consideration in selecting an appropriate tool. An audiotaped track that emits an electronic beep every minute can serve as an accurate prompt for the observer to collect interval-recording data on a student's behavior. However, such a "beep-prompted" data collection protocol is more intrusive and disruptive in a classroom than would be a daily behavior report card containing check marks to indicate the behaviors that were or were not displayed during a class period.

Classroom teachers need to weigh each of these determining criteria in light of the learning environment and severity of the academic or behavioral difficulty experienced by the student in order to select assessment tools that will provide the most appropriate data to make meaningful instructional decisions.

A COLLABORATIVE TEAM APPROACH

Introduction to Working as a Team

A *team* has been defined by Katzenbach and Smith as "a small number of people with complementary skills who are committed to a common purpose, performance goals, and approach for which they hold themselves mutually accountable" (1993, p. 45). The team comes together for the purpose of supporting the student, and the student is the central focus of all decisions. Federal law requires that all important assessment decisions in special education be made by a team of professionals, either the prereferral team that supports the general education teacher when academic or behavioral concerns appear or the student's IEP team after he or she is identified as having a disability.

The special education team is usually composed of the parent, the student, and school personnel, such as the general and special education teachers, a school psychologist, an administrator, therapists, paraprofessionals, and possibly outside support providers, including the student's physician, mental health counselor, and others. Parents often may be overwhelmed trying to navigate the different services that their child requires, and a school-based liaison or case manager could be a useful resource facilitating communication and decision making within the team. The case manager's role is to convene team meetings, keep participants apprised of student progress, and integrate the various supports that a child may need.

The research literature has established that effective collaboration and ongoing communication among various team members are key to ensuring ongoing student success. An effective education team engages in collaborative problem solving and shares goals, resources, and decision making (Friend & Cook, 2000). Finally, strong administrative leadership and support as allows the team to schedule the time needed for members to meet, ensures adequate professional development, and provides needed clerical assistance allow the team to function effectively (Rafoth & Foriska, 2006).

Team Approaches to Assessment

Multidisciplinary teams include the parents and various school-based personnel, including the teachers, administrator, psychologist, and therapists, each representing a different disciplinary background, who come together for the purposes of determining a student's eligibility for special education. This team often becomes the child's IEP team and continues to meet at least annually to revisit the IEP goals and progress made and to make decisions about future goals and needed services. Generally, each of the team members on a multidisciplinary team views the student from his or her own disciplinary area of expertise.

Transdisciplinary teams frequently have been assembled in early childhood special education settings and are composed of a group of professionals, often from different disciplines, who work together to help the student. Generally one of the team members takes on the role of being the contact with the child's family. Often the transdisciplinary team members cross disciplinary roles and boundaries as they work to assess and intervene with the child. For instance, the speech pathologist, psychologist, and special education teacher may conduct an *arena assessment* at the home of the toddler being referred for special education; the speech pathologist may interview the parents about the child's developmental history, strengths, and needs, while the special education teacher and psychologist engage the toddler with different toys and test materials to assess his or her development across motor/mobility, speech and language, social-emotional, and cognitive domains. Such an approach facilitates a holistic view of the child and also reduces duplication of services (Kilgo et al., 2003).

Collaboration with Parents and Families

Parents and family members are valued partners in the educational system, and their cultural context and familial preferences must be taken into account when making educational decisions for students. It is always critical to keep in mind that the parent or primary caregiver knows the child best and keeps an eye on the child's holistic strengths and needs that may not always be evident in academic settings. Parents provide important information about students' prior educational and medical history; their current functioning in school, home, and community settings; and their preferences, hopes and dreams for the future.

IDEA mandates parental participation at all stages of the special education process, from seeking informed consent prior to assessing the student to determine eligibility, to participating as a key member on IEP teams, to keeping parents informed on a regular basis about their student's progress at school. The collaborative partnership between parents and other family members and school personnel enables improved outcomes for the student and is of paramount importance.

In an RTI model, regular progress reports are sent home to make parents aware of any concerns that the teacher has about the student and of interventions being implemented. Parents are invited to share their insights and are encouraged to support school efforts in the home. The parents have the right to request that a multidisciplinary team evaluation be conducted at any point in the intervention process, if they believe that the interventions are not meeting their child's needs.

End-of-Chapter Questions

1. What are the different reasons for assessment in the special education process?
2. What are some important teams that convene to discuss the learning and behavioral difficulties experienced by students?
3. In what ways does the RTI model differ from the traditional teach-test-place model of special education service delivery?
4. What is the purpose of assessment in an RTI model?
5. What is the importance of developing a collaborative partnerships with families?

References

Algozzine, B., Christenson, S., & Ysseldyke, J. (1982). Probabilities associated with the referral to placement process. *Teacher Education and Special Education, 5,* 19–23.

Artiles, A., Rueda, R., Salazar, J., & Higareda, I. (2005). Within group diversity in minority dispro- portionate representation: English language learners in urban school districts. *Exceptional Children, 71*(3), 283–300.

Chalfant, J., & Pysh, M. (1989). Teacher assistance teams: Five descriptive studies on 96 teams. *Remedial and Special Education, 10*(6), 49–58.

Friend, M., & Cook, L. (2000). *Interactions: Collaboration skills for school professionals* (3rd ed.). White Plains, NY: Longman.

Fuchs, L. S., & Fuchs, D. (2007). A model for implementing responsiveness to intervention. *Teaching Exceptional Children, 39,* 14–23.

Katzenbach, J. R., & Smith, D. K. (1993). The discipline of teams. *Harvard Business Review, 71,* 111–120.

Kilgo, J., Aldridge, J., Denton, B., Vogtel, L., Vincent, J., Burke, C., et al. (2003). Transdisciplinary teaming: A vital component of inclusive services. *Focus on Inclusive Education, 1.* Retrieved July 1, 2008, from http://www.udel.edu/bateman/acei/inclusivefall03.htm

Klingner, J., & Harry, B. (2006). The special education referral and decision making process for English Language Learners: Child study team meetings and placement conferences. *Teacher's College Record, 108*(11), 2247–2281.

MacMillan, D. L., & Reschly, D. J. (1998). Overrepresentation of minority students: The case for greater specificity or reconsideration of the variables examined. *The Journal of Special Education,* 32, 15–24. President's Commission on Excellence in Special Education (2002). *A new era: Revitalizing special education for children and their families.* Washington, D.C.: U.S. Department of Education.

Rafoth, M., & Foriska, T. (2006). Administrator participation in promoting effective problem-solving teams. *Remedial and Special Education, 27*(3), 130–135.

Riley-Tillman, T. C., Kalberer, S. M., & Chafouleas, S. M. (2005). Selecting the right tool for the job: A review of behavior monitoring tools used to assess student response to intervention. *The California School Psychologist, 10,* 81–91.

Salvia, J., Ysseldyke, J., & Bolt, S. (2007). *Assessment in Special and Inclusive Education* (10th ed.). Boston: Houghton Mifflin.

Wehmeyer, M., & Schwartz, M. (2001). Disproportionate representation of males in special education services: Biology, behavior, or bias? *Education and Treatment of Children, 24,* 28–45.

Yell, M., & Drasgow, E. (2007). Assessment for eligibility under IDEIA and the 2006 regulations. *Assessment for Effective Intervention, 32,* 202–213.

CHAPTER 3

Legal and Ethical Issues in Assessment

Sara Boyce teaches English and Spanish at Cesar Chavez High School. She is deeply concerned about practices that are prevalent at her school. The school is considered to be in "program improvement" per the No Child Left Behind Act (NCLB) mandates because it has not met its adequate yearly progress (AYP) targets for 3 years in a row. There is a lot of pressure on teachers to get their students to meet AYP targets this year, and the principal has asked teachers to do "what it takes" to achieve this goal.

An alarming trend that Sara has observed is a lack of tolerance for individual student differences. Disciplinary referrals and transfers as well as special education referrals have increased exponentially, fewer students are earning needed academic credits, and the student dropout rate has risen. Teachers are being forced to adopt and follow scripted curricula with very stringent guidelines that determine when each lesson must be introduced, reviewed, and completed. Consequently, they have been resistant to differentiating instruction or to making instructional modifications and accommodations for students in their general education classrooms.

Particularly troubling to Sara is the fact that a large number of youngsters being referred for special education are from culturally and linguistically diverse backgrounds or from low socioeconomic status groups, and their parents generally have had less formal education. The school psychologist is flooded with referrals and has been using short forms of test batteries in order to complete his assessments per required timelines. Many of the youngsters who are referred are being found eligible for special education. Although individual teachers have made isolated attempts to address these concerns, there has not been a systemic effort to develop professional development and intervention plans to address the core underlying needs of the students and teachers at the school.

Reflections on the Scenario

1. What do you see as the key needs at this high school?
2. What are the accountability requirements of the NCLB legislation?
3. What do the Individuals with Disabilities Education Act (IDEA) mandates call for regarding nondiscriminatory assessment of students?
4. What are some ethical issues that are raised in this scenario?

COUNCIL FOR EXCEPTIONAL CHILDREN (CEC) STANDARDS

This chapter addresses the following CEC standards:

ICC8K1—Basic terminology used in assessment.

ICC8K2—Legal provisions and ethical principles regarding assessment of individuals.

GC8K2—Laws and policies regarding referral and placement procedures for individuals with disabilities.

GC8K3—Types and importance of information concerning individuals with disabilities available from families and public agencies.

It has been a long and hard struggle for individuals with disabilities to obtain equal access in our public education system (Dunn, 1968; Kavale, 2002). Historically, persons with disabilities have been delegated to institutions where they lived out their lives, and where minimal efforts at normalization and mainstreaming were undertaken on their behalf. Children and youths with disabilities were excluded from attending public schools because people doubted that schooling would provide any "educational benefit" for them. Changes in services available to individuals with disabilities were brought about by advocacy efforts, including litigation, by parents, community members, and individuals with disabilities themselves. These efforts have led to legal mandates securing the right of people with disabilities to have access to schooling.

Both legal mandates and ethical principles guide day-to-day assessment practices. This chapter will review key litigation leading up to landmark federal legislation in special education that has affected how students are assessed and served in schools. More recent litigation around the issues of high-stakes assessments will also be discussed. Finally, the ethical principles that guide assessment of students in the public schools will be reviewed.

LANDMARK LITIGATION IN SPECIAL EDUCATION AFFECTING ASSESSMENT

1. *Brown v. Board of Education of Topeka, Kansas (1954)*—Acclaimed as landmark civil rights litigation that had a widespread impact on how students are educated in public schools across the United States, *Brown v. Board of Education* did not directly pertain to students with disabilities. It was a class action lawsuit on behalf of African American students in Topeka, Kansas, where students attended racially segregated schools; the suit charged the state with providing a substandard education to African American students. Supreme Court Justice Warren delivered the decision overturning the 1896 *Plessy v. Ferguson* ruling. *Plessy* stated that as long as the separate educational facilities that were being offered were otherwise considered equal, segregation in and of itself did not violate the students' constitutional rights. In his landmark ruling on *Brown*, Justice Warren declared that separate schools are inherently unequal and that state laws supporting segregation deny equal educational opportunities to African American children. He found that *Plessy v. Ferguson* violated the 14th Amendment of the Constitution, the right to equal protection under the law. *Brown v. Board of Education* opened the doors for equal access and catalyzed other communities whose members

had been segregated from mainstream education, including individuals with disabilities, to fight against segregation of their students in public schools.

2. *Hobson v. Hansen* (1967)—This class action lawsuit was brought about on behalf of African American students who were being tracked into low-ability educational tracks on the basis of standardized intelligence (IQ) tests in the District of Columbia public schools. Tracking, a common practice in the past, involved placing students into classes on the basis of their ability, which usually was determined using IQ tests. Research indicates that there was disproportionate representation of students from low socioeconomic and culturally and linguistically diverse backgrounds in low-ability "tracks," thereby perpetuating the inequalities that were already present in society.

In *Hobsen v. Hansen,* Judge Wright ruled to end the tracking system that was based on ability grouping as determined by IQ tests. He declared that the IQ tests being used were not measures of innate ability. Environmental factors played a role in how students performed on the IQ tests, thereby invalidating their use to track students.

3. *Diana v. Board of Education* (1972)—A class action lawsuit was brought about in California on behalf of Mexican American children, many of whom spoke little to no English but, as was common practice at the time, were given intelligence tests in English. Not surprisingly, large numbers of Mexican American students underperformed on these intelligence tests. On the basis of their test results, the students were labeled as having mental retardation and were placed in special education classes.

As part of the *Diana v. Board of Education* consent decree, students from linguistically diverse backgrounds were allowed to choose the language that would be used when they were being assessed. Verbal sections of IQ tests could no longer be used to test students from linguistically diverse backgrounds. Furthermore, the state was charged with developing an IQ test that included items that were appropriate for Mexican American and other non-English speaking students, and that was normed on a diverse group of students, including students from Mexican American backgrounds.

4. *Larry P. v. Riles* (1979)—Another class action lawsuit brought about on behalf of African American students in San Francisco, California, contested the use of IQ tests, the use of which resulted in decisions to place these students in classes for the educable mentally retarded. Such class placements resulted in inadequate education and stigmatization of these students (Turnbull, Stowe, & Huerta, 2007). In *Larry P. v. Riles,* the Ninth Circuit Court of Appeals found these tests to be racially and culturally biased and to have a discriminatory effect on African American students. The Ninth Circuit Court, which has jurisdiction over states including California, Alaska, Arizona, Idaho, Montana, Nevada, and Washington, declared a moratorium on the use of standardized IQ tests with African American students.

In the meantime, the field of learning disabilities was growing. In order to be found eligible for a learning disability, a student was required to demonstrate a significant discrepancy between IQ and achievement. This moratorium on using IQ tests for African American students unfairly denied them access to services under the learning disability classification. Consequently, in 1984, at the request of African American parents, Judge Peckham lifted the moratorium on IQ tests for the purpose of determining eligibility for learning disabilities.

5. *Parents in Action on Special Education (PASE) v. Hannon (1980)*—In response to the *Larry P.* ruling, parents in another segregated school district in Chicago, Illinois (part of the jurisdiction of the Seventh Circuit Court of Appeals) sued the district for its use of racially biased intelligence tests to classify students with disabilities. The ruling in this case was different, partly due to the fact that landmark federal special education legislation (PL 94-142) had been authorized in 1975, as discussed in the next section, and this new federal legislation included a nondiscriminatory assessment clause. In *PASE v. Hannon*, the court ruled that although the IQ tests were mildly discriminatory, they were used in conjunction with other measures, and that the school district practices required careful consideration of other classification criteria in making eligibility decisions (Turnbull et al., 2007). Consequently, the court ruled that the use of IQ tests was permissible with African American students in Illinois.

SPECIAL EDUCATION LEGISLATION AFFECTING ASSESSMENT

Case law, as described in the previous section, has influenced federal legislation providing educational and civil rights to individuals with disabilities, particularly as it relates to assessment. This section reviews three federal laws that directly affect how services are provided to students in public schools: Section 504 of the Vocational Rehabilitation Act of 1973, IDEA and its subsequent reauthorizations (1975, 1986, 1990, 1997, and 2004), and the Elementary and Secondary Education Act (ESEA), later called NCLB (2001).

Section 504 of the Vocational Rehabilitation Act (1973)

Section 504, which is primarily civil rights legislation, prohibits discrimination against individuals with disabilities in any program that receives federal financial assistance. Section 504 mandates the granting of reasonable accommodations to persons with special needs. Such reasonable accommodations may include extended time on tests, a sign language interpreter, behavioral supports, etc.

Individuals with Disabilities Education Act (IDEA)

Originally authorized in 1975 as the Education for All Handicapped Children Act (PL 94-142), this landmark legislation has significantly changed how children and youth with disabilities receive access to schooling and services in public schools. Mandates to guide fair and unbiased assessment have been an integral part of this legislation. This nondiscriminatory assessment clause addresses eight provisions entitled Protection in Evaluation Procedures that call for assessments measures and practices to meet the following criteria:

1. Be racially and culturally nondiscriminatory,
2. Use the student's native language or mode of communication,
3. Be validated for the purpose for which they are used,
4. Be administered by trained professionals according to appropriate instructions,
5. Provide information about the student's specific educational need, and not be limited to intelligence testing,

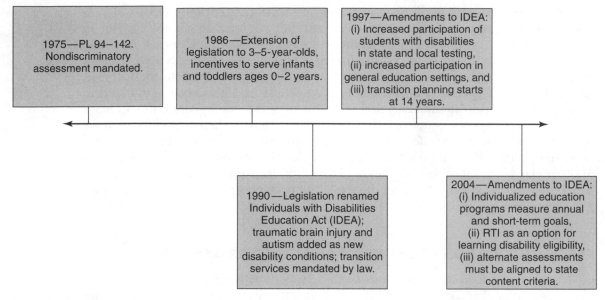

FIGURE 3.1   IDEA Timeline

6. Be based on more than one measure of student performance,
7. Involve a multidisciplinary team representing teachers and specialists, and
8. Be comprehensive, assessing the student in all areas related to the disability including cognitive, academic, motor, sensory, communication, and more.

The timeline presented in Figure 3.1 highlights mandates regarding assessment in reauthorizations of IDEA.

No Child Left Behind (NCLB, 2001)

NCLB was the 2001 reauthorization of ESEA. ESEA originally passed in 1965 and described federal mandates for prekindergarten to grade 12 education in the United States. NCLB aimed to improve performance of students in public schools by requiring schools to be staffed with highly qualified teachers who use scientifically based instructional techniques and monitor progress toward predetermined educational goals. NCLB increased accountability for the outcomes of education by having states, school districts, and schools set goals for student achievement that are referred to as AYP targets. The performance of different subgroups (e.g., English Language Learners, students from low socioeconomic backgrounds, students with special needs) is monitored to determine their achievement with reference to established AYP targets. The overall goal of NCLB is that all students will be proficient in reading and math by the 2013–2014 school year. Schools that do not meet their AYP targets will be sanctioned and parents whose children attend low-performing schools will have the right to enroll their children in a different public school.

OTHER IMPORTANT FEDERAL LAWS AFFECTING INDIVIDUALS WITH DISABILITIES

Americans with Disabilities Act (ADA, 1990)

Passed by the 101st Congress, the ADA is civil rights legislation that prohibits discrimination against individuals on the basis of their disability. It ensures that individuals with disabilities receive free and fair access in employment situations, public accommodations services and transportation, and telecommunications.

Assistive Technology Act (1998)

Passed by the 105th Congress and signed into law by President Bill Clinton, the Assistive Technology Act recognizes the rights of individuals with disabilities to live independently, participate in meaningful education and career opportunities, and be fully included in mainstream society. The legislation also recognizes the advances in the field of assistive technology (AT) but acknowledges that many people lack resources to pay for these devices and there is a shortage of skilled personnel to promote and facilitate the use of such devices. Consequently, this legislation provides federal financial assistance to promote public awareness, interagency coordination, and technical assistance for increased use of AT by individuals with disabilities.

ONGOING LITIGATION IN ASSESSMENT

Whereas much of the litigation in the 1970s and 1980s involved nondiscriminatory assessment, more recent litigation in special education revolves around the issue of high-stakes assessments, typically high school exit examinations that determine whether students will earn a high school diploma. The key issues at stake have been 1) whether the schools taught students the content and skills they needed to take and pass these assessments, and 2) whether students received the necessary accommodations or adaptations needed to successfully take the test. For instance, in the class action law suit *Noon v. Alaska State Board of Education and the Anchorage School District* (2004), the plaintiffs charged the state with not adequately preparing the students to take this test, not providing needed accommodations, and not offering an appropriate alternate assessment. Similarly, in *Chapman/Kidd v. California Department of Education*, which was filed on behalf of high school students with disabilities in California, the 2008 settlement required that the state appoint a neutral expert consultant to evaluate the extent to which high school students who had met all other graduation requirements but did not pass the High School Exit Exam had received necessary accommodations during the test.

ETHICAL GUIDELINES FOR ASSESSMENT

Legal mandates must be followed when assessing students; ethical questions also arise during day-to-day practice around testing and assessment. Assessment activities have a significant impact on the lives of children and youth, and professionals are advised to consider the gravity of these outcomes as they engage in assessment activities. In order to guide ethical conduct in professional assessment practices, leading educational organizations came together to develop the Standards for Educational and Psychological Testing (American Educational Research Association, American Psychological Association, and National Council on Measurement in Education, 1999). Then professional organizations such as the American Counseling Association, the American Educational Research Association, the American Psychological Association, the American Speech-Language-Hearing Association, the National Association of School Psychologists, the National Association of Test Directors, and the National Council on Measurement in Education came together to develop a Code of Fair Testing Practices that was based on the broader standards for testing and that provides guidelines for both test developers and users in the educational fields. Details on these guidelines may be found at http://www.apa.org/science/programs/testing/fair-code.aspx. Above all, the ethical guidelines call for assessments to be multifaceted, comprehensive, fair, useful, and valid (Burns, Jacob, & Wagner, 2008).

Here are some of the key guidelines for ethical conduct among professionals that are based on the Code of Fair Testing Practices:

1. *Select measures that are designed for the purpose for which they are used, and that are appropriate for the population being tested*—It is critical that assessments be selected on the basis of their appropriateness in assessing the knowledge, skills, behavior, or other variables of interest, that the measure accommodates for the special needs of the test taker (e.g., Braille, extended time, typed responses), and that it has strong technical qualities as described in Chapter 4.

2. *Follow professional standards for administration and scoring of tests*—Educators should administer only the measures that they are qualified to administer (the test manual usually states who is qualified to administer a particular test), be prepared with all testing materials, practice administration prior to giving the test to a student, maintain the security of the test by not publicly sharing test items, document any modifications made to testing procedures, correct any errors made in the testing situation, and maintain confidentiality of test results.

3. *Report and interpret test results accurately and without bias*—Educators should accurately interpret results using the test manual, be fair in interpreting results on the basis of the data obtained, maintain objectivity with reference to the student being assessed, ensure that the testing situation and test modifications are considered in the interpretation of test scores, and be sure to base conclusions on multiple measures rather than a single test.

4. *Inform test takers about their rights and responsibilities*—Informing test takers of their rights includes obtaining parental or student consent for testing and providing information about the purpose of the test, the types of items that will be tested, the importance of following test directions, what will be done with the test scores, how scores will be stored and kept confidential, and procedures for challenging test scores.

The Family Educational Rights and Privacy Act (FERPA)

This federal legislation was passed in 1974 to protect the privacy of students' education records in all federally funded educational agencies including preschools, public schools, colleges, and universities. Generally, written parental consent is required in

Activity: Ethical Behavior in Assessment

Identify the ethical dilemma associated with each of the following scenarios and suggest the steps that you would take to resolve the issue.

1. You are a new special education teacher who has recently earned her credential. You will be sharing a classroom with a teacher who has taught special education for 12 years. You observed this teacher giving standardized tests to her students. She did not read test questions verbatim from the test manual, assisted students with answering questions by giving prompts, did not use a stopwatch when administering timed subtests, and made errors in calculating the chronological age of some students.

2. An intern will be working with you for a month. She will be observing you and might be working with some the students that you serve. You are not sure whether to share the students' assessment reports and individualized education programs with her.

3. You are a special education teacher. You are concerned that your 5-year-old nephew may have autism, so you discuss your concerns with your sister. She is afraid of sharing these concerns with the teachers at her son's school because she thinks that their behaviors toward him might change as a result and she wants you to do some preliminary assessment with him.

4. The school psychologist at your school is on medical leave and several students are due for an initial referral for special education. Your principal has asked you, a speech therapist at the school, to assist with this backlog and administer cognitive measures to the students.

order to release a student's education record to another party. Under FERPA, parents have the right to inspect and review their children's education records, and if necessary to request that corrections be made to these records if they are found to be inaccurate. When the student reaches the age of 18 years, these FERPA rights transfer from the parent to the student.

LEGAL AND ETHICAL IMPLICATIONS OF AN RTI APPROACH

Legal mandates require that all eligibility decisions must adhere to the IDEA principle of nondiscriminatory assessment, even with an RTI model. Key among these nondiscriminatory evaluation principles is the use of multiple measures that are fair and appropriate for the target student, meet high professional standards for reliability and validity, are administered by trained personnel, and assess the student in all areas related to the suspected disability. Informed parental consent and participation is another consideration. Parents must be kept apprised of the interventions used and their child's progress. Parents have the right to request that their child be evaluated for special education eligibility at any point during the intervention process.

Because the empirical basis for RTI is still under investigation, some ethical and legal issues must be raised when considering its use. Burns, Jacob, and Wagner (2008) reviewed our current state of knowledge and practice in the field and identified four legal and ethical concerns around RTI:

1. The lack of research-based interventions across academic content areas, age groups, and ethnic backgrounds. Most of the empirical strategies that currently are available are in the areas of reading and math, and most are at the elementary school level, which leaves some gaps in our knowledge and skills for implementing RTI in secondary schools, across content areas, and with diverse learners.

2. There are no clear-cut scores that indicate whether a student is indeed responsive to intervention. Such scores could inform the team when in the intervention process to make a referral for special education eligibility. This situation raises a dilemma as the team must decide whether to continue with the interventions or to refer the student for special education.

3. Limited resources place constraints on how effectively schools can prepare all their staff members to adopt the RTI model. Resources also determine how many personnel are available to support the RTI process and affect the purchasing of curricular and progress monitoring resources, the hiring of external consultants, and the provision of teacher stipends for professional development.

4. Treatment fidelity data tell us whether the interventions were implemented as planned. Although it is often very difficult to obtain these data, fidelity information allows educators to make conclusive interpretations regarding a student's responsiveness to intervention. If, for instance, Max did not meet his established goal, it is difficult to state whether he did not progress because his teacher did not implement the intervention correctly and/or consistently or whether Max was nonresponsive to that level of intervention.

Treatment Fidelity in RTI

Treatment fidelity addresses the extent to which the interventions are implemented in the manner in which they were developed. In order for a research-based intervention to be effective, data collection and intervention should be implemented consistently and accurately to all students over time. Several variables affect the extent to which interventions are implemented with fidelity in real-world school settings (e.g., competing demands on the teacher's time, lack of skill in implementing the intervention, lack of resources or time, student tardiness or absenteeism, unexpected events such as a fire drill, concert practice).

In order to ensure that RTI interventions result in the desired outcomes, it is integral for schools to train their teachers, psychologists, and other support staff who are involved in providing these interventions so that they are proficient in their use. The interventions selected need to be logistically feasible and able to be accommodated effectively within the daily school schedule. It is also important for a trained observer to conduct ongoing observations to monitor how effectively these interventions are being implemented. The process for monitoring fidelity of interventions should be approached as a positive professional development opportunity to alleviate teachers' concerns that they may be penalized if interventions are not delivered as planned.

Web Resources on Special Education Legislation

Americans with Disabilities Act   *http://www.ada.gov/*

Code of Ethics in Assessment and Testing   *http://www.apa.org/science/programs/testing/
fair-code.aspx*

Individuals with Disabilities Education Act   *http://idea.ed.gov/*

Special Education Law   *http://www.wrightslaw.com/*

End-of-Chapter Questions

1. Why was *Brown v. Board of Education* considered to be landmark civil rights legislation in public education?
2. Explain any two pieces of litigation that had a direct impact on how special education services are provided today.
3. What was a common theme for litigation on behalf of individuals with disabilities from the 1950s to 1970s? How has that theme changed over the years with the passage of IDEA?
4. Which federal laws safeguard the rights of individuals with disabilities? Discuss.

5. What are the Protection in Evaluation Principles of IDEA?
6. How does NCLB affect how students with disabilities are served in schools?
7. Why should ethical principles and issues be of utmost importance when assessing children and youth?
8. What are the key provisions of FERPA?
9. What are some ethical issues raised as a result of adopting an RTI model of early intervention and eligibility determination? Discuss.

References

American Educational Research Association, American Psychological Association, and National Council on Measurement in Education. (1999). *Standards for educational and psychological testing* (2nd ed.). Washington, D.C.: American Educational Research Association.

Burns, M. K., Jacob, S., & Wagner, A. R. (2008). Ethical and legal issues associated with using response to intervention to assess learning disabilities. *Journal of School Psychology, 46,* 263–279.

Dunn, L. (1968). Special education for the mildly retarded: Is much of it justifiable? *Exceptional Children, 34,* 5–22.

Kavale, K. (2002). Mainstreaming to full inclusion: From orthogenesis to pathogenesis of an idea. *International Journal of Disability, Development, and Education, 49,* 201–214.

Turnbull, H. R., Stowe, M. J., & Huerta, N. (2007). *Free appropriate public education: The law and children with disabilities.* Denver, CO: Love Publishing.

CHAPTER 4

Traditional Norm-Referenced Testing

Lucy Nguyen is a beginning special education teacher who is getting ready for her first individualized education program (IEP) meeting. She wants to be well prepared for the meeting so that it goes off successfully. She has obtained information from the general education teacher, speech pathologist, and adaptive physical education teacher who serve the student and has written up their assessment findings in a report to share with the parents. She remembers from her special education certification program courses that it is really important to communicate with the parents prior to the team meeting to get their input regarding the goals and objectives on which they would like their child to focus. She also remembers that it is very important to explain assessment results clearly and concisely to her student's parents, as these concepts are difficult at times for parents to comprehend. Lucy pulls out the textbook from her assessment course to review key terms such as standard scores, percentile ranks, reliability, and validity.

Reflections on the Scenario

1. What are some factors that Lucy should consider when she is deciding which assessment measures would be most appropriate to collect data on the student's progress?
2. What are some variables she should consider as she prepares to administer, score, and interpret the assessments?
3. What variables did she consider in order to write the assessment report?
4. In what types of collaborative activities does Individuals with Disabilities Education Act (IDEA) legislation require IEP teams to engage?

COUNCIL FOR EXCEPTIONAL CHILDREN (CEC) STANDARDS

This chapter addresses the following CEC standards:

ICC8K1—Basic terminology used in assessment.

GC8K1—Specialized terminology used in the assessment of individuals with disabilities.

ICC8S1—Gather relevant background information.

ICC8S2—Administer nonbiased formal and informal assessments.

ICC8S5—Interpret information from formal and informal assessments.

ICC8S6—Use assessment information in making eligibility, program, and placement decisions for individuals who have exceptional learning needs, including those from culturally and/or linguistically diverse backgrounds.

ICC8S 7—Report assessment results to all stakeholders using effective communication skills.

ICC8S10—Create and maintain records.

GC8S2—Use exceptionality-specific assessment instruments with individuals who have disabilities.

Meaningful assessment uses technically sound tools to learn about a student's optimal performance levels in multiple domains of functioning, at the same time as it provides clear implications to guide educational programming. There are multiple measures, including norm-referenced tests (NRTs) and alternative assessments. This chapter introduces the reader to essential measurement concepts that assist in selecting, administering, scoring, and interpreting test data and in understanding the technical qualities of NRTs. The chapter goes on to review how to administer, score, and interpret NRTs and how to effectively communicate test results with parents, students, and other educational professionals. The purpose of NRTs in a Response to Intervention (RTI) model will also be discussed.

INTRODUCTION TO BASIC MEASUREMENT CONCEPTS

This section provides a review of the psychometric qualities of NRTs. It is important for educational professionals to be conversant with these psychometric variables so that they may correctly interpret test scores and effectively communicate their findings to students, their families, and other school professionals.

Distributions

A distribution shows how a number of participants performed individually on the test. The distribution is a compilation of raw scores earned by a group of test takers. A student's *raw score* is the number of items that the student got correct on a test. These scores can be represented as a list of scores, in a table, or graphically in the form of charts and graphs to demonstrate the spread of scores within the group.

A frequency distribution displays the number of participants who earned a particular test score. Scores are arranged in ascending or descending order from lowest to highest, or from highest to lowest. Table 4.1 shows a frequency distribution that is based on spelling scores for 20 students in Ms. Granger's second-grade class. Students could earn a maximum of 10 points on the test. Scores are arranged from highest to lowest with the highest earned score being 10 and the lowest being 2.

Measures of Central Tendency

The average performance of individuals on a test can be determined using measures of central tendency, including the mode, median, and mean.

TABLE 4.1	Frequency Distribution of Scores on Spelling Test in Ms. Granger's Class
Test Score	**Frequency**
10	2
9	5
8	8
6	3
4	1
2	1

The *mode* is the most frequently occurring score in a distribution and can usually be determined quickly by scanning the scores in the distribution visually. For instance, the modal score on Ms. Granger's spelling test is 8. Some distributions may have more than one mode. If there are two modal values, the distribution is termed *bimodal*.

The *median* is the score that divides the distribution into exactly two equal halves, with 50% of test takers scoring above and 50% scoring below the median score. It is possible for the median score to be a value that was not actually earned by a test-taker within the distribution. For instance, the median score in Ms. Granger's class is 7, a score that no student earned. The median value is often used when one is concerned that extreme scores in a distribution will have an undue influence on the average. For instance, the average selling price of homes in a neighborhood is usually presented as a median score so that the price of the multimillion-dollar mansion at the top of the hill that looks down upon the more modest homes below does not disproportionately affect the average price within that neighborhood.

The *mean* is the arithmetic average of scores in the distribution that is obtained by adding the individual raw scores and dividing them by the total number of scores. The formula for computing the mean score is

$$M = \frac{\Sigma X}{N}$$

where M = mean, Σ = sum; X = individual scores; and N = number of scores in the distribution.

Using the data in Table 4.1, we find that the sum of student scores in Ms. Granger's class amounts to 153. When the sum of scores is divided by the 20 students in the class, the result is a mean score of 7.65.

The mean is the most commonly used measure of central tendency and is usually the most useful measure when further statistical computations are to be conducted. Extreme high or low scores can unduly influence the mean.

Measures of Variability

Measures of variability or dispersion tell us about the spread of scores around the average score in a distribution. For example, imagine that you are a high school teacher who recently completed a parent education workshop at your high school on home-school literacy programs. You administered a survey to determine how satisfied parents were with your workshop. Parents could rate their satisfaction on a 5-point scale,

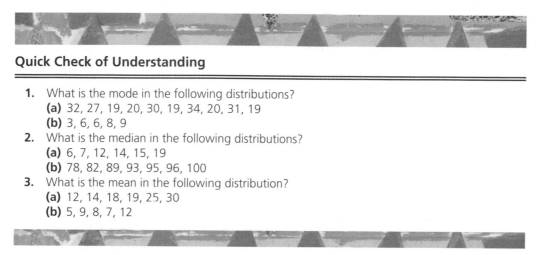

Quick Check of Understanding

1. What is the mode in the following distributions?
   (a) 32, 27, 19, 20, 30, 19, 34, 20, 31, 19
   (b) 3, 6, 6, 8, 9
2. What is the median in the following distributions?
   (a) 6, 7, 12, 14, 15, 19
   (b) 78, 82, 89, 93, 95, 96, 100
3. What is the mean in the following distribution?
   (a) 12, 14, 18, 19, 25, 30
   (b) 5, 9, 8, 7, 12

where 5 indicates "extremely satisfied" and 1 is "extremely dissatisfied" with the workshop. The average satisfaction score on the survey was 4.5, which leads you to think that you led a pretty good workshop. However, the average score is only part of the information you need to truly evaluate the effectiveness of your workshop. It is possible that although the workshop catered to the majority of the parents in attendance, it did not address the needs of all the parents who were present. Your school has a growing population of English Language Learners, and you may well need to modify your workshop to better meet their needs. A measure of variability tells you whether the individual scores in the distribution were closely clustered around the average score or whether they were spread quite far apart from one another. So, you would need to review the standard deviation to determine whether you met the needs of all the parents present or whether some parents were less satisfied with your workshop.

Range and standard deviation are two commonly used measures of variability. The *range* provides a quick estimate of variance and is the difference between the lowest and highest scores in the distribution. The *range* is calculated by subtracting the lowest score from the highest score in a distribution. For instance, the range of scores on Ms. Granger's spelling test was $(10 - 2) = 8$.

The *standard deviation* is the average distance of scores from the mean score in a distribution. Distributions with higher variability or a greater spread of scores will have higher standard deviations. Those with lower variability will have lower standard deviations. The standard deviation expresses whether the mean is indeed reflective of the scores within the distribution. Standard deviations are computed with the formula

$$SD = \frac{\sqrt{\Sigma(X - \overline{X})^2}}{N}$$

where $\sqrt{}$ = square root, Σ = sum, X = raw score on test, $\overline{X}$ = mean of the test, and N = number of scores.

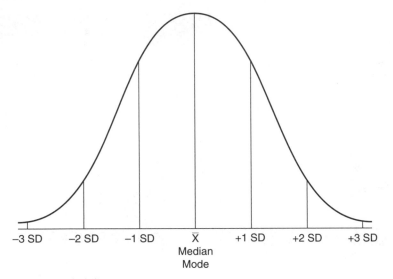

FIGURE 4.1   Normal Probability Curve

The mean and standard deviation are used in interpreting test scores. The test manual for a standardized test usually lists the mean and standard deviations for that test.

Normal Distribution of Scores

When you measure a variable such as reading skills or intelligence across a very large number of individuals from the general population, the resulting scores tend to form what is known as a *normal distribution*. In such a distribution, the scores cluster at the center of the distribution around the average score, with fewer individuals earning very high or very low scores. When this distribution is graphically displayed (see Figure 4.1), it is symmetrical or bell-shaped and is called the *normal probability curve*. The modal, median, and mean score in a normal distribution fall at the same value, with 50% of the sample scoring above and 50% scoring below the average score.

Not all distributions are normal. When the scores are clustered toward either end of the distribution, the distribution is *skewed*. For instance, when data are collected from a smaller sample within the population, their performance may not reflect the normal distribution. Let us assume that a reading test is administered in a classroom that serves gifted students in a language arts magnet school. The majority of students in the class earned high scores on the test and the resulting distribution was negatively skewed to the left, as displayed in Figure 4.2. But when the same test is administered in a special day class for students with mental retardation, the resulting distribution of scores was positively skewed with a majority of students earning low scores, as is displayed in Figure 4.2.

Standard Error of Measurement and Confidence Intervals

Another concept that is important for interpreting test scores is the standard error of measurement (SEM). A test score is the combination of the student's true score on the

A Negatively Skewed Distribution

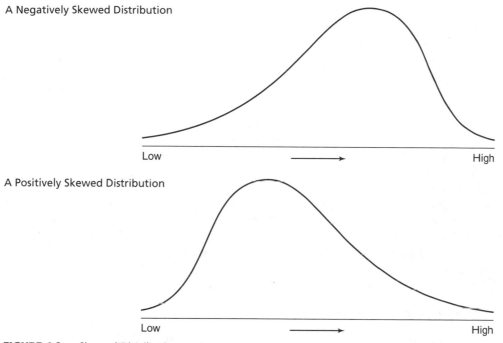

Low ⟶ High

A Positively Skewed Distribution

Low ⟶ High

FIGURE 4.2   Skewed Distributions

test and random error that stems from the test. For instance, if Raj takes the same test on more than one occasion under consistent testing conditions, he is likely to earn slightly different scores each time he takes the test, even if there have been no changes in his skill level. Some of his scores will be slightly above his true skill levels, and others will be slightly below. SEM is the statistic that estimates the range of scores that a student might earn if he were to take the same test on multiple occasions. It allows for the determination of the difference between the obtained score and the true score on multiple administrations of the test. Since it is close to impossible to determine one's true score, the SEM is considered to be an estimate of the amount of error in the test score.

The SEM usually results from error that is inherent within the test, but it also could result from errors in how a test is administered (e.g., student is given time over the normal limit) and factors unique to the student taking the test (e.g., the student is feeling unwell). The SEM can be added and subtracted from the student's obtained score to estimate what his or her true score would be. This is the reason why students' test scores are usually reported as a range. For example, if a student obtained a score of 95 on a reading test and the SEM was + or −3, the student's true score lies between 92 and 98.

The following formula can be used to calculate the SEM:

$$SEM = S_x\sqrt{1 - r_{xx}}$$

Here, S_x = standard deviation of the test, $\sqrt{\ }$ = square root, and r_{xx} = reliability coefficient of the test.

A teacher who uses a test is not required to compute the SEM of the test. The SEM is usually provided in the test manual. The SEM is taken into consideration when interpreting a student's performance on a test and especially when basing important decisions on test results. The SEM tells the reviewer how reliable a test is and suggests how much confidence one can have in the test scores.

A *confidence interval* is a range of scores within which it is highly likely that the individual's true score will lie. As noted in the preceding discussion on standard error of measurement, it is close to impossible to determine a student's true score on a test. Consequently, rather than presenting a student's obtained score on the test as an exact point value, it is better to represent a student's test performance as a range of scores. One can select either a high or low confidence interval, depending on the level of certainty one wishes to have with regard to the range within which the true score lies. Typically, a 68%, 90%, or 95% confidence interval is considered acceptable. A 68% confidence interval indicates that the true score falls within the given confidence band 68% of the time and outside of this range of scores 32% of the time. In order to be very confident about the true score falling within the band of scores, one must use either the 90% or 95% confidence band. The range of scores in the confidence interval is tighter at the 68% interval than at the 90% or 95% interval, so the 68% confidence interval is frequently used.

TYPES OF SCORES ON NRTs

A raw score on an NRT does not mean very much in and of itself. Raw scores on NRTs are converted to derived scores to facilitate interpretation. Derived scores include scores of relative standing, such as percentile ranks and standard scores, and developmental scores, such as age and grade equivalents. Using derived scores allows us to compare the target student's performance with that of others in the norm group and the student's performance on one test with his or her performance on a different test.

Percentile ranks indicate the relative position of a student's score on a test in comparison with scores obtained by other students in the norm group of the test. Percentile ranks differ from the percentage of items correct. They indicate the percentage of scores in the norm group that were at or below that test score. For instance, in Table 4.2, a student who scored 85 points on the test earned a percentile rank of 78, which indicates that she did as well or better than 78% of students of the same age or grade in the norm group who took the test. Percentile ranks range from 1–99. (It is possible for percentile ranks to contain decimals.) The 50th percentile rank is the median score.

TABLE 4.2 Test Scores and Corresponding Percentile Ranks

Test Scores	Percentile Ranks
97	90
95	89
91	88
89	85
88	80
87	79
85	78

There are some limitations to using percentile ranks. A majority of individuals in any population score toward the middle and fewer individuals score at the extreme ends of the score distribution, and percentile ranks mirror these trends. Percentile ranks are unequal units; the distance between any two scores at the middle of the distribution generally is smaller than the distance between any two scores at the ends of the distribution. As a result, percentile ranks tend to exaggerate the differences in scores at the center of the distribution and minimize the differences in scores toward the extremes of the distribution. In addition, percentile ranks are not amenable to further statistical manipulations because they are not on an equal interval scale.

Quartiles and deciles are part of the percentile family of scores. *Quartiles* are used when the distribution is divided into 4 parts with percentile ranks from 1–24 comprising the first quartile, 25–49 comprising the second quartile, 50–74 comprising the third quartile, and 75–99 comprising the fourth quartile. *Deciles* are used when the distribution is divided into 10 parts, with percentile ranks from 1–9 comprising the first decile and so on, up to percentile ranks from 90–99 forming the 10th decile.

STANDARD SCORES.   In order to facilitate comparisons of performance across individuals and across tests, one must convert raw scores to standardized score values. For example, when Sheri gets a standard score of 109 on the Wechsler Intelligence Scale for Children (WISC-IV) and a standard score of 72 on the Woodcock-Johnson Test of Achievement in the area of reading, one can determine that she exhibits a significant discrepancy of 37 points (or over two standard deviations) between IQ and achievement in the area of reading. When Joseph obtains a standard score of 89 on the Kaufman Test of Educational Achievement and his younger sister Anne obtains a standard score of 81 on the same test, he can retain bragging rights due to his superior performance.

Tests scores on NRTs are standardized so that the mean and standard deviation assume a predetermined value. Resulting scores on distributions that have been standardized in this fashion are called *standard scores*. Standard scores tell you how far a particular score is from the test mean in terms of standard deviation units. Commonly used standard scores in education include a z-score, deviation IQ score, T-score, normal curve equivalent, and stanine. Each of these scores is briefly explained in the following section and their relationships to one another are presented in Figure 4.3.

1. *Z-scores* have a mean score of 0 and a standard deviation of 1, where a z-score of +1 indicates performance that is one standard deviation above the mean and a z-score of −1 indicates a score that is one standard deviation below the mean. It is sometimes confusing to interpret the negative z-score values. Z-scores are often used for research purposes when additional statistical analyses are needed.

2. *Deviation IQ scores* have a mean of 100 and a standard deviation of 15. (A few outliers like the Stanford-Binet Intelligence Scale–IV have a standard deviation of 16, so be sure to check the test manual!) These deviation scores are derived from the intelligence quotient, which is why they are called deviation IQ scores. They are very frequently used in NRTs that assess achievement, behavior, motor skills, and other domains. For instance, an obtained deviation score of 93 is within one standard deviation of the mean (the range of scores between −1 and +1 standard deviation of the mean is 85–115) and suggests average performance. A standard score of 125 falls between +1 and +2 standard deviation units above the mean (between 115 and 130) and indicates above-average performance. A standard score of

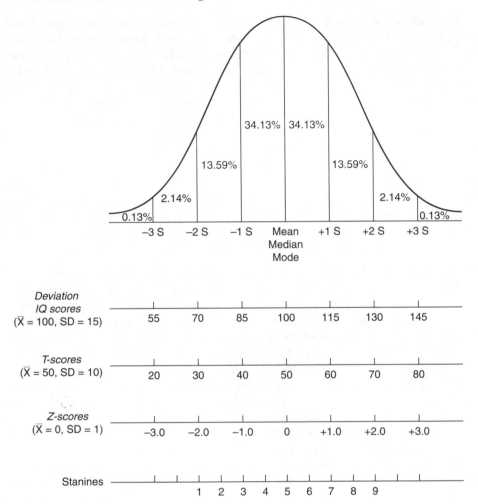

FIGURE 4.3   Normal Probability Curve and Standard Scores

67 is more than two standard deviations below the mean and suggests significantly below-average performance.

As is evident in Figure 4.3, 68% of all scores in a normal distribution fall within −1 and +1 standard deviations of the mean score, with 34% of scores falling between the mean and +1 standard deviation, and another 34% of scores falling between the mean and −1 standard deviation. An additional 14% of scores fall between +1 and +2 standard deviations above the mean, with a corresponding 14% of scores between −1 and −2 standard deviations below the mean. Two percent of scores fall between −2 and −3 standard deviations, and a corresponding 2% fall between +2 and +3 standard deviations of the mean score.

3. *T-scores* have a mean of 50 and standard deviation of 10. Consequently, a T-score of 60 indicates above-average performance, and a T-score of 40 is indicative of below-average performance. T-scores are often used on tests measuring behavior and emotional functioning.

4. *Normal Curve Equivalents (NCEs)* have a mean of 50 and standard deviation of 21.06. The NCEs divide the normal distribution into 100 equal intervals and express where the individual's score falls on the normal curve. NCEs correspond with the percentile rank and range from 1–99. The advantages of using NCEs over a percentile rank is that they are on an equal interval scale where the distance between each NCE is consistent and scores do not cluster toward the mean, and that they can be averaged.

5. *Stanines* have a mean of 5 and a standard deviation of 2. Short for standard nines, the stanine was developed during World War II when punch card computing was at its peak. This type of computing required single-digit scores, hence stanines divide the distribution into nine parts.

DEVELOPMENTAL SCORES.   Raw scores obtained on NRTs can be converted to age or grade equivalents to facilitate comparisons with other students of the same age or grade level as the target student. They indicate the average performance of students at a particular age or grade level. Age and grade equivalents serve as an indicator of student progress over the course of the year. Because they are intuitive and easily understood by parents and teachers alike, they are commonly used in the schools. Unfortunately, these measures are also easily misinterpreted and misused.

Age equivalents describe the student's score in terms of years and months, separated by a hyphen. For example, an age-equivalent of 11-3 indicates that the student's score was equivalent to the performance of an average 11-year, 3-month-old student.

Grade equivalents are presented in terms of grades and tenths of grades, separated by a decimal point. So a grade equivalent of 4.6 indicates that the student's score was equivalent to the performance of an average student in the sixth month of fourth grade.

Although there are merits to using these scores with young children, particularly children under age 6, their use with older children and adolescents has raised serious concerns and has even resulted in resolutions by professional organizations against their misuse (International Reading Association, 1982). Some of the key limitations follow.

1. Although age or grade equivalents give you scores that are equivalent to those obtained by an average student of a particular age or grade, they do not suggest a profile of correct or incorrect responses (Salvia, Ysseldyke, & Bolt, 2007). For example, a 14-year-old student who is reported to do math at a 7-year-old level will not demonstrate the same math profile as an average 7-year-old student. It is likely that the student is able to comprehend and apply higher-level mathematical reasoning skills but makes computation errors that bring down his score.

2. Test publishers tend to estimate the score that would be earned by students at a particular age or grade level using either interpolation or extrapolation techniques (Salvia et al., 2007. Because gathering a large norm sample that represents youngsters of every age or grade level is close to impossible, test publishers often estimate the scores that would be earned by, say, a 9.7 grader by obtaining normative data for students at the 9.5 and 10.0 grade levels.

3. Young children generally meet their developmental milestones in a well-defined sequence, which makes it easier to predict performance on the basis of age or grade at an early age. As children mature, their skill development is more erratic and individualized and consequently is harder to predict. For instance, whereas a baby learns to sit, then crawl, and then walk in a predictable sequence, a seventh

Activity

Test scores have just come back on a formal assessment instrument that was administered to students at the very beginning of the school year. Some parents have questions about their children's scores. Explain the misconceptions in the following items and describe for each case what the score really means.

1. Emily is in the fourth grade and received a grade equivalent score of 1.6 on reading comprehension. Her mother is concerned that Emily will now be placed in the first grade for all of her reading instruction.
2. Luisa scored in the 60th percentile in math computation. Her parents can't understand why she only got 60% of the items correct when she was always so good at math before.
3. On one of the subtests of an achievement test, LeAndre scored in the second stanine. His mother doesn't know how to explain to his dad that he only passed two out of the nine tests.
4. Jack took a popular achievement test that has a mean standard score of 100 and a standard deviation of 15. Jack's standard score on the reading subtest was 58. His mother thinks that this represents the number of items he got correct; she wants to know how many items there were altogether.
5. Dolce is a 15-year-old bilingual student. She scored an age-equivalent score 8-4 on a standardized vocabulary measure. When this measure was administered earlier in the year, her age equivalent score was 7-6. Dolce's father doesn't understand the scores.

grader may have excellent listening and reading comprehension but limited decoding skills. Thus, age or grade equivalents are less reliable and less meaningful for older students (Venn, 2007).

4. Age and grade scores obtained on different tests cannot readily be compared in order to determine students' performance across tests, due to variability in how the tests were constructed and standardized (Venn, 2007). This fact limits the utility of these developmental scores.

TECHNICAL CONSIDERATIONS IN SELECTING AN NRT

Lucy Nguyen, the special education teacher in this chapter's opening vignette, is looking for a test that she can use to monitor her students' progress in math. She wants to find out which math skills her students have mastered and which ones they are having difficulties with. Lucy wants a measure that will cover the scope and sequence of the math curriculum and give her consistent and accurate results regardless of whether it is administered by her or by Frank Jones, the third-grade general education teacher with whom she works closely. Lucy also wants to be sure that the test is appropriate for her many English Language Learner students with a range of disabilities; this population often is not included in the normative sample of NRTs.

Teachers must consider three critical elements when they are evaluating the technical qualities of any test. These elements include the reliability of the test, the validity of the test, and the appropriateness of the normative sample.

Reliability

The reliability is the consistency or accuracy of the test. So, in the preceding example, if Lucy selects a reliable test, it will yield similar results when it is administered on more than one occasion and by different examiners. If Mary earns a standard score of 94 the first time she takes the test, Lucy would expect Mary to earn a similar score if she took the test again the next day or the day after. The reliability coefficient (r) on a test ranges from 0 to 1, where 0 indicates a completely unreliable test and 1 indicates perfect reliability. Given that Mary is a human being, Lucy could not expect her to earn the exact same score on multiple administrations (i.e., reliability of 1.0), but she would expect a reliable test to produce consistent results. Most tests are considered to be reliable if the reliability coefficient is 0.90 or higher. This means that 90% of the variability in test scores can be accounted for by the student's true performance on the test and 10% of the variability is due to random error variance.

A reliability coefficient for tests of achievement and ability should be in the 0.90s. Acceptable tests of behavior, adaptive behavior, social skills, and self-perceptions tend to have lower reliability coefficients, often in the 0.80s.

There are a few ways to compute the reliability of a test:

1. *Test-retest reliability*—Test-retest reliability is computed by administering the same test items on two occasions in close succession to the same group of participants. If the retest is administered too quickly after the initial test, practice effects or boredom could affect the students' performance. If too much time elapses before the test is readministered, change in performance could be accounted for by learning and maturation. Ideally, the retest is administered within 2–3 weeks of the initial test administration. Test-retest reliability is time intensive and fairly expensive to conduct.
2. *Alternate forms reliability*—Two alternate forms of the same test with items of equivalent difficulty levels are developed and administered to the same group of participants in order to determine the alternate forms reliability coefficient. Usually half the participants receive Form A of the test first and then Form B, and the other half receive the test forms in counterbalanced order (i.e., Form B first and then Form A). Test publishers must develop enough items of equivalent difficulty to limit error variance. Yet the reliability coefficient can be obtained fairly quickly after the test administration, and this technique is not as time intensive as the test-retest method.
3. *Internal consistency reliability*—Still another type of reliability is the internal consistency or split-half reliability that requires administering a single test to the same group of participants at the same time and then correlating the performance on the two halves of the test. Usually, the odds-evens method is used, in which all the odd numbered test items are sorted to compose half of the test, and the even numbered items comprise the second half. Internal consistency reliability is quicker and less expensive, and it introduces less error variance because the same test is administered to the same sample.
4. *Interrater reliability*—Interrater reliability is computed by having two independent observers rate the student's performance on a test and correlating their individual ratings to determine reliability. Alternatively, the level of agreement

between the observers' ratings is computed as in the percentage-of-agreements formula presented here:

$$\text{Level of agreement} = \frac{\text{Number of agreements}}{\text{Number of agreements} + \text{number of disagreements}} \times 100$$

Interrater reliability is very important when the variable that is being tested is subjective and open to interpretation by the observer (e.g., performance on a writing rubric, observation of classroom behavior). In the example provided at the beginning of this section, interrater reliability is a factor when Lucy expects her students to perform consistently on the test, regardless of whether it is administered and scored by herself or by Frank, the general education teacher.

The reliability of a test is influenced by the following factors:

1. *Type of test*—Forced choice tests (e.g., multiple choice, true/false) that use objective scoring tend to be more reliable than open response tests (e.g., essay tests).
2. *Test length*—Shorter tests (e.g., screening measures) are inherently less reliable than longer tests that have more test items.
3. *Test–retest time interval*—As time passes between the administration of the test and administration of the retest, there is a greater likelihood that the student's performance will improve and the true score will change. Consequently, the less time that elapses between the administration of the original test and the retest, the more trustworthy the test is considered to be (Salvia et al., 2007).
4. *Controlling random error*—Consistency in test administration and scoring and controlling for extraneous variables in the testing environment, such as noise and temperature disturbances, can enhance test reliability.
5. *SEM*—Test reliability is inversely related to the SEM. Highly reliable tests have lower SEMs than do less reliable tests.

Validity

Validity is probably the most critical technical concept that needs to be closely scrutinized in order to select an appropriate test. It is the extent to which the test measures what it is intended to measure. For instance, a valid test of reading performance would require a student to read and comprehend material presented, rather than being quizzed on the art and science of reading. A test that requires a student to listen to questions presented orally and to construct a verbal response would not be considered a valid measure of nonverbal intelligence. In our example, Lucy is looking for a valid math test that covers the scope and sequence of the math curriculum and tells her which specific math skills her students have and have not mastered.

IDEA legislation requires that tests which are used in the nondiscriminatory assessment process be validated for the purpose for which they are used. Both the test publishers and the test users must ensure that tests being used are valid, that they are used for the purpose for which they were developed, and that prescribed testing procedures are followed. Some of these guidelines are described in the Standards for Educational and Psychological Testing (American Educational Research Association, American Psychological Association, & National Council on Measurement in Education, 1999) presented in Chapter 3.

There are four types of validity:

1. *Face validity* is not a technical construct, but it is critical to securing buy-in from test users and test takers. Also called "armchair validity," it refers to the user's sense, after he or she has reviewed test items, that it is worth investing time and energy in this test.

2. *Content validity* is the extent to which the test measures all the components of the content domain that is being assessed. For instance, a valid test of math would include adequate representation of items testing math facts, knowledge, concepts, computation, and application. Content validity is determined by a panel of content area experts who review the test items and ascertain the extent to which they agree that these items are representative of the content that should be included on the test. The test is then field tested by teachers in the classroom and the items are modified on the basis of their findings.

3. *Criterion-related validity* is the extent to which the new test that is being validated correlates with other existing measures of the same construct. There are two ways to determine criterion-related validity:

   a. *Concurrent validity* can be obtained fairly quickly by correlating test performance on the new test with performance on another established measure that assesses the same variable of interest. For instance, a test publisher who is developing a new vocational aptitude test would administer the test to a group of students, then after a few weeks administer an existing, valid measure of vocational aptitude to the same group of students. The publisher would then review the means and standard deviations of the scores and compute a correlation coefficient determining the extent to which student performance on the two measures is correlated. The higher the correlation, the stronger the concurrent validity of the test.

   b. *Predictive validity* is intended to determine how well the students' performance on the measure that is being validated correlates with real-life tasks and activities. It predicts how the student would perform in these real-life activities at a future point in time; consequently, it is longitudinal in nature and takes time to complete. The criterion in this case is a future measure of the construct that is being measured by the new test. The publisher of the vocational aptitude test in our example could determine predictive validity of the test by monitoring how well a student actually does in his chosen career as, say, an auto mechanic, on the basis of test results that indicated aptitude in this area. If future performance is highly correlated with the test results, the test has high predictive validity.

4. *Construct validity* is probably the most difficult type of test validity to comprehend and compute. Construct validity allows one to make inferences about the individuals tested in terms of their performance on the theoretical construct as it is operationalized and measured in the test administered. Generally, construct validity involves a systematic review and statistical analyses of how test performance relates to the theoretical basis for the test. For instance, the Wechsler Intelligence Test for Children (WISC-IV; Wechsler et al., 2004) was based on David Wechsler's construct of intelligence, which is defined as " the aggregate or global capacity of the individual to act purposefully, to think rationally, and to deal effectively with his environment" (Wechsler, 1944, p. 3). Items on the WISC-IV measure intelligence in

keeping with Wechsler's construct of intelligence. In contrast, the Teele Inventory of Multiple Intelligence (TIMI; Teele, 1996) is based on Howard Gardner's theory of multiple intelligences and adopts a very different theoretical orientation. Consequently, it assesses intelligence in ways that are very different from the WISC-IV. Test items on these measures look very different from each other, yet both are considered valid measures of the construct of intelligence.

There are two methods for determining construct validity: 1) *convergent validity*, in which the test results on the new test correlate with other independent measures of constructs that should be related to each other (e.g., high correlation between verbal ability and intelligence), and 2) *discriminate validity*, in which the test results on the new test do not correlate with other independent tests that measure different constructs and with which they are not expected to correlate (e.g., low correlation between body strength and obesity).

Several factors affect the validity of a test:

1. *Test reliability*—A test must be reliable in order to be valid. The reverse is not necessarily true, as a test could be very accurate and consistent yet still not measure the variable of interest.
2. *Test procedures*—Deviating from standardized test procedures through actions such as giving prompts that are not permitted, incorrectly timing a timed test, and changing the phrasing of test items can invalidate the results that are obtained using a valid test.
3. *Test norms*—If the test is normed on a relatively homogeneous sample that does not adequately represent the larger population, even if the test appears to have high validity it will likely be invalid when it is used with individuals who were not represented in the normative sample.

Appropriateness of Test Norms

Another key consideration in selecting a test is to review the sample on which the test was originally standardized. This review allows the test user to determine whether the norm group for the test represents the general population and whether it includes adequate numbers of individuals who share common characteristics with the target students who will be assessed. Ideally, the norm group of any test would include sufficient numbers of people from various demographic groups to represent the percentage of each group found in the most recent U.S. census data. Demographic variables of interest that are relevant to reviewing a test include age, grade, gender, ethnicity, language background, intelligence, disability, geographic region, parental income, and educational level. Generally this information about the demographics of the norm sample is provided in the test manual.

It is important to consider two elements of representativeness when reviewing the norm group data: 1) whether the norm sample includes individuals who share common experiences and backgrounds as the target students, and 2) whether there are adequate numbers of individuals in the norm group who share these traits as in the sample that you will be testing (Salvia et al., 2007). Selecting a test that has a norm sample that represents the target students being tested allows for a meaningful interpretation of test results. It is also important for there to be a *large enough number of individuals represented in the norm group at each age or grade level tested,* so as to increase the probability that the norm group represents the general population and includes participants from groups that are underrepresented in the general population. Salvia and colleagues recommend a minimum of 100 participants from each age or grade level in the normative sample.

Another consideration when reviewing the normative data of a test is its *currency*. The population of the United States is rapidly changing and these changes are reflected in the demographics of the students attending our schools. In addition, students are being exposed to information literacy at an earlier age and are performing better on tests than the generations that preceded them. Norms for achievement tests are considered to be current for a period of 7 years, and norms on ability tests are current for 15 years (Salvia et al., 2007). Older norms often artificially inflate student performance and should be updated. Revising the entire test and updating test items is a very costly and time-intensive task. Test publishers often save this time and expense by renorming the test on a new sample of participants such that the norms better reflect the current population and publishing normative updates of existing tests.

ADMINISTRATION, SCORING, AND INTERPRETATION OF NORM-REFERENCED TESTS

After an appropriate test has been selected, the examiner must prepare to administer, score, and interpret the test findings. He or she also needs to prepare the testing environment and the students in order to ensure optimal test results.

Preparation of the Examiner

Before selecting the test, the examiner will need to become familiar with the educational and family background of the target student, his or her needs and strengths, and the purpose for the testing. The examiner should obtain parental consent to assess the student and then obtain information through the following means:

1. *Reviewing the student's records*—The student's cumulative file, which is stored in the school office, contains important documents about his or her schooling history, changes in school placement, and any previous evaluations. The student's

Resources to assist in selecting NRTs:

1. Buros Mental Measurement Yearbook provides in-depth objective reviews of published tests and is available in hard copy at reference libraries, through subscriptions to its electronic database, and online at http://buros.unl.edu/buros/jsp/search.jsp
2. TestLink is a library of tests and measures put together by the Educational Testing Service and is available online at http://www.ets.org/test_link/about

record verifies information that is provided through other data sources. For instance, the date of birth in the file is likely to be more accurate than the student's own statement.

2. *Interviewing the student's family, former teachers, and other school professionals*—Interviews can provide information about the child's health, medical, and developmental history, educational background, social-emotional-behavioral adjustment, language skills and preferences, and areas of strength or concern.

3. *Observing the student*—Naturalistic observation of the student in his or her school or home environment provides very important information about the student. Ideally, this observation should be conducted without the student's knowledge in order to minimize reactivity effects and obtain an authentic sample of the student's behavior. It is an opportunity for the examiner to learn about the student's language and communication skills, behavior, academic competence, use of assistive devices or other accommodations and modifications, and more.

When selecting the test, the examiner should choose the measures on the basis of the purpose for the assessment, the information that is already known and available about the student, and the measures that will provide the most meaningful information to guide ongoing decision making. It is important to select a test that is suited to the student's language background and physical and cognitive functioning level and that allows for the necessary accommodations required to allow the student to perform optimally on the test.

In addition to considering the needs of the student, examiners should select a measure that is accessible to them and that they are qualified to use. The test manual usually clarifies the qualifications needed to administer and score the test. Most achievement tests and some behavior measures do not require specialized training and can be administered by special education teachers who have preparation in individual and group testing. Most ability tests, including cognitive, processing, and memory tests, call for specialized skills and advanced preparation and are administered by psychologists.

As discussed in Chapter 2, legal mandates and ethical guidelines require that qualified examiners administer tests according to prescribed guidelines. Incorrect administration produces misleading results that cannot be correctly interpreted. Life-changing decisions may be made on the basis of these incorrect test results. If a test is administered incorrectly the first time, it could be invalidated for later use. It is inadvisable to readminister a measure until several months have passed in order to eliminate error due to practice, repetition, boredom, etc. The examiner should be familiar with the test, practice its administration and scoring under supervision from a qualified professional, and receive feedback, particularly if he or she makes an error in test administration.

Preparation of the Testing Environment

After the examiner is qualified to administer the test, he or she needs to prepare the environment in which the student will be tested. The testing room should be quiet and free from distractions. Furniture should be comfortable (of the right height and

The following concepts are related to preparing to administer a test:

Chronological age—A student's chronological age must be correctly calculated to interpret test scores. This figure is determined by subtracting the student's birth date from the date on which the test was administered. In order to simplify the calculation, a month can be replaced by 30 days and a year can be replaced by 12 months (as in example 2 that follows). More than 15 days are rounded up to an additional month.

1.	Year	Month	Day		2.	Year	Month	Day
Test Date	2008	10	20		Test Date	~~2005~~ 2004	~~10~~ 21	~~09~~ 39
Birth Date	2001	08	14		Birth Date	1989	12	22
CA	7	2	6		CA	15	9	17
		7 years and 2 months					15 years and 10 months	

Starting point—The test manual recommends starting administration of the test (or individual subtests) at a specific item number that varies depending on the age, grade, cognitive ability, and language proficiency of the student.

Basal—The basal is the point in the test at which the examiner can assume that the student will receive credit for all easier items. Having a basal eliminates the need to administer every test item to all test takers. If a student gets a certain number of items correct beyond the recommended basal, the examiner can safely assume that he or she would get all easier items correct. The basal rules vary with different tests and different subtests so it is important to familiarize yourself with the test manual.

Ceiling—The ceiling is the point in the test at which the examiner can assume that the student will not get credit for more difficult items. Generally, the ceiling is reached after a student records a certain number of incorrect responses in a series of test items. After the ceiling is reached, the examiner stops test administration. Ceiling rules vary, so be sure to check the test manual.

size to allow the student and examiner to sit and write comfortably) and arranged with chairs across the table from each other or at a right angle to the table. This arrangement allows both the examiner and student to clearly see the testing materials without the student seeing his or her test protocol. The *test protocol* is the test record form on which the examiner reports the student's responses and scores. The examiner must ensure that all needed testing materials and supplies (e.g., examiner's manual, test record booklets, pencils, stopwatch) are readily available in the testing room so as not to waste time and distract the student by having to leave the room to secure the needed materials.

Lighting and temperature also need to be monitored to ensure optimal performance. For example, glare can impair a student's ability to use an assistive device to respond to the test. Similarly, if the room is either too hot or too cold, a test taker's performance could be adversely affected. Any distractions in the room (e.g., computer, toys) should either be concealed or removed from the room prior to the start of testing.

Preparation of the Student

Ideally, tests should be administered at the time of the day when the student performs best and when they are most alert and responsive. For some students the administration of the test should be determined on the basis of their medication schedule; others may perform best after breakfast or lunch. The examiner should work with the student, parent, and teacher to determine this time and scheduling the testing. The length of the testing session is determined on the basis of the amount of time the student will tolerate being tested. A testing session could be broken up into shorter sessions as needed. In order to ensure maximum participation, it is important not to pull the student out of their favorite class or during recess to conduct the testing.

If an examiner other than the classroom teacher is assessing the student, it is advisable for the examiner to touch base with the teacher to find out whether there are any extenuating circumstances that may require the testing session to be postponed or canceled. For example, a student may be having a particularly difficult morning, may be unwell, may have experienced a death in the family, or may have forgotten to bring his or her glasses or hearing aid to school that day.

Students are understandably anxious when they are taken by a psychologist or therapist with whom they may be unfamiliar to an unfamiliar testing environment. Test anxiety may also result if a special education teacher or specialist with whom the student is familiar conducts the testing in an unfamiliar location. Establishing rapport with the student helps alleviate some of this anxiety. Rapport is established by taking some time prior to the testing situation to introduce the student to the examiner, asking questions to get to know the student, and explaining to him or her the purpose of the testing in terms that are easy to comprehend. The box lists some suggestions for building rapport.

Tips for building rapport with a student:

1. Introduce yourself to the student and tell them what you will be doing together. Explain the test in simple terms at a level that the student can comprehend. Provide information about the number and types of tests that you will administer and the types of items on the test.
2. Take some time to get to know the student by asking about his or her interests, hobbies, favorite school activities, what he or she likes to do at home, plans for the summer vacation, an event coming up at the school, etc. This interchange can be conversational and relaxed with the examiner sharing information about himself or herself with the student too.
3. Alleviate performance anxiety by telling the student that the items will become increasingly difficult and that you do not expect him or her to know the answers to all the items. You just want the student to do his or her best on the test. Clarify how long you anticipate the testing to take. Give the student an opportunity to ask you questions about the test before testing starts.
4. Set the rules for the testing session by telling the student that you are not allowed to help him or her during the test or to confirm whether answers were correct. There will be a time for sharing the test findings at a later meeting. Tell the student that he or she should let you know if he or she needs to take a break.

Even when an examiner conceals the test protocol while noting responses, students regularly observe the examiner and make a note of his or her hand movements, thereby concluding whether they received a check mark or a zero score on test items. When they observe zeros or no marking, they may get discouraged. It is good practice for the examiner to affix the test protocol to a clipboard so that the student cannot easily discern what he or she is writing. The examiner should follow the scoring protocol described in the test manual (e.g., + or −, numerical scoring) so that others reviewing the test protocol can make sense of it. It is recommended for the examiner to note all student responses on the test, marking both correct and incorrect responses to facilitate later interpretation of test results. Using a pencil rather than a pen allows for cleaner and quicker corrections, when needed. Notes should be taken on the student's behavior, attention span, communication style, level of anxiety, and distractibility.

In addition to monitoring the student's behavior, it is also important for the examiner to monitor his or her own behavior, particularly the use of nonverbal head nods or gestures indicating approval when items are correct and disapproval or disappointment when the student does not score a correct response. Prompting must be limited to the verbal and physical prompts that are permissible according to the test. Feedback given to the student must be limited to encouragement of effort with comments such as, "I like how hard you are working," or "you are doing so well with following my instructions." The student may ask whether he or she got an item correct. The examiner may reassure the student that he or she is trying really hard and that the results will be shared with him or her at a later time.

COMMUNICATING ASSESSMENT FINDINGS

A multidisciplinary assessment is conducted to make educational decisions on the basis of the assessment results. A collaborative team that includes the student, family, teachers, administrators, and other school professionals should make all education decisions. A person-centered summary of assessment findings that focuses on the student's strengths and skills is suggested to guide ongoing instruction.

Assessment data is shared with the student and the family orally, in a face-to-face meeting, and followed up by a written report. In order for all members to participate fully at the team meeting, it is important to empower the student and family members so that they feel comfortable about expressing their opinions in a room full of experts who are usually pressed for time. In order to assure participation when sharing results, the team members must be positive about the student and focus on strengths and skills rather than deficits in comparison with others in a norm group (Sommerstein & Smith, 2001). The team members must be respectful of the family needs, schedule meetings at times that are convenient to the family, and listen empathetically to the family perspective. The student should be encouraged to participate in the meeting and may be given a role (e.g., preparing invitations for team members, introducing them at the team meeting, reading a short statement on the progress he made that year). A verbal summary of the findings allows the family members to have time to digest the information and formulate any questions that they may have. A draft of the written report should be presented to the family for their input before the report is finalized.

An outline for a written assessment report follows. In this report, assessment findings should be reported objectively, without ambiguity or judgment. Only relevant information should be presented, and examples should be used to illustrate the points that are being made in the report. The report should be written professionally and should be readable by multiple audiences rather than using technical jargon. The focus of the report is the student's current performance, and it should suggest interventions, modifications, and skills to be targeted for future instruction. A strengths-based approach to report writing facilitates planning for ongoing instruction.

Outline for an Assessment Report

The following are recommended components of an assessment report (Sattler, 1992):

1. *Identifying information*—This information includes the student's name, gender, school, grade, age, date of birth, and contact information; the date of the test; the date of the report; and the name of the examiner.
2. *Reason for the referral*—This statement clarifies who initiated the referral and why the student is being assessed.
3. *Background information*—Such information includes family status, cultural and language background, developmental history, medical background, educational history, and social-emotional adjustment.
4. *Observations during assessment*—This section includes key observations of the environment and the student's behavior during the assessment. It is important to include a cautionary note in the report if the behaviors observed indicate that the test results may not be valid due to student anxiety, distractibility, inability to comprehend test directions, or other reasons.
5. *Present levels of performance*—This section describes the student's current performance and includes a summary of test results with a written description of the student's strengths and areas of need. Data from each assessment used, both formal and informal, are presented separately and then synthesized into an overall summary of strengths and needs across the areas in which the student was assessed.
6. *Summary*—This is a brief review of the student's present levels, strengths, and needs.
7. *Implications of the assessment findings*—This section includes recommendations for services, programs, curriculum, instruction, adaptations, and other supports for the student in the school, home, and community settings.
8. *Signatures*—The last section contains the signatures of persons preparing the report

A Strengths-Based Approach:

"When I receive formal written reports from my daughter's psychologist, speech therapist, physician, neurologist, or whomever, I always consider them a draft. The first thing I did was sit down with a yellow highlighter and highlight every positive comment about her. If the report was not at least 50% yellow, I made additions about my daughter's strengths and talents, and asked that they be inserted in the report." *(Sommerstein, 1994, as cited in Sommerstein and Smith, 2001, p. 194)*

THE ROLE OF TRADITIONAL NORM-REFERENCED TESTING IN THE RTI FRAMEWORK

Traditional norm-referenced testing continues to have a place in the RTI framework. Schools may choose to use NRTs (i.e., group achievement tests such as the California Achievement Test) as a screening measure to determine which students are struggling in various academic areas in order to identify the students who will receive intervention support. Generally, NRTs are not used as progress monitoring measures for RTI purposes, as these progress monitoring tools need to be quick, efficient, sensitive to student growth, and amenable to frequent use.

Although a multidisciplinary team assessment will not be implemented in an RTI model until after the student is found to be nonresponsive to increasingly intensive interventions, NRTs will continue to be used as part of the psychoeducational evaluation that is conducted to rule out various reasons for the lack of responsiveness (L. S. Fuchs & D. Fuchs, 2007). So a student would still be evaluated using cognitive, processing, memory, language, behavior, adaptive behavior, motor skills, and other measures to determine the nature of his or her disability.

End-of-Chapter Questions

1. When might school personnel need to use measures of central tendency? What information would these measures provide?
2. When might school personnel need to use measures of variability? What information would these measures provide?
3. What are some characteristics of a normal distribution of scores?
4. What is the SEM? Why is it important to understand this concept?
5. What is a confidence interval and why is it important in interpreting test results?
6. Explain the following measurement concepts:
   (a) Percentile ranks
   (b) Quartiles
   (c) Deciles
   (d) Standard scores
   (e) z-scores
   (f) T-scores
   (g) Deviation IQ scores
   (h) Normal curve equivalents
   (i) Stanines
   (j) Age equivalent
   (k) Grade equivalent
7. What are the limitations to using developmental scores with students above the age of 6 years?
8. What are three technical characteristics that must be reviewed when selecting a NRT?
9. What does it mean for a test to be reliable? Why should a test be reliable? Explain the different types of test reliability.
10. What is test validity? Why is it an important consideration in selecting a test? Explain the different types of validity.
11. What factors should one consider in reviewing the appropriateness of test norms for a particular sample?
12. How could an examiner prepare to administer and score an NRT?
13. How could the examiner prepare the testing environment so that the student has an opportunity for optimal performance on the test?
14. In what ways could the student be prepared so that he or she may demonstrate optimal performance on a test?
15. What are some guidelines for communicating assessment findings to students and family members? What are the sections of a written assessment report?
16. In what ways are NRTs used in an RTI framework?

References

American Educational Research Association, American Psychological Association, & National Council on Measurement in Education. (1999). *Standards for Educational and Psychological Testing* (2nd ed.). Washington, D.C.: American Educational Research Association.

Fuchs, L. S., & Fuchs, D. (2007). A model for implementing responsiveness to intervention. *Teaching Exceptional Children, 39,* 14–23.

International Reading Association. (1982). Misuse of grade equivalents: Resolution passed by the Delegates Assembly of the IRA, April 1981. *Reading Teacher,* January, p. 464.

Salvia, J., Ysseldyke, J., & Bolt, S. (2007). *Assessment in special and inclusive education* (10th ed.). Boston: Houghton Mifflin.

Sattler, J. (1992). *Assessment of children* (3rd ed.). San Diego, CA: Sattler Publications Inc.

Sommerstein, L. (1994, November). *Curricular adaptations/classroom modifications.* Paper presented at Launching the Dream Conference, Rochester, NY.

Sommerstein, L., & Smith, J. (2001). Summarizing and communicating assessment information: Empowering students and families. In S. Alper, D. L. Ryndak, & C. Schloss (Eds.), *Alternate assessment of students with disabilities in inclusive settings* (pp. 183–198). Needham Heights, MA: Allyn & Bacon.

Teele, A. (1996). Redesigning the educational system to enable all students to succeed. *NASSP Bulletin, 80*(583), 65–75.

Venn, J. (2007). *Assessing Students with Special Needs* (4th ed.). Upper Saddle River, NJ: Pearson.

Wechsler, D. (1944). *The measurement of adult intelligence* (3rd ed.). Baltimore: Williams & Wilkins.

Wechsler, D., Kaplan, E., Fein, D., Kramer, J., Morris, R., Delis, D., et al. (2004). Wechsler Intelligence Scale for Children-Fourth Education Integrated. San Antonio, TX: Psychological Corporation.

CHAPTER 5

Alternative and Informal Assessments

Ms. Laura Gambini is a veteran sixth-grade teacher who taught at the same school in an affluent school district for 20 years. Her family recently moved to a different state, and since the start of the school year she has taught a combined fifth- and sixth-grade inclusive class at an urban school with a high proportion of English learner students. A special education teacher coteaches with Laura for two class periods, but she is alone with her students for the rest of the school day. In many ways, Laura feels like a beginning teacher once again. She is excited about learning better ways to meet her students' needs. She knows that she must assess each of her students to learn more about their present skill levels and modify the school-adopted curriculum accordingly. Laura is reviewing multiple assessment techniques, both norm-referenced achievement tests such as the Wechsler Individual Achievement Test and informal teacher-made tests, to determine her students' performance levels.

Reflections on the Scenario

1. What are some factors that Laura must consider when selecting appropriate assessments for her students?
2. In what ways could conducting ongoing assessments affect the performance of students in Laura's class?
3. What are the different types of assessments that Laura could select from?
4. What are some reasons for her to use norm-referenced tests (NRTs) with her students?
5. What are some reasons for her to use criterion-referenced tests (CRTs) and other alternative assessments?

COUNCIL FOR EXCEPTIONAL CHILDREN (CEC) STANDARDS

This chapter addresses the following CEC standards (from Standard #8 Assessment):

ICC8K1—Basic terminology used in assessment.

ICC8K4—Use and limitations of assessment instruments.

ICC8S8—Evaluate instruction and monitor progress of individuals with exceptional learning needs.

ICC8S9—Develop or modify individualized assessment strategies.

ICC8S10—Create and maintain records.

GC8K1—Specialized terminology used in the assessment of individuals with disabilities.

GC8S2—Use exceptionality-specific assessment instruments with individuals with disabilities.

GC8S3—Select, adapt, and modify assessments to accommodate the unique abilities and needs of individuals with disabilities.

Historically, tests in the field of education have been classified as either *NRTs or CRTs*. As discussed in earlier chapters of this book, NRTs are administered, scored, and interpreted in standard ways, using objective criteria, and the scores are compared with those of a national normative sample. CRTs, on the other hand, are designed to assess whether a student has mastered specific instructional objectives as demonstrated by performance of specific tasks. A student's performance on a CRT is scored on the basis of predetermined performance criteria that are indicative of mastery of the task. The student's performance in comparison with that of age- or grade-level peers is of secondary importance. CRTs are a type of informal assessment and are widely used in schools, as they allow teachers to find out which skills need to be the focus of ongoing instruction.

Several years ago, another type of assessment, *minimum-competency tests (MCTs)*, was introduced into the educational lexicon as a result of the accountability movement in the field. MCTs assess whether students meet minimum standards for graduation from high school. State Departments of Education or local school districts identify minimum standards that a student must meet prior to graduation in the areas of reading, writing, math, and sometimes content areas such as science and social studies. Tests that assess these minimum standards are also known as high school exit exams. Many states require students to pass these tests in order to earn a high school diploma. For the most part, these tests are traditional standardized tests.

This chapter will focus on assessment tools other than traditional standardized tests. Often termed *informal* assessments, these measures are systematic, authentic, and student-centered ways of evaluating student learning. The use of the term informal in this context describes measures other than formal standardized tests. It does not imply that the measures are selected without deliberation, that they lack technical adequacy or instructional utility, or that they are administered in a haphazard fashion. Some of the informal and alternative assessments that will be explained in this chapter include performance assessments, curriculum-based assessments, portfolios, and ecological inventories. Observation and interviews as assessment tools are more fully discussed in Chapter 7 of this book.

THE NEED FOR INFORMAL OR ALTERNATIVE ASSESSMENTS

Traditional standardized testing, particularly in the domains of intelligence and achievement testing, have been the hallmarks of American public education for many years. They have been found to be expedient measures for classifying and sorting students, making placement decisions, determining individual student strengths and needs, and determining the teaching effectiveness of schools and teachers. Despite their widespread acceptance, standardized tests have been associated with many problems:

1. Standardized tests contain items that are relatively quick to administer and easy to score so that administrators can sort large numbers of students as efficiently as

possible (Bowers, 1989). Consequently, standardized tests use items such as multiple-choice, matching, and true and false questions that can be scored quickly. Important life skills that should be taught in schools, such as speaking and writing, are seldom assessed by these tests due to the high cost and large amount of time associated with constructing, administering, scoring, and interpreting measures that assess such skills.

2. Standardized testing also does not take into consideration individual student learning styles and differences, and consequently it does not level the playing field for students who require accommodations for their linguistic, cognitive, attention, or motor needs (Goh, 2004). Students requiring accommodations often are penalized on standardized measures.

3. There has been much controversy surrounding intelligence testing, which is based largely on the use of standardized NRTs (Donovan & Cross, 2002). Intelligence tests have played a critical role in the overrepresentation of minority students in special education and have been critiqued as being biased and discriminatory.

4. Standardized tests do not consistently and accurately monitor student learning and have limited utility in informing instructional interventions (Deno, 1985; Elliott & Fuchs, 1997). Standardized tests are lengthy and expensive to administer, so they cannot be used as frequent checks of student progress, and they are not designed to be sensitive measures of smaller gains in student performance. An added limitation is that standardized tests are not based on the local curriculum.

Traditional assessments generally rely on paper-and-pencil tasks in which there is one correct response to a question. In order to obtain credit, students are required to choose or generate a response that matches the correct response. In contrast with traditional assessments, *alternative assessments* are performance based and require students to generate their own response to a question or assigned task, often using higher-order thinking and problem-solving skills [National Capital Language Resource Center (NCLRC), 2008; North Central Regional Educational Laboratory (NCREL), 2008]. The learning that is assessed using alternative assessments is considered to be more meaningful, more authentic, and more directly applicable to real-world experiences. In addition, alternative assessments allow students to show what they can do, so they are particularly meaningful for English learners and students with various disabilities who find it difficult to demonstrate their knowledge and skills in standardized ways.

PERFORMANCE ASSESSMENTS

Performance assessment and authentic assessment are terms that are used synonymously with alternative assessment. The NCREL (2008) defines performance assessment as "the direct, systematic observation of an actual student performance and the rating of that performance according to previously established performance criteria." Performance assessments are considered to be valid indices of what students know and can do. Students complete authentic tasks that are similar to situations which they would encounter in real life (e.g., write a letter, solve a math problem, make an oral presentation on the stock market, design a shopping mall, create a software program).

Performance assessments fall along a continuum ranging from a single focused and well-defined task (e.g., writing a letter to the editor), to a prolonged task that calls for the integration of multiple skills (e.g., building a solar-powered car), to a collection of student work (e.g., an art portfolio taken to an audition) (Elliott & Fuchs, 1997). Trained evaluators rate student work using predetermined criteria. The quality of student work is rated on the basis of both the process and product.

Performance assessment stems from a constructivist approach to learning in which the student is viewed as an active participant in the construction of knowledge (Elliott & Fuchs, 1997). Generally, teachers present the task that they want students to complete together with the criteria that will be used in judging their performance. Students are partners in their learning and are able to evaluate their own learning and areas of improvement as they proceed.

Teacher-Made Tests and Quizzes

As the name suggests, these performance assessments are developed by teachers to determine a student's mastery of materials taught. Teachers use measures such as short-answer tests, multiple-choice quizzes, word problems, and essays to identify whether students have mastered the content taught. Teacher-made tests also are used for the purpose of grouping students for instruction.

Teacher-made tests generally are formatted to either require *recognition* responses in which students select the correct response from a list (e.g., true or false, matching, multiple choice), or *recall* responses in which the student generates an original response to a prompt either orally or in writing (e.g., short-answer tests, math problems, critical essays). Tests that require recognition responses usually are laborious and time consuming to develop but quick to score. Tests that require recall responses are quick to construct and allow for the assessment of higher-order thinking skills, but they are more difficult to score.

Because teachers are in control of selecting the items on teacher-made tests, they choose items that best monitor student gains in knowledge and skills that are founded on the content that was actually taught in the classroom. These tests generally are sensitive to small changes in student performance and provide rich data for teachers to plan instruction. A limitation of teacher-made tests, however, is that their reliability and validity are usually unknown. Teachers are not consistent about using similar types of test items or the same number of items when they construct tests, and they do not necessarily follow standard procedures when they administer and score these tests. It therefore is difficult to compare student scores on two different teacher-made tests. In order to compare student progress over time, it is essential for the teacher to follow consistent administration procedures, keep the time limit constant, and use consistent scoring criteria. Teacher-made tests can be universally designed such that they are amenable to needed modifications or accommodations for individual students (e.g., reading aloud test items, allowing students to type their responses, providing extended time to work, limiting the number of test items).

Curriculum-Based Evaluation (CBE)

CBE is a type of performance assessment that directly assesses a student's performance on their local school curriculum. CBE assesses how instructional interventions affect student performance (Jones, Southern, & Brigham, 1998).

Hall and Mengel (2002) describe four characteristics of CBE:

1. The student is assessed in the basic skills taught in the local school curriculum, rather than using commercially published materials.
2. CBE employs the use of *academic probes*, short assessment tools that can be quickly administered (in 1–5 minutes) and scored to assess a student's progress (e.g., reading passages, spelling lists, writing prompts, solving math problems).
3. CBE calls for frequent and repeated assessment of student performance using these techniques (usually every 2 weeks) for ongoing monitoring of student progress.
4. Resulting student data are graphically presented to demonstrate trends in student progress.

There are various types of CBE (e.g., curriculum-based assessment, curriculum-based measurement, precision teaching), all of which measure student skill development using instructional materials and curricula that teachers use in their classrooms (Deno, 2003). Although these techniques vary, they all involve the following steps: 1) careful review of the curriculum to identify skills that must be learned, the sequence in which these skills are learned, and appropriate instructional experiences to facilitate skill acquisition, 2) analysis of individual students' current levels of functioning to determine the starting point for instruction, 3) identification of target behaviors in observable and measurable terms and developing criteria for determining mastery, 4) development of assessment instruments that can be used frequently and that fit into the instructional routine, 5) collection and display of data, and 6) use of these data to make instructional decisions (Jones et al., 1998). Unlike the global data obtained from standardized tests, CBE tests yield fine-grained information on student performance that can be analyzed and used to tailor specific interventions.

Curriculum-based measurement (CBM) is a type of CBE that employs standardized procedures. CBM has been used widely in the schools and has been supported empirically in the research literature.

Curriculum-Based Measurement (CBM)

INTRODUCTION TO CBM   CBM has been defined as ". . . a set of specific measurement procedures that can be applied to quantify student performance in reading, written expression, spelling, and arithmetic" (Deno, 1989, p. 15). CBM adopts standardized procedures for developing academic probes from the local curricula, for administering and scoring these probes, and for graphically presenting these data such that they can be understood by teachers, students, parents, and other interested parties (Elliott & Fuchs, 1997). These probes are administered frequently, usually weekly or at least monthly, to get an index of student performance. The student's performance, in turn, is compared both with his or her own performance over time and with the performance of grade-level peers.

CBM was developed in the late 1970s and early 1980s by Stanley Deno and his colleague Phyllis Mirkin at the University of Minnesota Institute for Research on Learning Disabilities, as a result of their work with teachers on using assessment data to plan instruction. The goal was to develop an inexpensive, reliable, and valid measure that could be administered frequently and efficiently within the classroom instructional routine, to provide data on student progress (Deno, 1985, 2003).

Students are assessed repeatedly over the course of the school year using CBM probes that are drawn from the annual curriculum and are of equivalent difficulty levels. CBMs are reliable and valid measures that adopt a standard measurement task to assess student growth frequently in the major academic areas. For instance, CBM *oral reading fluency* calls for a student to read aloud a passage of text. An alternate reading fluency (and comprehension) task consists of administering maze passages that require the reader to select words which are deleted from the text of the passage. CBM *written expression* typically requires the student to write sentences in response to a story starter or picture. CBM *spelling* requires the student to spell a word or part of a word that is dictated by the examiner. Finally, CBM *math* requires the student to solve arithmetic problems, including single-skill problems (e.g., addition, subtraction) and multiple skill problems (e.g., mixed arithmetic problems that call for mixed operations). The number of digits, letters, or words correct in a specified time limit (usually a minute) are added to obtain the student's score (Deno, 2003). Students can earn partial credit on the tasks, which makes the scoring criteria sensitive to student growth. When these probes are administered frequently, the data provide a meaningful snapshot of the student's academic profile over time. Figure 5.1 demonstrates a sample academic profile for a student in reading using CBM data.

More than 25 years of empirical data exists on CBM. Research indicates that when teachers consistently use CBM data to drive instruction, students make academic gains

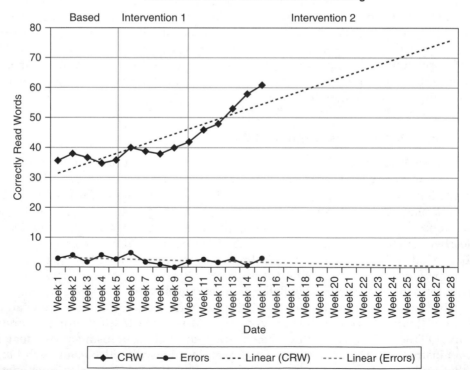

FIGURE 5.1 Student Reading Profile Using Curriculum-Based Measurement

and teachers make improved instructional decisions. These results have been proven for both dominant English speakers (Marston, 1989) and bilingual students (Baker & Good, 1995).

COMMON USES OF CBM   Deno (2003) identified some of these common uses of CBM:

1. *Enhance instruction for individuals and groups*—CBM can be used to track student performance over time and in response to interventions. As is shown in Figure 5.1, CBM allows the teacher to monitor student response to a range of interventions and modify instruction in response to student performance.

2. *Predict performance on high-stakes tests*—research indicates that a student's performance on CBM is highly correlated with performance on high-stakes standardized tests (Good, Simmons, & Kame'enui, 2001). Thus, CBM data allow early implementation of academic interventions without needing to wait for the scores on the high-stakes tests.

3. *Enhance instructional planning*—Teachers using CBM determine the performance levels of their students more accurately, and they make instructional changes with greater accuracy (Fuchs, Fuchs, & Hamlett, 1993).

4. *Develop local norms*—Normative performance for students taking the same CBM measures can be used to develop norms for an individual classroom, a grade level, a school, or even an entire district or state. Local norms allow teachers to compare the student's performance with that of other students in the same neighborhood who generally share similar educational experiences and life circumstances as the target student.

5. *Enhance communication*—Graphic displays of data are easily understood and enhance communication of student performance among the teacher, student, family members, and other parties.

6. *Screen students who are at risk for academic difficulties and track their progress*—CBM is commonly used as part of universal screening at school districts. It allows the school to determine reliably which students will benefit from academic interventions and allows teachers to track student responsiveness to preferral interventions.

7. *Reduce bias in assessment*—In a problem-solving or Response to Intervention (RTI) model, teachers are required to use objective, curriculum-based data to track interventions and make referrals on the basis of actual student performance. CBM measures help reduce bias in referrals for ongoing assessment.

8. *Serve as an accountability measure*—Student progress data using CBM can be used to evaluate the appropriateness of different instructional programs or inclusive models, and the data can be used either to justify their effectiveness or to make a case for the need for change.

9. *Accurately assess various populations of students*—While CBM measures originally were developed for use with elementary school students, research supports the use of these measures with secondary school students and in content areas like social studies and science (Muyskens & Marston, 2002). CBM also has been used effectively in assessing English language learners (Baker & Good, 1995), and it also can be used to predict success of early reading interventions with children in early childhood education programs (Good et al., 2001).

DIFFERENTIATION BETWEEN CBM AND MASTERY MEASUREMENT   Teachers use a variety of assessment data to instruct students effectively. When teachers want to know whether students have mastered a specific, usually isolated, skill that has been taught, they often use CRTs that measure students' mastery of the short-term instructional goal. If the student has mastered the skill, the teachers move on to teaching and then assessing the next skill in the instructional hierarchy. For instance, when using mastery measurement teachers test for mastery of multidigit addition with regrouping before introducing multiplication of 2-digit numbers by 2-digit numbers, a skill that requires the student to regroup correctly. An example of a mastery measure in reading would be testing students on their ability to read word families that end with "an." Different skills are assessed using a mastery measurement model at different times of the year. Mastery measures provide diagnostic data on whether the specific skill has been met, and if it has not been met, they indicate the types of errors the student is making. These data are useful in informing the teacher about remedial instruction and helping them decide when to reteach a skill and when to move ahead with the curriculum.

CBM, on the other hand, assesses a student's functioning in broad academic domains on the basis of long-term instructional goals that sample various skills covered in the annual curriculum. The student may have mastered some skills, may be in the process of acquiring some skills, may be gaining fluency with other skills, may have forgotten other skills, and may not have been introduced to a final group of skills. Consequently, CBM allows the teacher to review scores that were obtained at different times in the year to determine the rate at which a student makes gains in the academic domain.

TYPES OF CBM   There are two types of CBMs: a general outcomes measure and a skills-based measure. A *general outcomes measure* holistically samples multiple skills and target behaviors in a single assessment (Hosp, Hosp, & Howell, 2007). An oral reading fluency measure is a good example of a general outcomes measure because a student needs to use multiple skills, including letter recognition, phonemic awareness, blending, decoding, vocabulary, and content comprehension to read fluently. A *single skills measure*, on the other hand, assesses a group of skills in an academic domain such as math computation, where it is not possible to monitor progress on multiple skills using an overarching capstone task. For instance, a single skills measure may monitor progress on two discrete skills of addition and subtraction, each of which must be measured directly. Such a measure would include items that involve addition facts, addition with regrouping, double-digit addition with regrouping, subtraction facts, and subtraction with borrowing. These items would be randomly presented in the probe, rather than according to an instructional hierarchy.

ADVANTAGES OF CBM   CBM has several advantages over traditional standardized tests and other informal measures of achievement:

1. *Improved communication between teacher, student and parent*—Data on a student's performance are easily interpreted and used by the teacher in making educational decisions. Trends in student performance can be easily understood using data graphs.
2. *Increased sensitivity to student growth*—CBM measures are sensitive to small changes in student performance, thereby allowing the teacher to make immediate

instructional changes in response to a student's growth trends. For instance, the teacher could increase the intensity of a reading intervention when a student's performance seems to be declining or move the student to a more challenging curriculum when he or she shows a steep incline in performance beyond the target objective.

3. *Technical adequacy*—Research data demonstrate the reliability and validity of CBM. Data obtained through CBM correlate with data obtained from NRTs.
4. *Cost effectiveness*—CBM probes are relatively inexpensive to prepare, and the costs in terms of labor and materials are significantly lower than those of NRTs.
5. *Ability to measure the breadth of knowledge and skills gained*—CBM samples the annual curriculum and probes include items that span the entire curriculum. Consequently, an examiner can assess the retention and generalization of skills taught using CBM.
6. *Ability to measure learning regardless of teaching approach*—CBM does not assess skills taught according to a specific instructional hierarchy. Consequently, it can be used to monitor progress regardless of the type of curriculum or instructional approach used.

DEVELOPMENT, ADMINISTRATION, SCORING, AND INTERPRETATION OF CBM The following steps and directions have been adapted from Jim Wright's (2008) manual for teachers on CBM. For detailed directions on the steps in developing, administrating, and scoring CBM the reader is referred to the free downloadable resources at CBM Warehouse at http://www.interventioncentral.org/index.php/cbm-warehouse.

1. *Identify the domain to be assessed*—Most research in CBMs is in the areas of reading, math, writing, and spelling.
2. *Identify a measurement pool of items to be selected*—Items are drawn from instructional materials to be covered during the year. For reading assessment, passages are randomly selected. For spelling assessment, words are selected from various instructional units covered during the year.
3. *Prepare the CBM probes*—The teacher randomly selects items from the item pool to develop probes of equivalent difficulty for administration at different times of the year. (See Boxes 5.1–5.4 for administration of CBM in different areas.)
4. *Administer the probes*—Follow consistent administration criteria in terms of giving directions, arranging the testing setting, allowing students time to take the test, choosing scoring criteria, etc.
5. *Use consistent scoring criteria*—Scoring criteria are set for different types of skills. For instance, a reading score is composed of words read correct in a minute, a math score of digits correct in a minute, a written expression score of written words per minute, and a spelling score of correct letter sequence per minute.

GRAPHING CBM SCORES CBM data is graphed so that it can be interpreted easily. Graphing can be done by hand or using a computer. The following guidelines will assist in graphing CBM data:

1. Clearly label the graph with the student's name, grade, domain being monitored, specific skill being monitored, dates when probes were administered, and

BOX 5.1

Directions for Administering and Scoring CBM in Reading

Materials needed: a teacher copy of the passage to be read (that has cumulative frequencies of the number of words on each line of the passage to the right side of the page), a student copy of the passage, a stopwatch, and a pencil to record errors.

Directions: "When I say begin, start reading aloud from the top of this page and read across the page. You want to read each word. If you come to a word you don't know, I will tell you what it is. Try to read as well as you can."

Begin the stopwatch and give the student a minute to read aloud. Records all errors made by drawing a line through the incorrectly read word. Hesitations lasting longer than 3 seconds are marked as errors; in these cases, provide the word. After 1 minute has passed, record the point that the student has reached and stop administering the reading probe. Administer three reading probes following the same procedures and record the scores. Use the median fluency score at each administration when plotting the student's progress graph.

Scoring: Use the total number of correctly read words (crw) in a minute for scoring. Mispronunciations, substitutions (e.g., "saw" for "was"), omissions, and reversing word pairs (e.g., reading "more are coming" as "coming are more") are counted as errors.

BOX 5.2

Directions for Administering and Scoring CBM in Writing

Materials needed: a story starter, a stopwatch, pencil, and paper to write on.

Sample story starters: *It was a hot summer night and I could not fall asleep. Suddenly, I heard a thumping sound on the roof . . .*

It was the last day of school and everyone was excited about the upcoming party. The students...

I was playing in the park when . . .

Directions: "I want you to write a story. I will read you a sentence first and then you will write a short story about what happens. You will have 1 minute to think about the story and then 3 minutes to write. Try to write as much about the story as you can. If you don't know how to spell a word, you should guess. "

Begin the stopwatch and give the student a minute to think about the story. After the minute, repeat the story starter and then tell the student to pick up his or her pencil and start writing. At the end of 3 minutes, tell the student to stop writing.

Scoring: You may use one of several scoring criteria, but be consistent about using the same criteria over time. Here are four possible options for scoring:

1. ***Count total words written***—A cluster of words separated by a space is considered to be a word. Disregard misspellings and reversals in writing. Numbers or other characters are not counted as words. Hyphenated words are counted as one word.

2. ***Count total words spelled correctly***—Proper nouns must be capitalized. Abbreviations (e.g., Dr., Mrs.) are counted as words. If a word is spelled correctly but not correctly capitalized, include it in the count (e.g., **m**y mother went to India).

3. ***Count total letters written***—Follow the same criteria as in counting total words written. Include letters in misspelled words in the count.

4. ***Count correct word sequences***—A word sequence is two adjacent correctly spelled and grammatically correct words, separated by the appropriate punctuation, or a word and a punctuation mark. Count the first word of the sentence as a word sequence. Do not include numerals in the word count. For example, the following sentence contains seven correct word sequences: ^ My ^ mother ^ wears ^ a ^ red ^ dress^.

BOX 5.3

Directions for Administering and Scoring CBM in Math

Materials needed: student copy of probes, stopwatch, and pencils.

Directions: "You have some sheets of math problems in front of you. Some of the problems are addition, some are subtraction, some are multiplication, and some are division. [Modify this statement according to the type of probe.] Look at the problem carefully before you answer it. When I say begin, turn the sheets over and start solving the problems. Start with the first problem on the left top row and work across the page to the next row. If you come across a problem you don't know, make an X over it, and move on to the next problem."

Tell the student to begin and start the stopwatch. Tell him or her to stop at the end of 2 minutes.

Scoring: Score according to the number of correct digits—the correct digit in the correct place is counted as correct. Numerals written reversed are counted as correct. Students get full points for a problem for which they got the answer correct, even if they do not show the work. Give credit for correct digits in a problem that the student may have started but then crossed out. Carry-over digits are not counted.

unit of measurement [e.g., words correct per minute (wcm), digits correct per minute (dcm)].

2. The date when each probe is administered is recorded on the *x*-axis (horizontal axis), and the unit of measurement is plotted on the *y*-axis (vertical axis). Ideally, data are collected weekly or biweekly and plotted at these intervals on the graph in order to make tier decisions in an RTI model.

BOX 5.4

Directions for Administering and Scoring CBM in Spelling

Materials needed: stopwatch, pencils, lined paper, and word list.

Directions: "I am going to read some words to you. Write the words on the sheet in front of you, starting with the first word on the first line, second word on the second line, and so on. You will have 7 seconds to write each word, and then I will go on to the next word. Please go on to the next word even if you did not hear me or do not know how to spell a word."

Say the first word and then start timing, calling out the second word after 7 seconds. Repeat each word twice and use homonyms in a sentence (e.g., I tied my long *hair* in a braid). Do not respond to student questions. Continue dictating words at this rate for 2 minutes (about 17 words).

Scoring: Mark a ^ for each correct letter sequence, including before the first letter and after the last letter in a word. Letter reversals are viewed as errors. Proper nouns must be capitalized to be viewed as correct. For example, the correctly spelled word "hello" is marked as ^ h ^ e ^ l ^ l ^ o ^ = 6 correct letter sequences. If it is spelled "helow," it is marked as ^ h ^ e ^ l o w = 3 correct letter sequences.

3. Develop a goal line that joins two points on the graph: the median score for the baseline data points and the end-of-year target performance goal. The target performance goal is usually a benchmark score that is based on the aggregated performance of students at the same grade level in each academic domain at the end of the year. National normative target performance data for oral reading fluency, writing, and math can be used to assist in developing the goal line. Norms for reading fluency may be downloaded at http://www.interventioncentral.org/index.php/cbm-warehouse.
4. Mark any changes in intervention using a vertical line. Clearly mark the baseline phase, separate that from the first intervention, and separate that from the second intervention.

Several computerized templates can assist in graphing CBM data. CBM Warehouse is a free online resource that is part of Intervention Central and that includes Microsoft Excel templates for graphing data and free software such as ChartDog to assist with graphing. See http://www.interventioncentral.org/index.php/cbm-warehouse

USING CBM GRAPHS FOR DECISION MAKING   The examiner reviews the student's progress data to make instructional changes. In Figure 5.2, Intervention 1 did not prove to be effective, so the examiner introduced a new intervention to promote math skills in Week 10. To determine the student's trajectory of growth, the examiner looks at the four most recent data points to make one of the following decisions:

1. If scores are above the goal line, the end-of-year goal needs to be increased.
2. If scores are below the goal line, the student's instructional program needs to be revised.
3. If the trend line and goal line are pretty much the same, no changes are needed.

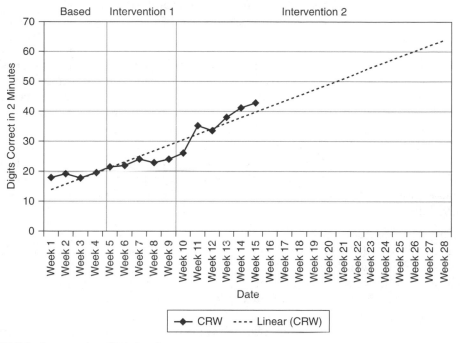

FIGURE 5.2 Interpreting CBM Graphs

In an RTI model, at the end of 8–10 weeks of intervention, trends in student data are closely examined to make tier decisions. Students who demonstrate that they meet their end-of-benchmark-period performance goal and who are making progress at an adequate rate may be moved out of Tier II interventions, as they have caught up to and are performing similarly to their grade-level peers. But students who are making progress at a slower rate, and who, while approaching, have not yet met their benchmark goals, may benefit from a second round of Tier II interventions. Other students may be demonstrating minimal growth and might need to receive more intensive, Tier III interventions or even receive a special education referral.

COMMERCIALLY AVAILABLE CBM PROBES The term CBM implies that teachers use the local school curriculum to develop probes, but the task of developing multiple sets of probes of equivalent difficulty is fairly time consuming and consequently is a disincentive for teachers. Research evidence suggests that equally accurate and meaningful data can be obtained using standardized CBM probes, such as the dynamic Indicators of Basic Early Literacy Skills (DIBELS), or other computerized CBM systems, such as AIMSweb or the Monitoring Basic Skills Progress software (Fuchs, Hamlett, & Fuchs, 1999). The National Center on Response to Intervention (NCRTI) website provides independent evaluations of the psychometric qualities and other features of various commercially available progress-monitoring tools, including the DIBELS and AIMSweb tools. The NCRTI is a technical assistance and dissemination center funded by the U.S. Department of Education, Office of Special Education Programs, and the website is http://www.rti4success.org/chart/progressMonitoring/progressmonitoringtoolschart.htm

Two frequently used commercially available CBM probes will be featured next: DIBELS and AIMSweb.

DIBELS   Roland Good and Ruth Kaminski at the University of Oregon developed DIBELS as a CBM of early literacy skills. DIBELS is composed of reliable and valid, brief, 1-minute probes in the area of early literacy, which can be downloaded free of cost from their website (http://dibels.uoregon.edu). These probes are best suited for children from kindergarten to sixth grade and have been widely used and empirically supported with this population. DIBELS probes parallel the five domains of literacy as defined by the National Institute of Child Health and Human Development's *National Reading Panel* (2000): phonological awareness, alphabetical principle, fluency, vocabulary, and comprehension. The following measures of the DIBELS are widely used to assess early literacy skills:

1. Phonological Awareness
   a. Initial Sound Fluency (assesses and monitors progress in identification of initial sounds in a word—e.g., *m* for mouse)
   b. Phonemic Segmentation Fluency (assesses and monitors progress in the production of individual sounds in a word—e.g., b-a-t=bat)
2. Alphabetical Principle
   Nonsense Word Fluency (assesses and monitors progress in letter sound correspondence and the ability to blend sounds to form nonsense words—e.g., m-e-k=mek)
3. Fluency in Connected Text
   Oral Reading Fluency (assesses and monitors progress in fluency in reading grade-level text).
4. Vocabulary
   Vocabulary is assessed through the Word Use Fluency measure, in which a word is called out loud by the administrator and the student uses that word accurately in a sentence or phrase that he or she speaks aloud.
5. Comprehension
   Comprehension has been found to be highly correlated with oral reading fluency and is measured by using the Oral Reading Fluency measure. An additional measure of comprehension is the Retell Fluency measure, in which the student retells the passage that he or she just read.

AIMSWEB   Developed by Dr. Mark Shinn and his associates, AIMSweb is a formative assessment system that is composed of CBM assessment probes in the areas of early literacy, reading, early numeracy, mathematics, spelling, and written expression, as well as a data management system that allows teachers and administrators to record student data on these probes, monitor progress over time, and generate reports on student progress. Probes are applicable for students in grades kindergarten through eighth grade. Reading and early literacy probes are available in both English and Spanish. AIMSweb supports the DIBELS probes as well, and it is possible to use the AIMSweb data manager with DIBELs probes. AIMSweb also offers a palm link software feature that allows the CBM probes to be administered and scored using PDA devices and electronically uploaded to the data manager. More information about AIMSweb is available at http://www.aimsweb.com/.

PORTFOLIO ASSESSMENT

Portfolios have been widely used for academic and professional purposes, particularly in specialized disciplines, such as art, architecture, and writing. Portfolio assessment is a dynamic process in which students and teachers jointly select samples of student work that demonstrate the progress made by the student over a period (Hancock, 1994). A review of the portfolio indicates the student's strengths and need areas.

Portfolios are a lot more than a random collection of student work samples. These work samples are purposefully selected in order to answer assessment questions and make ongoing instructional decisions. For instance, a language arts portfolio could include audio samples of reading fluency, sample pages from a writing journal, and sample spelling tests to determine the student's progress in reading, writing, and spelling multisyllabic words. Student participation in item selection and self-reflection is paramount in the portfolio assessment process and distinguishes portfolios from other student records (e.g., cumulative records). A portfolio includes a range of items, such as videos, audio samples of student reading, quizzes, diary entries, art work, photographs, rubrics, work logs, self-assessments, and peer and teacher comments on work completed.

Determining the Purpose and Contents of the Portfolio

The teacher generally determines the purpose of the portfolio and the type of assessment questions that the portfolio will be designed to answer. The contents of the portfolio are then identified accordingly. Portfolios are used for a wide variety of reasons, some of which are discussed here.

A *process portfolio* includes works in progress and serves as a meaningful progress monitoring tool to review a student's development in an area such as writing or math over a period of time. The teacher can modify instruction on the basis of included student artifacts, and the student can review these artifacts to reflect on his or her growth. A *product portfolio* includes completed work that is indicative of the student's typical skills across different areas. It serves as a valuable tool to facilitate communication about a student's performance between school and home and between teachers from one to the next grade level. A *celebratory or showcase portfolio* includes completed works that represent the student's finest work. Such a portfolio is proudly displayed at parent–teacher meetings, job interviews, and other forums, and students are given a fair amount of autonomy in selecting items for inclusion in these portfolios. *Accountability portfolios* have been used by states such as Vermont and Kentucky as part of their statewide competency assessment system (the alternate assessment system to track the progress made by students with significant disabilities over the course of the year).

Portfolios could be contained in a variety of formats. Hard-copy portfolios could be contained in a three-ring binder, a closable container, plastic crate, or other format. *Electronic portfolios* allow a student to use technology to present their work to a wider audience. Electronic portfolios are also called digital portfolios or e-portfolios, and may be saved to a CD or posted to a website. An e-portfolio is an electronic record of the student's achievements and, like other types of portfolios, facilitates self-reflection and artistic expression. The creation of the e-portfolio also displays students' advanced technological skills, such as graphic design, blogs, multimedia presentations, and hyperlinks. An e-portfolio is typically managed by the student and can be readily updated and used for multiple purposes.

Portfolio Evaluation Procedures

A portfolio includes multiple work samples to allow the reviewer to evaluate a student's performance. A well-organized portfolio that is amenable to easy review and evaluation is a meaningful and feasible assessment tool. A table of contents allows the reviewer to navigate the portfolio contents. The portfolio may be organized by subject area (e.g., reading samples followed by writing samples), or chronologically by month in the school year. Having a standardized set of requirements for what is to be included in a portfolio makes it easier for teachers to develop scoring criteria for evaluating the portfolio. See a sample list of requirements in Figure 5.3.

SCORING RUBRICS   Rubrics are scoring guidelines that allow raters to evaluate various performance assessments, including portfolios, according to a set of predetermined scoring criteria. Using rubrics allows the rater to make fair, objective, and informed judgments regarding the students' performance. Training more than one rater to use the same rubric can minimize bias in ratings and increase interrater reliability. In order to further reduce subjectivity in ratings, raters may conduct blind reviews of portfolios of students who attend a different class or even a different school than the one at which they teach.

There are several advantages of using scoring rubrics:

1. Rubrics enhance reliability in scoring. Clear scoring criteria allow more than one rater to consistently evaluate the product.
2. Rubrics enhance validity in scoring. When scoring criteria on the rubrics are developed by consensus from experts in the content domain, the validity of the performance assessment is enhanced.
3. Rubrics enhance effective communication. Rubrics communicate to both the student completing the task and the rater evaluating the task the criteria that will be used in evaluating the final product. Parents and other stakeholders also may have access to the rubric that informs them about how their students' work was rated.

Rubrics used to score portfolios could be holistic or analytic (Venn, 2007). A *holistic rubric* requires the reviewer to look at the portfolio in its totality and generate an overall rating for the portfolio. An *analytic rubric* is more detailed and involves rating various components of the portfolio and using these ratings to arrive at an overall rating of the portfolio. Sample holistic and analytic rubrics are included in Figure 5.4.

Some online resources for developing rubrics:

Rubistar at *http://rubistar.4teachers.org/index.php*

Teachnology.com's Teacher Rubric Makers at *http://www.teach-nology.com/web_tools/rubrics/*

Kathy Schrock's Guide for Educators: Assessment Rubrics at *http://school.discoveryeducation. com/schrockguide/assess.html*

Elementary School Reading Portfolio

Content	Date included	Date Reviewed	Comments
List of books read Teacher observation log Audiotape of student reading Conference forms Formal and informal test results			

Elementary School Writing Portfolio

Content	Date included	Date Reviewed	Comments
First piece of writing in the year Teacher observation log Writing samples: personal narrative, exposition, letter, essay, report, poem Formal and informal test results			

High School Alternate Assessment Portfolio

Content	Date included	Date Reviewed	Comments
Daily Routine—Two completed observations using individualized checklist with student engaging in daily routine Reading—Audiotape of student reading at instructional level at three times in the year Writing samples—Three samples from different times in the year Math—Math problem-solving checklists completed three times in the year based on observation of student using functional math skills Communication—Video sample of authentic communication exchange; list of augmentative communication devices used, if applicable social-emotional—Observation log of student engaging in social relations with peers and adults Vocational—Task analysis with completed observation of student performing a job task Self-assessment—Narrative reflection (could be a drawing or written or dictated response) of student's accomplishments over the year Parent–teacher—Student communication log with sample entries from daily log included			

FIGURE 5.3 Portfolio Content Selection Criteria

Holistic Writing Rubric

Rating	Criteria
5	Clear organization—definite introduction, body, and conclusion Varied and descriptive vocabulary Smooth transition between ideas Correct grammar and spelling Engaging writing
4	Logical organization of ideas Adequate and accurate use of vocabulary Fair transition of ideas Some grammar and spelling errors but none that detracts from meaning
3	Mostly organized response—sometimes difficult to follow Simple vocabulary, accurate use Transition between thoughts is mostly missing Several grammatical and spelling errors Writing style affects meaning
2	No coherence in writing—series of sentences that often do not flow together Repetitive vocabulary, not always used accurately Grammatical and spelling errors throughout response Meaning not clear
1	Jumbled incomplete sentences Lots of grammatical and spelling errors Meaning not coherent
0	No response

Analytic Rubric for Oral Presentation

Criteria	4 points	3 points	2 points	1 point
Organization	Logical and engaging sequence	Logical sequence	Some jumping around between thoughts	Unclear sequence
Content	Sound knowledge of topic, good answers to questions	Fair knowledge of topic, most questions answered	Not comfortable with topic, answers only very basic questions	Seems unfamiliar with topic, not able to address questions
Presentation	Appealing graphics, good eye contact, engaging	Relevant graphics, mostly gives eye contact	Minimal graphics, minimal eye contact, reads from notes	No graphics, reads from notes, no eye contact
Elocution	Clear voice and articulation	Clear voice, some articulation errors	Soft, unsure of self	Difficult to hear, unclear diction

FIGURE 5.4 Sample Portfolio Grading Rubrics

Student's Name: Julio Sepulveda

Teacher and Grade: Mrs. Roberts, Grade 2

Date of Review: June 14, 2010

	I used to:	Now I can:
Writing	Not write clearly Not use correct punctuation Use big letters	Read my writing Use capitals and commas Use big and small letters
Spelling	Guess Give up	Sound out the word Write neater

Reading
 	
question
	Read slowly
	Not stop or ask a
	    at a full stop
	Get angry
		Read faster
		Read so it sounds like I am talking I stop
		
		Use the tricks my teacher taught me to
		    sound out words

I have improved the most in:

Sounding out words, stopping and thinking about what I am reading, not getting angry, trying harder

I still need to work on:

My handwriting

FIGURE 5.5 Sample Student Reflection on Portfolio

Portfolio Conferences

Given the importance of student participation in the portfolio process, it is evident that ongoing conferences between students and teachers are a key component of developing portfolios. The conference is a venue for students to engage in guided reflection on their learning goals and their progress toward meeting these goals, on the basis of the evidence included in their portfolio. It is recommended that the teacher hold portfolio conferences with each student four times during the school year. These meetings can be time consuming and difficult to schedule. In order to make the process more efficient, teachers could meet with a small group of students at the same time or could assign students a task that requires them to produce a written reflection on their portfolios prior to meeting with the teacher (Venn, 2007). Figure 5.5 shows a sample student reflection on his portfolio.

Guidelines to Using Portfolios

There are several benefits to using portfolios. Portfolios review student performance over time using authentic measures. Students play a key role in the portfolio assessment process, which in turn increases their self-esteem and ownership of their learning. Data from portfolios are fairly intuitive to comprehend and facilitate communication about a student's performance between school and home.

Despite these benefits, some experts have questioned the use of portfolios in education (Barrett, 2007; Gearhart & Herman, 1998; Herman & Winters, 1994). First, there are insufficient data on the technical qualities of using this technique. Portfolio assessment is time consuming and it is cumbersome to develop rubrics and to train raters to use them accurately. Users are urged to limit educational decision making that is based on portfolio assessment to decisions at the individual student level and not to use this tool to make large-scale accountability decisions. Portfolios are not suited for decisions that call for comparison of a particular student with age peers (e.g., when determining a student's eligibility for special education).

The following are recommended guidelines for using portfolio assessment (Barrett, 2007; Gallagher, 1998; Salvia, Ysseldyke, & Bolt, 2007):

1. *Identify and clearly state the purpose for the portfolio*—Portfolio contents, scoring criteria, rubrics, and so on will be determined on the basis of this expressed purpose. This purpose needs to be shared with the students, parents, and others who review the student portfolio.
2. *Be sure that portfolio content aligns with the articulated purpose of the portfolio*—There should be sufficient work samples to provide evidence of the student's performance. Items included should be relevant and meaningful.
3. *Ensure student participation in the selection, review, and reflection components of the portfolio*—Encourage maximum student participation in and ownership of the process, according to the student's developmental level. It is also important for students to receive feedback on their reflections on their growth.
4. *Include narrative explanations for why items were included in the portfolio*—These explanations increase their alignment with the learning goals and facilitate portfolio review and self-reflection.
5. *Scores and grades on individual artifacts are not a required component of portfolio assessment*—Scores on individual assignments can bias the reviewer, particularly if holistic scoring criteria are used.
6. *Have clear scoring criteria and train raters*—Clear scoring criteria reduce bias and increase objectivity. Using raters who are trained in this technique increases the credibility of the portfolio data.

ECOLOGICAL ASSESSMENTS

A student's learning is influenced by many variables that relate to the student, the teacher, and the learning environment. Students are idiosyncratic, and they respond in varied ways to the same teacher and the same instructional style. Most assessment techniques tend to focus on student-specific variables, but it is clear that the instructional context and learning environment must also be examined, and if necessary altered, to ensure optimal learning.

Observing the Classroom Environment

Ecological assessments allow school personnel to observe environmental variables that affect a student's performance within the context of the authentic learning environment (Haney & Cavallaro, 1996). These assessments allow team members to identify the learning environments within which a student interacts and to assess the individual's strengths and needs within these contexts for the purpose of planning instructional interventions. Observations using checklists, rating scales, and ecological inventories are some assessment techniques that are used in examining the relationship between students and their instructional environment.

Ecobehavioral Assessment

Ecobehavioral assessment is a technique that analyzes a multitude of variables which have an impact on the teaching and learning that occurs in a classroom. Among these variables are student behavior, teacher behavior, classroom rules, instructional time, questioning techniques, instructional tasks and strategies, peer groupings, and social relationships. Salvia, Ysseldyke, and Bolt define ecobehavioral assessment as "educational assessment to describe observations of functional relationships between student behavior and its ecological context" (2007, p. 216). Identifying these relationships allows teachers to reflect on their classroom environment and make modifications in order to positively affect student learning.

Greenwood, Carta, Delquadri, Arragea-Meyer, Utley and their colleagues at the Juniper Gardens Children's Project in Kansas developed one of the first ecobehavioral assessments, the Code for Instructional Structure and Student Academic Response (CISSAR; Stanley & Greenwood, 1981). Using observations by trained coders, CISSAR collects data on student behaviors (e.g., student response to an academic task, competing responses such as distraction or inappropriate talk), teacher behaviors (e.g., teacher position in the classroom, teacher actions) and the classroom ecology (e.g., class grouping, type of task, instructional activity).

Another type of assessment, the Ecobehavioral Assessment System Software (EBASS; Greenwood, Carta, Kamps, & Delquadri, 1995) is based on a similar premise as CISSAR. EBASS allows raters to conduct systematic classroom observations using their laptop computer or handheld device.

Another ecobehavioral assessment that investigates variables in the school and home environments that affect student learning is the Functional Assessment of Academic Behavior (FAAB; Ysseldyke & Christenson, 2002). FAAB uses classroom observation, interviews, and checklists with the target student, parents, and teachers to collect data on student needs and available supports so that instructional interventions may be planned on the basis of these data.

Ecological Inventories

Ecological inventories are a commonly used ecological assessment tool. Lou Brown and his colleagues developed ecological inventories in 1979 as an informal assessment of the different domains within which an individual functions and the skills required to be proficient in those domains. The five domains in which humans typically interact are domestic, vocational, school, community, and leisure (Brown & Snell, 2000). An ecological inventory is an individualized assessment that investigates the skills which a student needs to develop in order to be functional in current and future environments within these life domains. Skills are determined through observation and interview with meaningful others in the student's life. Students are then provided instruction in areas of discrepancy and provided with supports and environmental modifications as needed so that they are better equipped to become fully functional in current and/or future learning environments. Skills that are found to be lacking in multiple domains, and those that are more critical for the individual's safety and physiological needs, are considered to be higher priority and are taught first.

Brown et al. (1979) identified five stages in developing an ecological inventory:

1. *Identify the curricular domains*—These could be one or more of the five domains listed, depending on relevance to the student. As an example, let us consider Mary, a 17-year-old student with Down syndrome who has several individualized education program goals in the "domestic" domain with a focus on independent living skills. An ecological inventory for Mary is presented in Figure 5.6.

Student: Mary VanderMeer

Environment: Home Kitchen

Date: March 12, 2010

Informants: Parents, teacher, grandmother, Mary

Methods: Interview and observation

Subenvironments/ Activities: Cooking and Cleaning in kitchen	Performance Level			Component Skills			Comments
	Assistance on all steps	Some assistance	Independent	Begins task	Selects required materials	Asks for help	
Preparation to cook							
• Wash hands			X	X			
• Gather ingredients	X					X	
• Gather needed utensils		X				X	
Cooking							
• Wash ingredients		X			X		Has difficulty with fine motor control
• Measure		X			X		
• Peel	X					X	
• Cut	X					X	
• Pour		X		X			
• Stir			X	X			
Clean up							
• Wash dishes		X		X			Familiar with clean up
• Wipe up area			X	X	X		

FIGURE 5.6 Sample Ecological Inventory for Mary (adapted from Brown & Snell, 2000)

2. *Identify and investigate current and future environments within the domain*—Use multiple informants and sources of data to arrive at the various environments within which a student currently lives, works, studies, and plays, and to determine those environments that they will likely find themselves in the future. For instance, Mary is in a high school transition program, and relevant environments for her are her home, school, recreation center, and grandmother's house. A future environment for her will be a job site. The environment of focus for Mary is the home.

3. *Identify subenvironments for each relevant environment*—Subenvironments are specific locations within the broader environment of focus. It is important to prioritize which of the subenvironments should be tackled first (e.g., the focus for Mary is assuming greater independence in the kitchen).

4. *Identify key activities for each subenvironment*—Determine specific activities in which the student will be required to participate within the selected subenvironment. Student preferences, situational demands, parental preferences, and other factors are considered in determining these key activities. In Mary's case, the focus is her preparation of her own meals in her kitchen at home.

5. *Identify the skills needed to perform each activity*—Generally activities are analyzed into their component steps and the student is asked to complete the activity. The student is taught whatever steps in which he or she was not proficient when observed. In Mary's case, she is being assessed (and instructed) on how well she is able to prepare to cook, cook her meal, and then clean up after herself.

Ecological inventories can be used to identify student needs and to plan instruction across domains and skills. Conducting interviews with multiple informants and using observations of the student in the current or future environment allow the professional to obtain an accurate picture of the student's skills and level of support needed.

ALTERNATIVE ASSESSMENT IN AN RTI MODEL

The RTI model is built on the premise that ongoing screening and assessment tools are in place to identify a student's performance levels and to determine which students need assistance in order to keep up with their peers. The performance assessments described in this chapter can be used to collect data on a student's performance and guide ongoing instructional planning. Portfolio assessments allow students to reflect on their own learning and share it with others. Ecobehavioral assessments help the teacher reflect on his or her teaching and show ways to modify the instructional environment to enhance student outcomes.

Progress monitoring using authentic measures is a key component of RTI. CBM is the preferred progress monitoring tool in an RTI model, primarily due to its strong technical qualities, ease and efficiency of administration, sensitivity to student progress, and ability to ascertain maintenance of skills learned over the course of the school year. CBM data are easy to graph and share with other team members, which facilitates decision making regarding the effectiveness of the instruction and intervention being provided. Trends in student data can be reviewed to determine whether a student is making adequate progress or needs more intensive interventions.

End-of-Chapter Questions

1. Why have standardized tests been criticized over the years? How do alternative assessments address some of these criticisms?
2. Explain the concept of alternative assessment. Give some examples.
3. What is meant by performance assessment? Describe some of the characteristics of these assessments.
4. Discuss the following assessment techniques:
   (a) Teacher-made tests
   (b) CBE
   (c) CBM
   (d) Portfolios
   (e) Ecological inventories
5. Explain the defining characteristics of CBE.
6. Describe the basic process of using CBM. What are its relative merits compared with other alternative and standardized measures?
7. What are some common uses of CBM?
8. When would teachers use a mastery measurement approach to assessment? Contrast such an approach with CBM and explain how they differ.

9. What are the various types of CBM?
10. What is the DIBELS?
11. What are some different reasons that students are asked to maintain educational portfolios? Discuss some of the common types of portfolios.
12. Why are scoring rubrics used in rating portfolios? Discuss.
13. Distinguish between holistic and analytic scoring rubrics used in rating a portfolio.
14. Why is it important to have regular student–teacher conferences when adopting a portfolio assessment system?
15. What are some guiding steps when using portfolio assessment?
16. Justify the importance of assessing the learning environment. What techniques are used in assessing environmental variables at school?
17. What is an ecobehavioral assessment? Describe some tools that can be used for this purpose.
18. Briefly discuss the process of conducting an ecological inventory.

References

Baker, S., & Good, R. H. (1995). Curriculum-based measurement of English reading with bilingual Hispanic students: A validation study with second grade students. *School Psychology Review, 24,* 561–578.

Barrett, H. S. (2007). Researching electronic portfolios and learner engagement: The REFLECT initiative. *Journal of Adolescent and Adult Literacy, 50*(6), 438–448.

Bowers, B. (1989). Alternatives to standardized educational assessment. Eugene, OR: *ERIC Clearinghouse on Educational Management, ERIC Digest EA 40.*

Brown, F., & Snell, M. (2000). Meaningful assessment. In M. Snell & F. Brown (Eds.), *Strategies for instructing students with severe disabilities* (pp. 69–114). Upper Saddle River, NJ: Merrill/Pearson Education.

Brown, L., Branston, M. B., Hamre-Nietupski, S., Pumpian, I., Certo, N., & Gruenewald, L. (1979). A strategy for developing chronological-age-appropriate and functional curricular content for severely handicapped adolescents and young adults. *Journal of Special Education, 13,* 81–90.

Deno, S. (1985). Curriculum-based measurement: The emerging alternative. *Exceptional Children, 52,* 219–232.

Deno, S. (1989). Curriculum-based measurement and special education services: A fundamental and direct relationship. In M. Shinn (Ed.), *Curriculum-based measurement: Assessing special children* (pp. 1–17). New York: Guilford Press.

Deno, S. (2003). Developments in curriculum-based measurement. *Journal of Special Education, 37,* 184–192.

Donovan, M. S., & Cross, C. T. (2002). *Minority students in special and gifted education.* National Research Council Committee on Minority Representation in Special Education. Division of Behavioral and Social Sciences and Education. Washington, D.C.: National Academies Press.

Elliott, S. N., & Fuchs, L. S. (1997). The utility of curriculum-based measurement and performance assessment as alternatives to traditional intelligence and achievement tests. *School Psychology Review, 2*(2), 224–233.

Fuchs, L., Fuchs, D., & Hamlett, C. (1993). Technological advances linking the assessment of student's academic proficiency to instructional planning. *Journal of Special Education Technology, 12,* 49–62.

Fuchs, L. S., Hamlett, B., & Fuchs, D. (1999). *Monitoring basic skills progress* (2nd ed.) [Computer software]. Austin, TX: Pro-Ed.

Gallagher, J. D. (1998). *Classroom assessment for teachers.* Pearson.

Gearhart, M., & Herman, J. L. (1998). Portfolio assessment: Whose work is it? Issues in the use of classroom assignments for accountability. *Educational Assessment, 5*(1), 41–55.

Goh, D. S. (2004). *Assessment Accommodations for Diverse Learners.* Boston, MA: Allyn & Bacon.

Good, R. H., III, Simmons, D., & Kame'enui, E. J. (2001). The importance and decision-making utility of a continuum of fluency-based indicators of foundational reading skills for third-grade high stakes outcomes. *Scientific Studies of Reading, 5,* 257–288.

Greenwood, C. R., Carta, J. J., Kamps, D., & Delquadri, J. (1995). *Ecobehavioral assessment system software.* Kansas City, KS: Juniper Gardens Children's Center.

Hall, T., & Mengel, M. (2002). *Curriculum-based evaluations.* Wakefield, MA: National Center on Accessing the General Curriculum. Retrieved July 11, 2008, from http://www.cast.org/publications/ncac/ncac_curriculumbe.html

Hancock, C. R. (1994). Alternative assessment and second language study: What and why? *ERIC Digest, ED376695.*

Haney, M., & Cavallaro, C. C. (1996). Using ecological assessment in daily program planning for children with disabilities in typical preschool settings. *Topics in Early Childhood Special Education, 16,* 66–81.

Herman, J. L., & Winters, L. (1994). Portfolio research: A slim collection. *Educational Leadership, 52*(2), 48–55.

Hosp, M. K., Hosp, J. L., & Howell, K. W. (2007). *The ABCs of CBM: A practical guide to curriculum-based measurement.* New York: Guilford Press.

Jones, E. D., Southern, T. W., & Brigham, F. J. (1998). Curriculum-based assessment: Testing what is taught and teaching what is tested. *Intervention in School and Clinic, 33*(4), 239–249.

Marston, D. B., (1989). A curriculum-based measurement approach to assessing academic performance: What it is and why do it. In M. R. Shinn, *Curriculum-Based Measurement: Assessing Special Children.* New York: The Guilford Press.

Muyskens, P., & Marston, D. B. (2002). *Predicting success on the Minnesota Basic Skills Test in reading using CBM.* Unpublished manuscript, Minneapolis Public Schools.

National Capital Language Resource Center. (2008). *Assessing learning: Alternative assessment.* Retrieved July 12, 2008, from http://www.nclrc.org/essentials/assessing/alternative.htm

North Central Regional Educational Laboratory. (2008). *Performance assessment.* Retrieved July 10, 2008, from http://www.ncrel.org/sdrs/areas/issues/methods/assment/as8lk5.htm

National Institute of Child Health and Human Development. (2000). *Report of the National Reading Panel. Teaching children to read: An evidence-based assessment of the scientific research literature on reading and its implications for reading instruction.* NIH Publication No. 00-4769. Washington, D.C.: U.S. Government Printing Office.

Salvia, J., Ysseldyke, J., & Bolt, S. (2007). *Assessment in special and inclusive education* (10th ed.). Boston: Houghton Mifflin.

Stanley, S. O., & Greenwood, C. R. (1981). CISSAR: Code for instructional structure and student academic response. Observer's manual. Kansas City, KS: University of Kansas, Bureau of Child Research, Juniper Gardens Children's Project.

Venn, J. (2007). *Assessing Students with Special Needs* (4th ed.). Upper Saddle River, NJ: Pearson.

Wright, J. (2008). *Curriculum-based measurement: A manual for teachers.* Retrieved July 10, 2008, from http://www.jimwrightonline.com/pdfdocs/cbaManual.pdf

Ysseldyke, J., & Christenson, S. (2002). Functional assessment of academic behavior: Creating successful learning environments. Longmont, CO: Sopris West.

CHAPTER 6

Universal Design, Assessment Accommodations, and Alternate Assessments

Mishi Ishimatsu's parents are concerned that her inability to communicate verbally is causing her to become frustrated at school. Mishi was labeled as having cerebral palsy with moderate mental retardation when she was a few months old. Since that time, Mishi has received early intervention services and attended a preschool special education program. She is now in kindergarten and her parents believe that she has higher cognitive skills than she is able to demonstrate. The school has placed her in a segregated special day class and she is instructed according to modified grade level standards. The teacher has made several modifications for Mishi. She primarily communicates using simple picture symbols, push-button switches that play prerecorded phrases, gestures, and grunts. Mishi's parents believe that she is not sufficiently challenged at school. They are looking for a more sophisticated communication system that is better suited to her cognitive and communication needs, but do not know who to ask for assistance. The family immigrated to the United States a few months after Mishi was born, and her mother does not speak English fluently. They have asked the special education teacher to help them find a better way to assist their daughter communicate with her peers, teachers, and family members. The special education teacher has asked the district Assistive Technology coordinator to assess Mishi for the appropriate assistive technology.

Reflections on the Scenario

1. In what ways could assistive technology help Mishi at home and school?
2. Who is responsible for assessing a student in the area of assistive technology and augmentative communication systems?
3. What role do her parents and family members play in the assessment process for identifying the most effective device for Mishi?
4. How might Universal Design for Learning assist students like Mishi who are nonverbal?
5. What are some guidelines for determining assessment accommodations for Mishi?
6. How do schools assess the annual progress made by students with moderate to severe disabilities? What are some assessment techniques that they could use?

COUNCIL FOR EXCEPTIONAL CHILDREN (CEC) STANDARDS

This chapter addresses the following CEC standards:

ICC8K1—Basic terminology used in assessment.

ICC8K2—Legal provisions and ethical principles regarding assessment of individuals.

ICC8K4—Use and limitations of assessment instruments.

ICC8K5—National, state or provincial, and local accommodations and modifications.

GC8K1—Specialized terminology used in the assessment of individuals with disabilities.

ICC8S2—Administer nonbiased formal and informal assessments.

ICC8S3—Use technology to conduct assessments.

ICC8S4—Develop or modify individualized assessment strategies.

GC8S3—Select, adapt, and modify assessments to accommodate the unique abilities and needs of individuals with disabilities.

GC8S4—Assess reliable methods of response of individuals who lack typical communication and performance abilities.

IMPORTANCE OF ASSESSING ALL STUDENTS IN SCHOOLS

National trends over the years indicate a move toward greater inclusion of students with disabilities in the general education classroom. General and special education teachers have had to work collaboratively to meet the needs of all learners. With the passage of the No Child Left Behind Act (NCLB) in 2001, greater attention has been paid to the ongoing academic achievement of all students in U.S. public schools, and student performance data have been disaggregated by subgroup. Students in all subgroups (e.g., English learners, students of low socioeconomic status, those with special needs), are required to make adequate yearly progress in order for a school to meet NCLB mandates. In addition, per the Individuals with Disabilities Education Act (IDEA, 2004), all students with identified disabilities must have access to the general education curriculum and must participate in state and district assessments. Schools are required to assess student performance using measures that demonstrate their proficiency in a curriculum that is aligned to rigorous grade-level content standards.

Although most students in the schools demonstrate proficiency using the same assessments that are administered to their peers, some students with individualized education programs (IEPs) and English learners require accommodations to participate in these assessments. Other students with more significant disabilities require completely different assessments known as alternate assessments. There is a great deal of controversy about the fairness of assessment accommodations and the extent to which they invalidate test results. As was discussed in Chapter 3, there has been much litigation around the use of standardized testing and more recently around test accommodations for diverse learners. One way to make the general education curriculum and assessments more accessible to a diverse group of learners is by applying universal design principles.

UNIVERSAL DESIGN OF LEARNING

The concept of universal design stems from the field of architecture. In the 1970s, an architect named Ronald Mace, who was a wheelchair user, recommended that physical environments be designed inclusively to allow diverse users to access them. Mace argued in favor of proactively designing physical environments and products so that they would be functional for a wide range of users. Retroactive accommodations are generally more cumbersome and costly in terms of both time and money. Universal design gained acceptance and has since become the norm in the design community, reinforced by the passage of the Americans with Disabilities Act (ADA, 1990) and more recently by the 2004 reauthorization of IDEA. Universal design is widely used in the design of public spaces today and appears in the use of curb cuts on sidewalks, handlebars in toilet stalls, lower sinks, ramps in entranceways, and other features. These features are beneficial not only to individuals with disabilities but also to elderly individuals, persons with baby strollers, skateboarders, and others (McGuire, Scott, & Shaw, 2006).

Universal Design for Learning (UDL) is a more recent application of universal design principles in the field of education, specifically curriculum development, instruction, and assessment of learners. Orkwis and McLane defined UDL as "the design of instructional materials and activities that allows the learning goals to be achievable by individuals with wide differences in their abilities to see, hear, speak, move, read, write, understand English, attend, organize, engage, and remember" (1998, p. 9). According to the Center for Applied Special Education Technology (2010), UDL has three basic premises:

1. Curriculum that provides *multiple means of representation of content*, presenting information through various means (e.g., printed text, electronic text, closed captions, audiotapes, Braille, ASL).
2. Curriculum that provides *multiple means of expression* of what the learner knows (e.g., through written response, typed response, drawings, photos, multimedia presentations).
3. Curriculum that provides *multiple means of engagement* through cognitive supports (e.g., summaries of information presented, questions to stimulate background information, use of strategy instruction, use of engaging instructional materials

The Assistive Technology Act (PL 108-364) defines universal design as "a concept or philosophy for designing and delivering products and services that are usable by people with the widest possible range of functional capabilities, which include products and services that are directly accessible (without requiring assistive technologies) and products and services that are interoperable with assistive technology." (2004, p. 118)

such as digital or graphic materials that capitalize on the learner's interests and increase motivation).

Basic Principles of Universal Design of Instruction

Instruction that is universally designed meets seven basic principles that are presented by the North Carolina State University's Center for Universal Design (2008):

1. *Equitable use*—Instruction is designed to maximize use by learners with a range of learning styles and preferences. Instruction is equally accessible to all students, regardless of their learning modalities and preferences (e.g., a teacher's presentation could be made using visuals to complement the lecture so as to be comprehensible to students with hearing disabilities, English learners, and other students).

2. *Flexibility in use*—There is a choice in methods of use that can be adapted to individual preference (for example, students can demonstrate their knowledge of a unit of study by developing a project on the topic in various forms such as a slideshow, a diorama, drawings, an essay, etc.)

3. *Simple and intuitive*—Instruction is easy to understand and accessible by learners regardless of their language skills, prior experiences, or knowledge (e.g., simple, 1-step directions are accompanied by written prompts directing students how to complete a task).

4. *Perceptible information*—Essential information is effectively communicated to the student (through, e.g., use of large font, few words, gestures, symbols, minimal text in a slideshow).

5. *Tolerance for error*—Instruction anticipates variability in learner responses (e.g., setting computer preferences so that a student cannot accidentally delete important documents or applications).

6. *Low physical effort*—Instruction maximizes student learning and minimizes fatigue (e.g., text-to-speech software to assist a student who has reading disabilities to decode large volumes of text, automatic sensors that open doors for people entering a building).

7. *Size and space for approach and use*—Instruction is designed to maximize physical access to required materials and activities regardless of the learner's body size or motor skills (e.g., classroom furniture that is wheelchair accessible, student materials on shelves that are within easy reach of students using wheelchairs).

Implications for Assessment

Universally designed assessment allows students to participate in curriculum and assessment activities in various ways that are suited to their learning preferences and modalities, while still producing meaningful and valid data about their academic performance (Thompson, Thurlow, & Malouf, 2004). IDEA (2004) requires states and districts to use universally designed assessments. The law mandates that "the state educational agency (or in case of a district-wide assessment, the local education agency) shall, to the extent feasible, use universal design principles in developing and administering any assessments. . . ." (§ 612(a)(16)(E)). After completing an extensive review of the literature on assessment as it relates to universal design principles, the National Center on Educational Outcomes published seven key elements of universal design of assessment (Thompson & Thurlow, 2002). These assessment design principles include

1. *Inclusive assessment population*—Consider the diversity of the populations that will be assessed prior to developing the assessment.
2. *Precisely defined constructs*—Design assessment items to provide a valid inference about the variable being assessed while still giving students the maximum opportunity for success.
3. *Accessible, nonbiased items*—Review items to ensure sensitivity to students from diverse cultural and language backgrounds, students with disabilities, etc. as the assessment is being developed.
4. *Amenable to accommodations*—Assessments are designed to be compatible with needed accommodations such as large font, assistive technology, auditory output, etc.
5. *Simple, clear, and intuitive instructions and procedures*—Instructions and test items should be simply stated and easy to understand.
6. *Maximum readability and comprehensibility*—Techniques such as using common words, simple vocabulary, clearly marked questions, and short sentences with few words, etc. should be used to increase readability and comprehension.
7. *Maximum legibility*—The text should be presented in a font and type size that is easy to read, leaving sufficient blank space, and graphs, tables, and illustrations should be clearly marked and placed by the descriptive text.

USING ASSISTIVE TECHNOLOGY FOR ASSESSMENT

Assistive technology facilitates the inclusion of individuals with disabilities in their schools and communities. By enhancing the functional capabilities of the individual with special needs, assistive technology helps level the playing field and increase that individual's meaningful participation in everyday life activities. The following definitions of assistive technology devices and services are taken from the Assistive Technology Act and will help the reader better understand the purpose and function of assistive technology.

Assistive technology device: "any item, piece of equipment, or product system, whether acquired commercially, modified, or customized, that is used to increase, maintain, or improve functional capabilities of individuals with disabilities." (2004, p. 118)

Assistive technology service: "any service that directly assists an individual with a disability in the selection, acquisition, or use of an assistive technology device." (2004, p. 118) This includes services for 1) evaluating an individual's assistive technology needs; 2) acquiring the assistive technology device; 3) selecting, designing, customizing, and repairing the device; 4) coordinating technology use with other therapies and interventions; and 5) training and providing technical support to the user/s, their family members, and other professionals.

Assistive technology solutions do not always require sophisticated technological solutions and high costs. *Low-technology* assistive devices usually do not require any electronic tools and are mostly low-cost devices that are also easy to use. Low-technology devices may be as simple as attaching a pencil grip to a pencil, using a clipboard to keep the paper from moving as a student writes, or gluing a popsicle stick to each page of a picture book to help a child turn the pages. *Mid-technology* devices use simple technology solutions such as a tape recorder, switch and button-operated device, data projector, audio output device, or other device to facilitate use by a wider audience. *High-technology* devices usually require fairly sophisticated technology, are more expensive to purchase, and usually require extensive training to use. Examples of high-technology devices include a sophisticated voice output system, dynamic display screen, head-mounted eye-control computer access device, etc.

Finding the Right Assistive Technology for a Student

The IEP team plays a key role in assessing a student for assistive technologies and ensuring that the technology selected best meets the student's needs. Team members evaluate the child's needs, environmental demands, and the family and cultural expectations. They investigate multiple solutions, from low-technology alternatives such as picture cards, spell checkers, tape recorders, or calculators, to high-technology devices such as computers, electronic organizers, and voice output devices. The IEP team continuously re-evaluates the need for and use of the assistive technology, with the overarching goal being to find ways to make it easier, more efficient, and less intrusive for an individual to complete a task. The Wisconsin Assistive Technology Initiative (http://www.wati.org) is an excellent resource for free downloadable assessment forms and lists other products that can be ordered to assess a student's assistive technology needs.

The use of assistive technologies affects the family routine and interactions in profound ways and it is critical to work closely with parents and the target individual to identify assistive technology needs and to determine the acceptability and fit with a device (Parette, Brotherson, Hourcade, & Bradley, 1996). Although the use of assistive technology has the potential to improve quality of life and relationships within the family, it also can increase stress levels in the home. For instance, devices such as a wheelchair may require structural modifications in the home. Other devices such as a voice output device may require parents to learn new, often complex skills.

When conducting an assistive technology assessment, the team is advised to seek information about five areas (Parette et al., 1996):

1. *The individual learner*—Her needs, interests, preferences, desires, and current functioning levels, as well as her emotional readiness to use assistive technology will help the team determine assistive technology needs.
2. *The device*—The ease of use, reliability, safety, practicality, cost, performance, and acceptability of the device are some considerations.
3. *The family*—Their needs, preferences, resources, routines, and willingness to adopt the technology will affect its use.
4. *The service system*—The financial support, technical assistance, medical, and other supports available to the family influence the adoption of a device.
5. *Cultural factors*—The family's customs, values, and beliefs that influence their worldview will influence their acceptance of the device (e.g., if the child's

disability is viewed as something shameful that should be hidden from others in their community, the use of an assistive device that will draw more attention to the child when the family members are out in the community so it is not likely to be used).

It is wise to adopt any new assistive technology device on a trial basis and have the individual practice using it in authentic environments, indoors and outdoors, at home, school, and in the community. The correct device is usually found only after much trial and error in multiple settings. The student's IEP should list the products, devices, and services that the student will receive to ensure that they are made available for the student to use. It is recommended that the IEP list only the generic product name rather than the specific brand name, in order to give the team some flexibility in securing the appropriate device for a student.

ASSESSMENT ACCOMMODATIONS

Students with disabilities often require instructional and assessment accommodations that help them to learn and to demonstrate what they have learned. These accommodations may be in the form of reading materials aloud to them, typing their responses on a computer, giving them extended time on a task, or having them use an assistive device to demonstrate learning. The IEP team identifies the accommodations that are beneficial for the student and lists these in the student's IEP.

Best practice dictates that these identified accommodations be provided to the student during day-to-day instruction, during ongoing student progress monitoring, and when the student is taking high-stakes assessments. For example, a student who uses a calculator during math class should be permitted to use a calculator when she is taking the end-of-the-year math test, and a student who has his weekly quizzes read aloud to him by his teacher should have test items read aloud to him by the proctor. It is not wise to introduce a new accommodation when a student takes a test, as it is possible that this accommodation will confuse or distract the student and hinder his test performance (e.g., permitting the use of a glossary of terms on a test, when the student is not familiar with using a glossary). Instead, the team should only identify accommodations that are of proven benefit to the student, and the student should practice using the accommodation prior to using it on a test.

Assessment Accommodations and Modifications

An *assessment accommodation* is a change in the testing materials or procedures that enables the student to demonstrate what he or she has learned and is able to do (Thurlow, Elliott, & Ysseldyke, 1998). An example of an accommodation is the use of a computerized test in which the student uses a text browser to read aloud test items on a science test and then clicks on the correct response on the computer, rather than using a paper copy of the test to color in correct responses on a scantron sheet. Accommodations help level the playing field for a student with special needs while allowing them to participate in the same learning activities as their grade-level peers. The task expectation, quantity, and difficulty level are not changed when accommodations are provided.

A *modification*, on the other hand, is a more intensive change to the learning task that alters the task expectation, quantity, and often the difficulty level. For instance, a student receiving modifications for a learning disability and distractibility may be given fewer math problems to complete than his grade-level peers on a math test (though the problems are of the same level of difficulty). Another student who has a cognitive disability may complete a different set of math problems at a lower difficulty level than those assigned to his grade peers.

Types of Assessment Accommodations

Thurlow et al. (1998) identify the following assessment accommodations:

1. *Setting accommodations*—Students with special needs may benefit from taking their assessments in a different location with minimum noise and distraction, where they are not likely to distract their peers (e.g., when using a tape recorder or computer).
2. *Timing accommodations*—Students who take longer to read instructions and organize their thoughts, or who have difficulties writing, may need extended time on tests. Students using specialized devices may need frequent breaks during testing. Extended time is one of the most frequently used accommodations for students with disabilities and English learners. Team members are cautioned not to overuse this accommodation, as it is not effective for all students. Some students may lose focus due to the extended time and get distracted or off-task, which will likely lower their test performance.
3. *Scheduling accommodations*—Some students may need to take the test at a different time in the day than their peers. Their test schedules may be dictated by their medication schedule or the time of the day when they are most alert and engaged. Other students may be unable to sit for long periods of time and may need to take their tests over the course of several days.
4. *Presentation accommodations*—Students may have their assessments presented to them in varied formats depending on their sensory, perceptual, or cognitive needs. For instance, tests may be presented using Braille, large print, fewer items per page, an interpreter, or assistive devices, such as audiotape, amplification device, read-aloud software on a computer, etc. Test directions may be clarified or translated for English learner students.
5. *Response accommodations*—Students may demonstrate their skills in varied ways, other than filling in a conventional scantron answer sheet. They may be permitted to have a scribe to mark their response in the test booklet, type their responses, or read them into a tape recorder.

Standard vs. Nonstandard Accommodations

Providing accommodations on norm-referenced tests (NRTs) poses unique challenges because such tests need to be administered, scored, and interpreted in standard ways that are usually not amenable to accommodations. Students who take NRTs under nonstandard conditions usually have their scores discarded because their scores cannot be compared with those of the norm group who did not receive any accommodations. Some NRTs may be administered with a few permissible accommodations such as use of large print, marking answers in the test booklet, oral administration of the test, and extended time. Test publishers conduct special norming studies that include data from students using these accommodations. Recently, states have started listing the accommodations that are permissible on specific statewide assessments on their Department of Education websites. Accommodations that are permissible on standardized tests are known as *standard accommodations*. Accommodations that are not permissible on the NRT, even if they are prescribed by students' IEPs, are called *nonstandard accommodations*. Scores obtained using these nonstandard accommodations usually are not included in the school and district aggregate scores.

Testing-of-Limits

A student who is having difficulty taking a standardized test according to the regular administration procedures may be tested-of-limits by re-taking the test with assistance to see whether he is able to improve his performance (Goh, 2004). This practice allows the assessor to determine what the student is able to do under altered conditions or with special assistance that compensates for the disability. Testing-of-limits is not frequently used and results of the test administered in this manner should be interpreted with caution and not compared with norm group data.

Guidelines for Assessment Accommodations

The following guidelines should be considered when determining which accommodations may benefit a student (Goh, 2004; Thurlow et al., 1998):

1. The IEP team is familiar with the students' strengths, preferences, needs, and learning style, so this team should make the accommodation decisions.
2. The instructional environment, learning challenges, types of learning activities, and other ecological factors should be considered in selecting the appropriate accommodations.
3. New accommodations should not be introduced during testing. Instead, the student should use the same accommodations during instruction and assessment.
4. All accommodations should be appropriate and individualized rather than being based on the label of the student's disability.
5. A systematic determination of the student's needs should be made prior to considering possible accommodations.
6. The accommodations that are to be used should be listed on the IEP to safeguard the student.
7. Accommodations should be determined in a fair manner—they are not intended to give the student an unfair advantage, but rather to give him or her an equal opportunity to perform.
8. An accommodation should not be provided when the student is being assessed to diagnose his or her disability. For example, a child would not wear eyeglasses when the optician is testing her visual acuity in order to prescribe glasses.

ALTERNATE ASSESSMENTS

In the past, students with moderate to severe disabilities often were excluded from participating in state and district-wide accountability assessments. The IEP team would commonly arrive at a determination that exempted these students from participating in high-stakes tests, and their test results were not included in the aggregated data for their school. As Ysseldyke and Olsen assert, when students are "out of sight in assessment and accountability systems, they are out of mind when policy decisions are made and when educational structures and programs are designed" (1999, p. 175).

It has been argued that in order to get a true picture of the state of education and to make effective policy decisions, policy makers need to review data for all students in the schools. In addition, the exclusion of large numbers of students with disabilities from accountability assessment systems resulted in a lack of motivation on the part of administrators to invest resources to improve the education received by this population of students. High expectations would only apply and required teacher professional development and curricular and instructional resources would only become available if these students' test scores mattered. When the performance of students with disabilities on statewide assessments is publicly reported, school systems are encouraged to evaluate the quality of educational programs and services, and if students are not making progress, to initiate changes in the educational system.

What Is an Alternate Assessment?

The 1997 reauthorization of IDEA made it mandatory for all students with disabilities to participate in state and district testing. Starting in 2000, states and local districts had to develop alternate assessment systems for students who had significant cognitive disabilities and who could not participate in the regular state and local assessments with accommodations.

Alternate assessments measure the annual progress made by students with disabilities toward modified general education standards or alternate general education standards. Alternate assessments are intended for students for whom participation in state- and district-level assessments, even with accommodations, usually is not a meaningful experience (Ysseldyke & Olsen, 1999). An alternate assessment is appropriate for students with significant cognitive disabilities who participate in a curriculum that covers life skills instruction along with academic content instruction (Ysseldyke & Olsen).

It is important to note that NCLB permits two types of alternate assessments:

1. Alternate assessment that is based on modified academic achievement standards (AA-MAS) is permitted for up to 2% of students in a district who are assessed on the same grade-level academic content standards as their grade level peers, but with modifications regarding expectations for content mastery.
2. Alternate assessment that is based on alternate academic achievement standards (AA-AAS) is permitted for up to 1% of students in a district with the most significant cognitive disabilities for whom regular or modified assessments are not meaningful (Cortiella, 2007).

The Secretary of Education sanctioned the first type of alternate assessment, AA-MAS, in 2005. This form has been used with students with disabilities whose current performance levels are below those of their grade-level peers but higher than the performance levels of students taking alternate assessments that are based on alternate standards. These modified assessments are more closely aligned to general education assessments in format, structure and content, but they permit needed modifications and accommodations (e.g., reduced number of test questions, simplified language for test questions, larger font size). States are gradually phasing in these modified assessments for students with disabilities who are learning grade-level content but are unable to participate meaningfully in statewide assessments. The next part of this chapter refers primarily to the second type of alternate assessment that is based on alternate achievement standards for students with the most significant cognitive disabilities.

Who Is Eligible for an Alternate Assessment on the Basis of Alternate Achievement Standards?

Determining who is eligible for an alternate assessment is tricky because the goal is to make individualized and objective eligibility decisions to the greatest extent possible. The IEP team would be ill advised to make categorical decisions about participation in alternate assessment that is based on a student's special education label. It has been proposed that alternate assessments based on alternate achievement standards are appropriate for students who are not on track to earn a high school diploma (Ysseldyke & Olsen, 1999). Yet it is difficult to make accurate predictions about whether a student is on track to earn a high school diploma, particularly if the student is in elementary school when the decision is being made (Kleinert & Thurlow, 2001).

Individual states have developed their own criteria for who will participate in an alternate assessment that is based on alternate achievement standards. Two of these state criteria are presented here:

- *Kentucky:* Students are eligible to participate if they have severe cognitive disabilities that prevent them from completing the regular program of study even with extended services and other modifications and adaptations. These students also require ongoing instruction in community-based settings to allow for the acquisition, maintenance, and generalization of learning.
- *California:* A team decision is made about eligibility of a student who demonstrates academic and cognitive ability and adaptive behavior that require substantial adjustments to the general curriculum. The student's learning objectives focus on functional applications of the general curriculum. The student is unable to participate in statewide assessment even with modifications and accommodations.

Alternate Assessment Techniques

There is consensus amongst stakeholders that the curriculum and assessment for students with severe disabilities include both academic and functional outcomes. States are required to assess students' performance in the general academic curriculum, and also to assess the functional curriculum and personal-social-vocational domains (Browder et al., 2002). An example of a curricular framework for alternate assessments that is based on alternate achievement standards is presented by the National Center on Educational Outcomes, who identified five curriculum-related domains: 1) academic and functional literacy, 2) personal and social adjustment,

3) contribution and citizenship, 4) responsibility and independence, and 5) physical health (Ysseldyke & Olsen, 1999). These domains may be assessed using multiple techniques like the following:

Performance assessment—The student being assessed completes a task or activity (e.g., taking a folder to the front office to meet a geography standard, washing his hands with soap to meet a health standard, writing a letter to the mayor to meet a language arts standard). Data could be collected using task analysis, observation, or a rubric that evaluates the product created.

Portfolio—The portfolio is a compilation of student products that depict competency across state standards. Electronic portfolios are another option that allow for easier review amongst raters who are not already familiar with the student and his or her work. The blind review reduces bias and increases credibility of this evaluation technique.

Interviews—Surveys, checklists, or rating scales are completed that reflect the responses of teachers, parents, therapists, and others who are familiar with the student and can answer questions about the student's performance.

Traditional paper and pencil test—The student is presented with a series of test items that inquire into his or her knowledge and skills in a content area. The student may receive accommodations or modifications to complete the test. The percentage of items scored correctly is the student's score, and it is compared with the score that the student earned during the previous year.

Guidelines for Alternate Assessments

Regardless of the alternate assessment technique selected, it is important for the assessment to be an authentic indicator of what a student has learned over the course of the year, as demonstrated with optimal supports (e.g., verbal prompts, physical prompts, assistive devices) (Kleinert & Thurlow, 2001). Furthermore, the alternate assessment that is based on alternate achievement standards should be based on a continuous assessment rather than being a single snapshot of the student's performance at a particular point in time. Often the assessment is integrated across multiple domains to allow a student to demonstrate multiple skills while completing a single task. For instance, Henry can demonstrate spatial orientation, communication, and mobility skills when he is asked to take a message from his classroom to the front office.

Kleinert, Green, Hurte, Clayton, and Oetinger (2002) have the following suggestions for teachers whose students will participate in state or district alternate assessments:

1. Develop standards-based IEPs that link student learning objectives to state standards. This linking helps clearly articulate how the student's instruction will connect to the alternate assessment.
2. Be sure that students can access state standards in multiple ways so that the instruction is guided by state standards. Students may participate in the general education curriculum with no modifications, with materials presented in a different format, with content modifications, or while meeting individualized goals (e.g., a

student could work on following directions while he assumes the role of "organizer" in a small group cooperative learning lesson in geography).

3. Plan for the alternate assessment starting at the beginning of the school year, giving students opportunities to practice and master skills that are tested on these assessments.

4. Use student self-monitoring to increase their ownership of their own learning. Students can check off tasks they have completed on a checklist, select items to include in their performance portfolio and reflect on them, identify areas where they improved and areas where they need more practice, and set goals for their own performance.

UNIVERSAL DESIGN AND ASSESSMENT ACCOMMODATIONS IN A RESPONSE TO INTERVENTION (RTI) FRAMEWORK

Although there is minimum mention of universal design in the RTI literature, it clearly makes sense to work toward ensuring that the curriculum, instruction, and assessments used with all students in the schools are universally designed. Specifically with regard to assessment, all tests and probes used to screen students, test for mastery of learning, assess their skill levels, and monitor progress need to be developed so that they are accessible to a wide variety of learners with a range of learning needs and styles. It is imperative that students be provided with the opportunity to demonstrate their optimal performance on these measures.

In an RTI framework, universal design principles are applicable at each of Tiers I, II, and III. Students at Tier I are provided with an accessible and meaningful curriculum, instructional techniques, and assessments to measure their learning. Students who struggle with the high-quality curriculum and instruction at Tier I receive needed accommodations, and if necessary assistive devices, to help them make progress at Tier II. Students who have not made adequate progress with the Tier II interventions will likely receive instructional and assessment accommodations and modifications at Tier III. Some struggling students will qualify for special education and may take alternate assessments that are based on modified achievement standards (AA-MAS). Most students with significant cognitive disabilities who qualify for alternate assessments using alternate achievement standards (AA-AAS) are identified early in their lives, often during infancy, and receive special education services when they begin school.

Web Resources

Center for Applied Special Technology—*http://www.cast.org*
Center for Universal Design—*http://www.ncsu.edu/www/ncsu/design/sod5/cud/*
National Alternate Assessment Center—*http://www.naacpartners.org/*
National Center on Educational Outcomes—*http://www.cehd.umn.edu/nceo/*

End-of-Chapter Questions

1. What events led to the increased focus on accountability that is evident in education today? What are the implications of this accountability movement for students with identified disabilities?
2. What is meant by "universal design for learning"? What are the basic principles of universal design? Select any four principles and suggest how they may be applied in a classroom setting.
3. Why should assessments be universally designed? What principles must be considered in order to develop universally designed assessments?
4. How can assistive technology assist students with disabilities?
5. Explain the legislation that mandates the use of assistive technology in public schools.
6. How can IEP teams go about selecting the appropriate assistive technology for a student with a disability? Explain the role of parents in this process.

7. Distinguish between an assessment accommodation and a modification. Give examples of each.
8. What are the commonly used assessment accommodations?
9. What are some guidelines that assist in the selection of appropriate accommodations for learners?
10. Explain what standard and nonstandard accommodations are.
11. What is an alternate assessment? What are the two types of alternate assessments? Explain the eligibility criteria for students to qualify for each type of alternate assessment.
12. What techniques could be used in designing an alternate assessment?
13. What are some considerations in designing an alternate assessment for students with moderate to severe disabilities?

References

Assistive Technology Act of 2004, Pub. L. No. 108-364, § 2 and 3, Stat. 1714 and 1710. Retrieved July 29, 2008, from http://frwebgate.access.gpo.gov/cgi-bin/getdoc.cgi?dbname=108_cong_public_laws& docid=f:publ364.108

Browder, D., Ahlgrim-Delzell, L., Flowers, C., Karvonen, M., Spooner, F., & Algozzine, R. (2002, April). *How states define alternate assessments for students with disabilities.* Paper presented at the annual meeting of the American Educational Research Association, New Orleans, LA.

Center for Applied Special Education Technology. (2010). *UDL Guidelines–Version 1.0: Examples and Resources.* Retrieved September 24, 2010, from http://www.udlcenter.org/implementation/examples

Center for Universal Design. (2008). *Principles of Universal Design.* Retrieved July 29, 2008, from http://www.ncsu.edu/www/ncsu/design/sod5/cud/about_ud/udprinciples.htm

Cortiella, C. (2007). *Learning opportunities for your child through alternate assessments: Alternate assessments based on modi?ed academic achievement standards.* Minneapolis, MN: University of Minnesota,

National Center on Educational Outcomes. Retrieved August 5, 2008, from http://www.cehd.umn.edu/nceo/OnlinePubs/Learning Opportunities.pdf/

Goh, D. S. (2004). *Assessment accommodations for diverse learners.* Boston, MA: Allyn & Bacon.

Kleinert, H., Green, P., Hurte, M., Clayton, J., & Oetinger, C. (2002). Creating and using meaningful alternate assessments. *Teaching Exceptional Children, 34*(4), 40–47.

Kleinert, H. L., & Thurlow, M. (2001). An introduction to alternate assessment. In H. Kleinert & J. Kearns (Eds.), *Alternate assessment: Measuring outcomes and supports for students with disabilities* (pp. 1–15). Baltimore: Paul H. Brookes Co.

McGuire, J. M., Scott, S. S., & Shaw, S. F. (2006). Universal design and its applications in educational environments. *Remedial and Special Education, 27,* 166–175.

Orkwis, R., & McLane, K. (1998). A curriculum every student can use: Design principles for student access. *ERIC/OSEP Topical brief.* Reston, VA: Council for Exceptional Children.

Parette, H. P., Brotherson, M. J., Hourcade, J. J., & Bradley, R. H. (1996). Family-centered assistive technology assessment. *Intervention in School and Clinic, 32,* 104–112.

Thompson, S., & Thurlow, M. (2002). *Universally Designed Assessments: Better Tests for Everyone!* NCEO Policy Directions Number 14. Minneapolis, MN: National Center on Educational Outcomes. ERIC Document Reproduction Service No. ED 467724.

Thompson, S., Thurlow, M., & Malouf, D. B. (2004). Creating better tests for everyone through univer-sally designed assessments. *Journal of Applied Testing Technology, 6*(1), 1–15.

Thurlow, M. L., Elliott, J. L., & Ysseldyke, J. E. (1998). *Testing students with disabilities: Practical strategies for complying with district and state requirements.* Thousand Oaks, CA: Corwin Press.

Ysseldyke, J., & Olsen, K. (1999). Putting alternate assessments into practice: What to measure and possible sources of data. *Exceptional Children, 65,* 175–185.

CHAPTER 7

Cognitive Assessment

Henrietta Odema is a second-grade student at Lee Elementary. She has struggled with all academic subjects since she started kindergarten and is usually the last student to complete assigned tasks. Henrietta evidences some speech and language delays, both with expressive and receptive language. Her reading is dysfluent, and she finds it difficult to keep up with the math and content area curriculum. Henrietta forgets skills that she has previously acquired and finds it difficult to generalize and apply new learning to unfamiliar tasks. She is well behaved, puts in a lot of effort, and tries very hard to please her teachers. Henrietta's peers tend to "baby" her and do things for her, as she often appears lost or confused and has difficulty completing everyday tasks for herself. Although she is generally well liked, recently she has been teased by some of her classmates. Her parents and teachers are concerned about her slow rate of growth across all academic subjects and would like her to be assessed for special education.

Reflections on the Scenario

1. What are some of Henrietta's strengths and needs as described in this vignette?
2. What apparent cognitive delays does Henrietta evidence?
3. What are some cognitive assessments that could be used to determine her cognitive functioning?
4. In order for Henrietta to be eligible for special education, what difficulties does she need to demonstrate in addition to delays in cognitive functioning?
5. How can data obtained from these cognitive assessments be used to assist her teachers and parents in developing a program plan for Henrietta?

COUNCIL FOR EXCEPTIONAL CHILDREN (CEC) STANDARDS

ICC8K1—Basic terminology used in assessment.

ICC8K2—Legal provisions and ethical principles regarding assessment of individuals.

ICC8S2—Administer nonbiased formal and informal assessments.

ICC8S5—Interpret information from formal and informal assessments.

ICC8S6—Use assessment information in making eligibility, program, and placement decisions for individuals with exceptional learning needs, including those from culturally and/or linguistically diverse backgrounds.

GC8S4—Assess reliable methods of response of individuals who lack typical communication and performance abilities.

Cognitive processes such as information processing, thinking, memory, language, intelligence, and learning distinguish human beings from other animals. These mental processes are critical to our survival and allow us to adapt to our environment. Cognition is seen as synonymous with "the ability to learn how to learn" or "thinking skills" (Barber, 2000). Students apply these processes to the sensory stimulation that they receive through their sense organs, thereby making meaning and learning new concepts, building knowledge, and gaining skills. Some students, such as Henrietta, experience delays in one or more cognitive process, which often results in academic and adaptive difficulties.

WHY ASSESS COGNITIVE FUNCTIONING?

Intelligence is one of the most studied cognitive processes in education and also among the most controversial. Intelligence test batteries are the most frequently used norm-referenced tests (NRTs) in school settings, and intelligence quotients (IQs) are seen as predictors of key life outcomes, such as academic achievement, performance in work settings, social and occupational status, and income (Floyd, Clark, & Shadish, 2008; Sattler, 1992). In addition, IQ tests are used routinely as part of a psycho-educational battery of tests to determine students' eligibility for services under the disability category of mental retardation and in making other special education eligibility decisions.

ISSUES IN COGNITIVE ASSESSMENT

Much of the controversy associated with intelligence testing stems from the debate over the relative contributions of heredity vs. environment, the definition of intelligence, and the accuracy of IQ tests, particularly when they are used with diverse populations (McLoughlin & Lewis, 2001; Sattler, 1992). Intelligence tests are designed to measure samples of human behavior in order to make predictions about future learning. The nature vs. nurture controversy is evident in the measurement of intelligence. Children inherit the genotype for intelligence from their parents, but this genotype interacts with a wide range of environmental influences including prenatal and perinatal factors, nutrition and health, richness of stimulation in the home environment, availability of language models, and schooling experiences to result in the manifestation of intelligence.

Theorists have proposed varying definitions of the construct of intelligence. Intelligence tests stemming from these varied theories assess intelligence in very different ways. For example, David Wechsler, who developed the Wechsler Intelligence Scale for Children (WISC-IV), defined intelligence as the "aggregate or global capacity of the individual to act purposefully, think rationally, and deal effectively with his environment" (Wechsler, 1958, p. 7). Howard Gardner took a different perspective when he proposed the multiple intelligence theory in 1983 on the basis of cognitive research, which viewed intelligence as a set of problem-solving skills. Gardner (1983) identified eight distinct intelligences: visual/spatial, bodily/kinesthetic, musical, interpersonal, intrapersonal, linguistic, logical/mathematical, and naturalist. He argued that schools tend to attach undue importance to the linguistic and logical/mathematical intelligences and to undervalue other intelligences. He encouraged schools to appreciate the multiple gifts and talents of their students.

The accuracy of IQ tests has been questioned, particularly because it measures the performance of students from culturally and linguistically diverse backgrounds and children from low socioeconomic status groups. As described at some length in Chapter 3, a series of lawsuits including *Larry P. v. Riles* (1979), *PASE v. Hannon* (1980), and *Diana v. Board of Education* (1972) illustrate examples of bias in the development, administration and use, and interpretation of assessment data obtained from intelligence tests for students from nonmainstream backgrounds.

The utility and applicability of intelligence testing in schools also has been questioned and critiqued. Much of this criticism stems from the lack of instructional utility of intelligence test data to guide educational interventions. The use of intelligence tests in school settings arguably can be limited to their role in diagnosing whether or not a student is determined to be eligible for special education services. Although intelligence tests are viewed as predictors of academic achievement, they do not provide explicit data to guide academic instruction and typically are not sensitive to gains in student achievement.

Variables Affecting Performance on Intelligence Tests

Several variables affect how a student performs on a cognitive assessment. The following are a few of the characteristics that significantly affect the assessment of intelligence:

1. *Acculturation*—A common set of background experiences that result in a shared opportunity to learn (Salvia, Ysseldyke, & Bolt, 2007). Acculturation is influenced by how long a student has lived in a particular country or city and the extent to which he or she has adopted the culture of this setting.
2. *Age*—Older children have had more opportunities than younger children to acquire the shared experiences that are typical to people within their cultural group. Consequently, it is difficult to obtain an accurate index of cognitive functioning in very young children.
3. *Sensory and motor disabilities*—Students with vision or hearing impairments require different types of tests or modified administration. For example, a student who is blind will likely have difficulties on the performance items of the WISC-IV, (i.e., the block design, picture completion, object assembly and other performance subtests). Similarly, students with motor and speech disabilities would need to be tested using an appropriate measure that accommodates their special needs.
4. *Race, ethnicity, socioeconomic status, and language background*—Test scores are indicative of the student's mastery of the norms and cultural values of the mainstream, middle-class culture. Verbal items have been found to be "culturally loaded" to a greater extent than nonverbal or performance items, so some psychologists prefer to use nonverbal tests of intelligence to equalize the playing field for students. Despite the strengths of nonverbal tests as a means to reduce the discrepancies between ethnic and socioeconomic groups, nonverbal reasoning is less closely related to academic performance. Consequently, verbal measures are still preferred predictors of academic achievement.

Variables that are unique to the particular test used affect student performance on an IQ test. According to the Buros Mental Measurement Yearbook, there are as many as 250 measures of intelligence and general aptitude. A student's performance has been found to fluctuate depending on the test used (Floyd et al., 2008). Clearly, an essential criterion in selecting an appropriate NRT is to ensure that the normative sample includes the demographic characteristics of the student who you will be assessing. In addition, it is important to administer a test that is current and whose norms reflect the most recent U.S. Census data. Recent normative updates of IQ tests suggest that the general intelligence levels of the population are on the increase. This increase in IQ scores in the general population over time, usually 3 IQ points per decade, is known as the Flynn effect (Flynn, 2007), because this trend was highlighted in a series of studies conducted by James Flynn in the 1980s. These gains in IQ scores over generations are a function of many variables, including improved health and nutrition, improved education, increased environmental and intellectual stimulation of youngsters, and greater exposure to test-taking skills and strategies early in a child's school career.

Psychologists are advised to carefully select the assessment measures to be used, and to validate and support the test data by gathering supplementary information on the student using interviews, observations, and document reviews including school records and developmental histories.

COMMONLY USED COGNITIVE ASSESSMENT MEASURES AND TECHNIQUES

Traditional, standardized NRTs have been widely used to assess human cognitive processes such as intelligence. Some decades ago, it was routine practice to administer group intelligence tests to all students in public schools, but that practice has been discontinued in most states. Group intelligence tests such as the Otis-Lennon School Ability Test (Otis & Lennon, 1995) and Cognitive Abilities Test (Lohman & Hagen, 2005) were generally composed of multiple-choice items that required strong reading skills and did not provide the most accurate index of global intelligence. Individual intelligence tests tend to be more accurate and comprehensive in focus and typically are used to determine eligibility for special education purposes. Dynamic assessments that rely on a test-teach-test model have been used less frequently but have potential for cognitive assessment. Commonly used assessments are described next.

COMMON NORM-REFERENCED TESTS (NRTs)

Wechsler Intelligence Scale for Children–Fourth Edition Integrated (WISC-IV Integrated; Kaplan, Fein, Kramer, Dells, & Morris, 2004*).* This individually administered test of intelligence is appropriate for children age 6 through 16 years and 11 months. The WISC-IV Integrated is the latest in a series of Wechsler Intelligence Scales that have been developed and widely used since 1949. There is a Spanish version of the WISC-IV that was normed on a predominantly Puerto Rican population (which could limit the validity of this test for use with students from other cultural Spanish language backgrounds). The lower extension of these scales, the Wechsler Preschool and Primary Scale of Intelligence (WPPSI-III, Psychological Corporation, 2002) is used with young children ages 2 years 6 months through 7 years 3 months. The upper extension of the Wechsler Scales, the Wechsler Adult Intelligence Scale (Wechsler, 1997) is appropriate for use with older adolescents and adults.

Earlier versions of the WISC provided two composite scores for verbal and perform-ance items. The WISC-IV Integrated has 10 core and 5 supplemental subtests that yield four composite scores: the Verbal Comprehension Index, the Perceptual Reasoning Index, the Working Memory Index, and the Processing Speed Index. The WISC-IV Integrated also measures test behavior, problem-solving style, and cognitive processes.

The test takes 60–90 minutes to administer. It requires a highly qualified exam-iner with advanced graduate training and supervision in assessment. The test has strong technical qualities and provides a good index of children's cognitive process-ing abilities.

Kauffman Assessment Battery for Children-II (KABC-II)

The KABC-II was designed to assess the processing and cognitive abilities of chil-dren ages 3 to 18 years (A. S. Kauffman & N. L. Kauffman, 2004). It is based on a dual theoretical model of neurological processing by Luria and the broad and narrow abilities model by Cattell-Horn-Carroll (CHC). The KABC-II includes 18 core and supplementary subtests. The administrator can select appropriate subtests on the basis of the child's age and the theoretical model that he or she wishes to use in order to interpret the test. The standardization sample was representative of the 2000 U.S. Census and has been found to have adequate technical qualities. The KABC-II is ap-pealing and motivating for younger children. A nonverbal scale is available for use with students with speech and language difficulties, those with hearing impair-ments, and English learners.

Universal Nonverbal Intelligence Test (UNIT)

This nonverbal test of cognitive processing was designed to reduce the language load and bias that is inherent in most cognitive assessments and to provide a culture-fair measure of children and adolescents' cognitive abilities (Bracken & McCallum, 1998). The test is individually administered and appropriate for children ages 5 to 17 years. The measure is completely nonverbal and particularly suited to students with speech and language delays, those with hearing loss, and English Learners.

The UNIT assesses students' memory and reasoning through six subtests: Symbolic Memory, Cube Design, Spatial Memory, Analogic Reasoning, Object Memory, and Mazes. The first two subtests could be administered as part of an Abbreviated Battery for screening purposes, while the first four subtests comprise the Standard Battery. The Extended Battery, which could be used for diagnostic pur-poses, is composed of all six subtests. The UNIT has strong reliability and validity data. The test has adequate basal and ceiling levels, making it a good measure for children who have very high and very low abilities (Bandalos, 2004). Test developers have taken great care to minimize bias in the test and attempt to make it a culture-fair measure.

Woodcock–Johnson III Test of Cognitive Abilities (WJ-III Cognitive)

Part of the WJ-III psycho-educational battery consisting of the cognitive and achieve-ment scales, this cognitive test is appropriate for individuals aged 2 to 90+ years (Woodcock, McGrew, & Mather, 2001). The WJ-III COG battery has 10 subtests, which combined with 10 additional subtests comprise the extended WJ-III COG. The test, which is based on the CHC theory of cognitive abilities, yields data on the following cognitive factors: comprehension knowledge, long-term retrieval, visual/spatial thinking, auditory processing, fluid reasoning, processing speed, and short-term memory. This is a comprehensive cognitive battery with strong technical qualities and two alternate forms. Scoring is computerized and fairly quick.

DYNAMIC ASSESSMENT

Most cognitive assessments, such as those described in the preceding section, are considered to be static measures of what a student already knows. Dynamic assessment (DA), on the other hand, measures a student's learning potential. DA focuses on the learning process rather than on the learning outcomes (Yeomans, 2008). DA has been researched and used for the past 75 years to identify a learner's strengths and weaknesses. DA stems from two theoretical bases: Vygotsky's zone of proximal development and Feuerstein's model of mediated learning experience (MLE). Vygotsky explains that each child learns at a different rate and the child's learning is scaffolded to the next step through adult prompts and assistance. Similarly, Feuerstein highlights the role of the "mediator" who observes how a person learns and solves problems. This information can help an educator set up future learning tasks.

Dynamic assessment consists of a "pretest-intervene-retest procedure" (Fabio, 2005, p. 42). It involves setting up a learning task, teaching the student how to complete the task, providing feedback to assist learning, and then collecting data on the student's responsiveness to the learning in order to measure his or her learning potential. By following this dynamic process, DA overcomes some of the inherent bias that has plagued traditional cognitive and intelligence measures, such as IQ tests. It also addresses the problem of many students with disabilities not demonstrating their optimal performance on standardized tests. Research data suggest that students from lower socioeconomic backgrounds, those from ethnic minority groups, and students with disabilities profit greatly from instructional interventions and mediation and perform better on dynamic measures (Fabio, 2005; Hasson & Joffe, 2007).

Campione (1989) discusses three dimensions along which DAs may vary:

1. *Index*—This measure captures the student's response to learning. The index could be the amount of change from an independently completed pretest to an independently completed posttest. Alternately, the index could be the amount of scaffolded assistance needed to help the student perform at the criterion level on the posttest.
2. *Style of interaction*—Some DAs are individualized to the student's needs where the examiner can modify the prompts in light of the student's responses. Others are standardized and the examiner must use the fixed prompts that are part of the assessment.
3. *Nature of skills assessed*—Earlier uses of DA targeted general domains such as cognition, whereas more recent research with DA has targeted academic skill development.

An example of a dynamic assessment is the Learning Propensity Assessment Device developed by Feuerstein, Rand, Jensen, Kaniel, and Tzuriel (1987) to be an interactive

Cross-Battery Assessment

Cross-battery assessment (XBA) was introduced by Flanagan, McGrew, Ortiz, and their colleagues in the 1990s as a time-efficient technique to assess cognitive abilities across intelligence and achievement tests. The XBA assessment is based on the validated CHC theoretical framework on cognitive abilities that looks at an individual's broad and narrow abilities. This multidisciplinary assessment battery includes cognitive, academic, and language tests; interviews; observations; and informal assessments that are selected to specifically suit the referral concerns and needs of the individual student. Because XBAs are tailored to the unique needs of the child, they are particularly appropriate for culturally and linguistically diverse learners and learners with a range of disabilities. For more information on this model, visit http://www.crossbattery.com.

process among the learner, the examiner, and the task. DA data can improve how we instruct students in our schools. For example, the state curricula can be examined to ensure that students have opportunities to build cognitive process skills such as creative thinking, information processing, enquiry, reasoning, and evaluation (Yeomans, 2008). Thinking skills programs could be implemented that include activities and problems which promote thinking skills in students.

INTERPRETATION AND USE OF COGNITIVE ASSESSMENT DATA FOR ELIGIBILITY DETERMINATION AND INSTRUCTIONAL PLANNING

Cognitive assessment data are useful for deciding whether a student qualifies for special education services. They also are used to shed light on a student's strengths and weaknesses and to guide initial instructional decisions.

Using Cognitive Assessment Data for Making Eligibility Decisions

Probably the main reason to administer intelligence tests is to identify whether a student has a disability. A complete psycho-educational battery of tests provides diagnostic information that is informative regarding the student's eligibility for special education. When they are used together with other measures, IQ tests provide a comprehensive picture of the child's learning ability and performance. These tests provide standardized test scores that readily allow the student's performance to be compared with that of age or grade-level peers. Individual intelligence tests, such as those previously described, generally are administered to determine eligibility. For instance, in order for a student to be identified as having intellectual disabilities, which is labeled mental retardation per the Individuals with Disabilities Education Act (IDEA), the student must demonstrate below-average intelligence and deficits in adaptive behavior that are evident during his or her developmental years. Similarly, students who are being tested to determine a possible learning disability, speech and language disability, or emotional disturbance often are administered an intelligence test to ascertain that their learning aptitude is within the average or above-average range and that their educational performance in not adversely affected due to low intelligence.

Using Cognitive Assessment Data for Instructional Planning

Knowing a student's cognitive functioning level provides the teacher with a starting point to plan instruction. Intelligence data guide the teacher about the rate of the student's learning and help with pacing of instruction. Knowledge about cognitive strengths and deficits assists the teacher to decide how to introduce new learning tasks.

Students whose cognitive functioning is well above that of their peers need to be challenged to engage in more creative and divergent ways of thinking. Such students benefit from receiving greater autonomy and choice in planning their learning, having the curriculum accelerated and compacted, and having opportunities to extend their learning beyond the classroom (e.g., real-world problem-solving situations, internships in the discipline of interest).

A student whose cognitive functioning is below average, on the other hand, should be introduced to one task at a time, after having mastered prerequisite skills. Such students benefit from opportunities for repetition and guided practice and need to be taught specifically how to generalize skills to apply them to new situations. For instance, Henrietta, who was described in the vignette at the start of the chapter, develops new knowledge and skills at a slower pace than her peers. Her teacher should provide her with concrete examples, break up the learning task into its subcomponents, and give her multiple prompts and scaffolds to support her learning. Her teacher also needs to provide specific direction for her to apply information that she has learned to new settings and contexts.

The instructional strategies used in the classroom need to be grounded in the theoretical framework about how students learn and think; ideally, this framework also guides the cognitive assessment approaches used. For instance, when teachers are using DA, they need to identify specific learning tasks and implement them with active opportunities for scaffolding and feedback from the teacher. Students need to be provided with repeated opportunities for skill development and mastery of the learning task. Similarly, if teachers adopt a Multiple Intelligence model, they must structure the classroom learning activities to provide ample opportunities to allow children to develop their talents in the various intelligences that were proposed by Gardner. The classroom might include centers for music, art, kinesthetic learning, reading and writing, and math and science, and students might have be allowed to work both independently and collaboratively on learning projects.

COGNITIVE ASSESSMENT IN A RESPONSE TO INTERVENTION (RTI) FRAMEWORK

Some psychologists and educators have viewed RTI as being incompatible with the traditional psycho-educational testing approach and consider the implementation of an RTI model as the harbinger of the end of the IQ testing movement (Willis & DuMont, 2006). In reality, these two approaches are not mutually exclusive. For a long time now the IDEA legislation has required that when a child struggles with academics, he or she must receive adequate and empirically validated instruction and interventions within a general education classroom setting before he or she is referred for special education. Per IDEA (2004) mandates, a local education agency may use either the traditional discrepancy approach to identify a student as having a learning disability or may use alternate, research-based procedures, such as RTI, to determine whether a student responds to scientifically validated and research-based interventions.

Universal screenings using whole-class administration of district benchmark assessments and curriculum-based measurement (CBM) probes seem to be time- and cost-effective measures that allow the early identification of struggling learners. CBM probes have been proven effective as progress monitoring tools for interventions at Tiers 1, 2, and 3. A psycho-educational battery is often administered in Tier 3 to determine a student's eligibility for special education, particularly if the student evidences multiple and complex difficulties in several domains of functioning (Willis & DuMont, 2006). Psycho-educational assessments are still the common tool that is used to rule out exclusionary causes for learning disabilities, such as below-average intelligence; vision, hearing, or other sensory deficits; and emotional-behavioral disabilities. A multidisciplinary psycho-educational assessment using multiple measures will assist in ruling out which learning problems are a function of language delays vs. cognitive delays and distinguish between emotional and behavioral difficulties that affect academic achievement and a general cognitive delay.

Some educators argue for the use of cognitive assessments in distinguishing whether the student being assessed truly has a specific learning disability (Olfiesh, 2006; Wodrich, Spencer, & Daley, 2006). The RTI model allows one to determine whether a student is falling behind age- and grade-level peers and whether he or she is responding adequately to interventions applied, but it does not provide sufficient diagnostic information to determine the nature of the student's disability.

End-of-Chapter Questions

1. Discuss some factors that have contributed to the controversy surrounding intelligence tests.
2. Which factors influence how a student performs on cognitive assessments?
3. What is DA? Describe the process.
4. How can IQ test data be interpreted in order to make decisions about eligibility and instruction?
5. Describe the role of cognitive assessment in an RTI model.

References

Bandalos, D. L. (2004). Review of the Universal Nonverbal Intelligence Test. In *Mental Measurements Yearbook*. Available from http://www.unl.edu/buros/.

Barber, M. (2000). Thinking for learning. *Managing Schools Today, 9*(8), 33–35.

Bracken, B., & McCallum, S. (1998). *Universal Nonverbal Intelligence Test*. Itasca, IL: Riverside Publishing.

Campione, J. C. (1989). Assisted testing: A taxonomy of approaches and an outline of strengths and weaknesses. *Journal of Learning Disabilities, 22*, 151–165.

Fabio, R. A. (2005). Dynamic assessment of intelligence is a better reply to adaptive behavior and cognitive plasticity. *The Journal of General Psychology, 132*, 41–64.

Feuerstein, R., Rand, Y., Jensen, M. R., Kaniel, S., & Tzuriel, D. (1987). Prerequisites for assessment of learning potential: The LPAD model. In C. S. Lidz (Ed.), *Dynamic assessment: An interactional approach to evaluating learning potential*. New York: The Guilford Press.

Floyd, R. G., Clark, M. H., & Shadish, W. R. (2008). The exchangeability of IQs: Implications for professional psychology. *Professional Psychology: Research and Practice, 39*(4), 424–423.

Flynn, J. R. (2007). *What is intelligence?: Beyond the Flynn Effect*. Cambridge, UK: Cambridge University Press.

Gardner, H. (1983). *Frames of mind: The theory of multiple intelligences*. New York: Basic.

Hasson, N., & Joffe, V. (2007). The case for dynamic assessment in speech and language therapy. *Child Language Teaching and Therapy, 23*(1), 9–25.

Kaplan, E., Fein. D., Kramer, J., Dells, D., & Morris, R. (2004). *Wechsler Intelligence Scale for Children Fourth Edition Integrated*. San Antonio, TX: Pearson.

Kauffman, A. S., & Kauffman, N. L. (2004). *Kauffman Assessment Battery for Children* (2nd ed.). Circle Pines, MN: American Guidance Service.

Lohman, D. F., & Hagen, E. P. (2005). *Cognitive Abilities Test (Form 6)*. Rolling Meadows, IL: Riverside Publishing.

McLoughlin, J. A., & Lewis, R. B. (2001). *Assessing students with special needs* (5th ed.). Upper Saddle River, NJ: Merrill/Pearson Education.

Olfiesh, N. (2006). Response to Intervention and the identification of specific learning disabilities: Why we need comprehensive evaluations as part of the process. *Psychology in the Schools, 43*(8), 883–888.

Otis, A. S., & Lennon, R. T. (1995). *Otis-Lennon school ability test* (7th ed.). San Antonio, TX: Psychological Corporation.

Salvia, J., Ysseldyke, J., & Bolt, S. (2007). *Assessment in special and inclusive education* (10th ed.). Boston: Houghton Mifflin.

Sattler, J. (1992). *Assessment of children* (3rd ed.). San Diego, CA: Jerome Sattler Publications.

Wechsler, D. (1958). *The measurement and appraisal of adult intelligence* (4th ed.). Baltimore: The Williams and Wilkins Company.

Willis, J. O., & DuMont, R. (2006). And never the twain shall meet: Can Response to Intervention and cognitive assessment be reconciled? *Psychology in the Schools, 43*(8), 901–908.

Wodrich, D. L., Spencer, M., & Daley, K. B. (2006). Combining RTI and psychoeducational assessment: What we must assume to do otherwise. *Psychology in the Schools, 43*(7), 797–806.

Woodcock, R., McGrew, K., & Mather, N. (2001). *Woodcock Johnson III Normative Update (NU) Tests of Cognitive Abilities*. Rolling Meadows, IL: Riverside Publishing.

Yeomans, J. (2008). Dynamic assessment practice: Some suggestions for ensuring follow-up. *Educational Psychology in Practice, 24*(2), 105–114.

CHAPTER 8

Assessment of Behavior and Social-Emotional Functioning

Misty and Suzy are twin sisters who attend 10th grade at Jefferson High School. Their parents have been actively involved in their education and their mother is on the school PTA. Suzy has been receiving special education services since third grade for a learning disability in math. She works hard to keep her grades up at school. Suzy is a warm and empathetic young lady with a ready smile and a positive attitude, always ready to assist others. She is a little self-conscious because she is very tall and wears braces, and she is generally shy around others outside her small close group of friends. Misty, on the other hand, is very attractive and is on the school cheer team. Other kids at school have called her arrogant and standoffish. She is often rude to her family, peers, and teachers, and has been verbally aggressive, teasing and bullying some of her classmates. Misty is quick to put her sister down any opportunity that she gets, though Suzy is usually forgiving of her sister's put-downs.

Reflections on the Scenario

1. In what ways are the two sisters in the vignette different from each other? In what ways do their social behavioral styles influence their lives?
2. Of what is the social-emotional-behavioral domain composed?
3. Why should schools focus on the social-emotional-behavioral competence of students? What are the implications of this domain for later life adjustment?
4. How does one's social-emotional-behavioral competence affect school behavior and academic performance?
5. What techniques are used to assess and monitor social-emotional-behavioral competence in youngsters?

COUNCIL FOR EXCEPTIONAL CHILDREN (CEC) STANDARDS

This chapter addresses the following CEC standards (from Standard #8 Assessment):

ICC8K1—Basic terminology used in assessment.

ICC8K4—Use and limitations of assessment instruments.

GC8K4—Procedures for early identification of young children who may be at risk for disabilities.

ICC8S1—Gather relevant background information.

ICC8S2—Administer nonbiased formal and informal assessments.

ICC8S4—Develop or modify individualized assessment strategies.

ICC8S8—Evaluate instruction and monitor progress of individuals with exceptional learning needs.

ICC8S10—Create and maintain records.

GC8S1—Implement procedures for assessing and reporting both appropriate and problematic social behaviors of individuals with disabilities.

GC8S5—Monitor intra-group behavior changes across subjects and activities.

THE IMPORTANCE OF SOCIAL-EMOTIONAL-BEHAVIORAL COMPETENCE

A student's social-emotional-behavioral competence has widespread implications for school success and later life adjustment outcomes. A child's social and emotional adjustment is a powerful predictor of his or her academic success and attitude toward school (L. K. Elksnin & N. Elksnin, 2006). Prosocial behavior in the classroom has been found to enhance academic outcomes, including performance on standardized tests (DiPerna & Elliott, 1999; Zins, Bloodworth, Weissberg, & Walberg, 2004). Several social-emotional challenges prevent students from performing well at school. These challenges can result in discipline issues, social rejection, alienation from peers and teachers, poor academic performance, and even dropping out of school (Zins et al., 2004). The impact of such challenges extends to later life adjustment as well. Empirical evidence suggests that 90% of jobs are lost due to social-emotional difficulties and not due to a lack of academic or vocational skills (Bullis, Nishioka-Evans, Fredericks, & Davis, 1993). Schools play a key role in assisting students to learn to navigate their social worlds by creating strong supportive classroom communities.

Between 10 and 15% of children have been reported to have problems with peer relationships (Asher & Rose, 1997). Having friendships seems to buffer children from environmental stressors and serves as a safety net that facilitates academic competence and emotional adjustment (Doll, 1996; Ladd, Kochenderfer, & Coleman, 1997). Feelings of social isolation during childhood have been found to influence social relationships throughout the life span.

Children and adolescents with social-emotional problems are at risk for externalizing and internalizing behavior problems. Externalizing behaviors occur when the child outwardly demonstrates inappropriate behaviors, either physically (e.g., aggressive and violent behavior), or verbally (e.g., verbal abuse, taunting, teasing).

Internalizing behaviors occur when the child demonstrates inappropriate behaviors that are not directed at others, such as excessive shyness, anxiety, withdrawal, and depression. Often, internalizing behaviors result in the individual experiencing physical symptoms (also called somatic manifestations), such as stomachaches and other illnesses.

Social-Emotional-Behavioral Competence in Children and Youth with Disabilities

There is general consensus that many students with disabilities experience difficulties in the area of social relationships with peers and adults (Bryan, 2005; Kavale & Mostert, 2004; Pavri & Monda-Amaya, 2000, 2001). Difficulties in the domain of affective functioning affect self-concept, attribution style, and self-efficacy (the belief that one can successfully take on and complete a task) and make an individual more prone to loneliness (Bryan, 2005; Margalit & Al-Yagon, 2002; Pavri & Luftig, 2000). A child's attributions and self-concept affect his or her social behavior, which in turn affects his or her social status and friendships with peers and lays the foundation for future social behavior. Specific difficulties that have been identified in youngsters with disabilities include problems reading social cues, problems following classroom rules, negative playground behavior, lower peer acceptance, and difficulties with social problem solving using effective social strategies (Leffert, Siperstein, & Millikan, 2000; Walker & Sprague, 1999).

Given the incidence and consequences of social-emotional-behavioral difficulties in children and adolescents, it is imperative that school professionals identify these difficulties as soon as they appear, develop appropriate interventions, and monitor students' responsiveness to these interventions. Research evidence suggests that early identification, prevention, and intervention reduce the risk of academic failure and facilitate later life adjustment (Lane & Menzies, 2003; Walker & Shinn, 2002).

AREAS OF SOCIAL-EMOTIONAL-BEHAVIORAL COMPETENCE

Social-emotional-behavioral competence is a broad area that is composed of many subdomains. School professionals are often unsure how to begin to identify difficulties and intervene in this area. Tanis Bryan, a leading researcher in the area of social relationships in students with disabilities, recommends adopting the following five-component model when assessing a student's functioning in the social-emotional domain (Bryan, 1997):

1. *Affective status*—One's emotional state and ability to regulate emotion to react to situations in a socially acceptable fashion influence one's affective status. Loneliness, depression, anxiety, and mood states may be among the variables assessed.
2. *Beliefs and attributions*—A student's beliefs and attributions affect his or her self-efficacy. A student's attribution of outcomes to either intrinsic factors (e.g., ability, effort) or extrinsic factors (e.g., task difficulty, luck) is considered to be his or her locus of control. Research indicates that many children with learning disabilities tend to have an external locus of control attributing positive consequences to external causes and negative outcomes to intrinsic causes (Pearl, Donahue, & Bryan,

1986; Tur-Kaspa & Bryan, 1993). For instance, Mark attributes his high score on a math test to the fact that the test being easy, and believes he was not selected to be in the school band because he did not practice enough for the band audition.

3. *Friendship and peer relations*—Friendships serve as a safe zone within which children learn to negotiate their social world, explore their social skills, and seek emotional intimacy and support. It is suggested that the assessment separately explores both whether the child has mutual friendships and also what their social status is within the peer group.

4. *Social skills*—Social skills are learned ways of interacting with others that are generally considered to be socially acceptable and that result in positive responses from others (Cartledge & Milburn, 1996). Social skills are developed within a sociocultural context, starting with early socialization experiences in the home. Consequently, it is important to consider the student's cultural context when assessing social skills and developing interventions. In a review of the literature on social skills interventions in schools, Caldarella and Merrell (1997) identified the dimensions of social skills that were most frequently addressed in research studies and found that social skills were classified into the following categories: 1) self management (e.g., self-control, following social conventions and rules, frustration tolerance, social independence); 2) peer relations (e.g., empathy, social participation, social interaction, peer preferred social behavior, leadership skills); 3) academic skills (e.g., task orientation, academic responsibility, independent work completion); 4) compliance (e.g., getting along with others, sharing and turn-taking, social cooperation); and 5) assertion (e.g., initiating conversation, acknowledging and giving compliments, etc.)

5. *Maladaptive behaviors*—Such behaviors include self-injurious actions such as biting and scratching, aggressive behaviors, bullying, teasing, and hyperactivity.

A RESPONSE TO INTERVENTION (RTI) FRAMEWORK IN THE SOCIAL-EMOTIONAL-BEHAVIORAL DOMAIN

Because of RTI's push for prevention and early identification of difficulties that appear in the classroom, and its focus on student outcomes, there has been a call to adopt this approach in the social-emotional-behavioral domain (Gresham, 2004, 2005; Harris-Murri, King, & Rostenberg, 2006). Researchers are investigating ways to adopt RTI as an alternative means of identifying youngsters with emotional disturbances. RTI is particularly appealing because it provides immediate services and supports for students, thereby preventing problem behaviors from becoming chronic and requiring more costly and intensive interventions down the road. In addition, it has the potential for more accurate eligibility determination, thereby reducing the disproportionately high minority representation in the special education category of emotional disturbance (Harris-Murri et al., 2006). Extensive research evidence indicates that students from minority backgrounds are overrepresented in the emotional disturbance category, compared with students from the same minority backgrounds in the general school population (Harry, Klingner, Sturges, & Moore, 2002; Patton, 1998).

Given the systematic and data-based nature of RTI and its compatibility with the tiers of prevention in a school-wide positive behavior support (PBS) model, RTI is considered to be a potentially viable alternative for the diagnosis of emotional disturbance as well (Gresham, 2005). Both RTI and PBS are based on the principles of differentiated instruction to address expressed needs of students in schools (Fairbanks, Sugai, Guardino, & Lathrop, 2007; Sandomierski, Kincaid, & Algozzine, 2008).

The Social-Emotional-Behavioral RTI Model

Generally speaking, a problem-solving model of RTI is best suited to tiered interventions in the social-emotional-behavioral domain. A team of professionals who work with the target student(s) and who have expertise in behavioral interventions assess the student, work closely with the family, and problem solve around the students' expressed difficulties. The team would meet regularly to review progress-monitoring data to determine the effectiveness of the interventions implemented and suggest changes as needed.

Starting with *universal screening*, an RTI approach will allow for early identification of children who are at risk for social-emotional-behavioral difficulties. Best practice dictates that universal behavioral screening techniques be accurate, sensitive, and specific enough to identify risk factors and incorporate multiple methods and informants, while also being cost efficient and easy to administer (Severson, Walker, Hope-Doolittle, Kratochwill, & Gresham, 2007).

The Office of Special Education Programs has worked with several leading researchers in the area of emotional and behavior disorders in an attempt to identify viable and technically adequate behavioral screening and assessment measures (Severson et al., 2007). The review panel considered six measures to be optimal:

1. The Systematic Screening for Behavior Disorders (SSBD; Walker & Severson, 1990), a comprehensive teacher rating measure that screens for externalizing and internalizing behavior problems at several points early in the child's school career
2. The School Social Behavior Scale (Merrell, 1993), a teacher rating scale that assesses for social competence and antisocial problem behaviors
3. The Revised Behavior Problem Checklist (Quay & Peterson, 1993), a teacher rating scale used to detect behavior disorders in school-age students
4. The Eyberg Child Behavior Inventory (Eyberg & Pincus, 1999; Eyberg & Ross, 1978) and the Sutter-Eyberg Student Behavior Inventory, which consist of parent and teacher rating scales that investigate problem behaviors at home and school
5. Drummond's School Risk Screening Scale (Drummond, 1993), a teacher rating scale for negative classroom behavior, attitude, and peer rejection
6. The Conners Rating Scales-Revised (Conners, 1997), which include parent, teacher, and student rating scales to assess disruptive behaviors at home and school.

The SSBD emerged as the most heartily endorsed measure, due to its strong norm sample, use of three levels of screening, and support from research studies. The SSBD allows for observation of academic engaged time and positive social behavior as recorded on the playground (Severson et al., 2007).

Tier 1 or universal interventions are implemented schoolwide or classwide, either daily or weekly, to all the children in a school. Universal interventions address the social behaviors that all students at a school are expected to demonstrate (Sandomierski et al., 2008). Generally, universal interventions target social and academic development

(Gresham, 2004). They could take the form of schoolwide expectations, rules, procedures, discipline plans, character building and violence-prevention programs such as Character Counts, and social skills curricula such as Skillstreaming. Generally, the goal of universal intervention is to teach prosocial behaviors that are necessary for academic and life settings. Sugai, Horner, and Gresham (2002) determine that approximately 80–90% of youngsters are well served by these universal interventions.

Simple measures may be used to determine which students are nonresponsive to the universal interventions and need additional support. For instance, office discipline referrals may indicate students who need more targeted interventions. In- and out-of-school suspensions are another indicator of behavior problems. Commercially available Internet-based information systems such as the School-Wide Intervention System (http://www.swis.org) could be adopted to gather information, enter data, and generate reports for on-site office discipline referral information. These measures are effective in identifying students who demonstrate externalizing behaviors, but a more systematic screening such as the SSBD may be necessary to identify youngsters who have internalizing problems. An important caution is that students are to be identified for selected interventions only if high-quality academic and behavior instruction and interventions have been applied at both the school-wide and classroom levels and students have not responded appropriately to these interventions.

Tier II or selected interventions are targeted at the 10–20% of students in the class who are not responsive to the universal interventions. It is important to note that a large number of students who demonstrate behavior difficulties also have academic difficulties that likely need to be remediated. Tier II interventions are implemented to build students' social-behavioral and/or academic-behavioral repertoire so that students will become more responsive to universal interventions. Behavioral interventions that are easy to administer in small groups and that are not too time and personnel intensive include social skills training, group counseling, or mentoring programs (Gresham, 2004; Sandomierski et al., 2008). Often, individually focused interventions, such as a behavior contract, self-management strategy, or behavior reduction techniques, such as response cost or differential reinforcement, might be employed (Gresham, 2005).

Ongoing progress monitoring should occur at least biweekly in order to ensure that the students are indeed responding appropriately to the intervention. Daily behavior report cards can be developed and used by the teacher to monitor the effectiveness of the interventions that are adopted.

Tier III or targeted interventions are provided to the group of students who exhibit chronic academic and/or behavioral difficulties and are not responsive to Tier II interventions; generally such students make up no more than 1–5% of a class (Sugai et al., 2002). At this point more in-depth data are collected on the student, including a review of interventions already used. The intensity and persistence of the problem behaviors in these students require individualized and comprehensive interventions that are resource intensive and often reach beyond the school system. Mental health, juvenile justice, and social service agencies may be involved. Generally, a functional behavior assessment is conducted to learn about the relationship between the student's behavior and the variables in his or her environment, and interventions are tailored to reduce the specific problem behavior and replace it with positive behaviors (Gresham, 2005). The purpose or communicative intent of the student's behavior is investigated. Again, the student's ongoing progress is frequently

Reflection

Mrs. Aimee Xu's third-grade classroom has 30 students and is in an urban school district. What kinds of universal screenings and interventions might be in place for all students? What selected interventions could Aimee implement for Jerry, who is out of his seat a lot, and for Valerie, who is constantly talking and disrupting the class? How could Aimee monitor these students' progress in response to these interventions? Another student in Aimee's class, Aaron, was an interschool disciplinary transfer and was sent to Aimee's class after physically assaulting his previous teacher. He is prone to angry outbursts, uses abusive language, and occasionally hits his peers and/or teachers. How might the school team work with Aimee to develop targeted interventions for Aaron and evaluate the effectiveness of these interventions?

monitored, either daily or weekly using more direct measures. For instance, teacher rating scales that report on shorter time intervals or direct observation of target behavior may be appropriate. A useful resource for PBS and planning is available at http://www.pent.ca.gov.

GUIDELINES FOR ACCURATE ASSESSMENT OF BEHAVIOR AND SOCIAL-EMOTIONAL FUNCTIONING IN DIVERSE STUDENTS

The six criteria to be considered when selecting an effective progress-monitoring technique (Riley-Tillman, Kalberer, & Chafouleas, 2005) were discussed in Chapter 2. Table 8.1 lists questions that must be asked along these six dimensions in order to select an appropriate assessment tool for diagnosing and monitoring a student's behavior.

There are some additional considerations when assessing students in the social-emotional-behavioral domain within an RTI framework:

1. *Ensure social validity of the assessment tools*—Social validity implies acceptability and perceived importance of the domain and assessment tool as appropriate and meaningful by various stakeholders (i.e., the respondents such as teachers, student, and parent) who provide the assessment data, as well as the student and family members who will be making decisions on the basis of the data obtained. For example, direct observation of the frequency of out-of-seat behavior would be considered socially valid, but a parent questionnaire might not be considered to be a meaningful indicator of this behavior.

2. *Use multiple sources of data across multiple informants*—Obtaining aggregated data across different informants and times of the day is particularly important when assessing a student in this domain. Children react differently in varied settings depending on the environmental stressors placed on them. For example, Alex is often defiant and disruptive during language arts class, but he emerges as a cooperative and confident class leader during physical education. Obtaining the perspective of the primary caregivers and family members and working closely

TABLE 8.1	Criteria to Be Considered When Selecting a Behavior-Monitoring Tool	
Criteria	**Considerations**	**Sample tools**
Goodness of fit	Does the assessment tool assess the target behavior effectively? Can the tool be adapted for frequent and accurate use in monitoring the students' behavior?	Systematic observation used to determine frequency of "shouting out" in class.
Directness	Does the tool provide an objective measure of the target behavior as it occurs?	Event recording of out-of-seat behavior; attendance records to indicate truancy.
Generalization	Does the tool yield data on the typical, day-to-day functioning of the target student?	Teacher behavior rating scale response on social skills.
Feasibility	Is it easy, quick, and cost effective to use the selected tool?	Daily Behavior Report Cards as an indicator of student response to an intervention.
Minimal need for training	What duration and intensity of training are required to utilize the tool effectively?	Tallying the number of "caught doing something good" positive behavior slips.
Minimal intrusiveness	What is the impact of using the tool on the teacher and students' daily classroom routines?	An external, unfamiliar observer visiting the class can be disruptive; attendance records as a measure of truancy are not intrusive.

Source: Information adapted from Riley-Tillman, Kalberer, and Chafouleas (2005)

with them through the assessment and intervention process will help reduce the difficulties in this domain.

3. *Use social comparison data* —It is prudent to collect comparison data on another peer of the same age, gender, and ethnic background who attends the same class as the target student when monitoring a student to determine whether the behaviors being demonstrated are truly atypical.

4. *Consider ecological variables* —External factors in the child's environment (e.g., external distracters such as noise or competing activities, internal distracters such as fear, hunger, or sleep deprivation) can have a significant impact on a child's behavior. These variables may result in dips or spikes in the child's performance.

5. *Select assessment tools that are authentic, feasible, and technically sound* —When using an RTI model it is key to select assessments that are brief and easily administered and that provide a valid and reliable index of the behavior being monitored. Some sample assessment techniques are described in the section that follows.

KEY ASSESSMENT TECHNIQUES USED IN AN RTI APPROACH

The following assessment techniques could be used to screen a student's behavioral and affective status, identify and diagnose behavioral difficulties, determine behavior intervention and support plans, and monitor student progress when behavioral interventions are implemented.

Observation

Probably the most widely used assessment technique is observation. A lot can be learned about students' social, emotional, and behavioral worlds by observing their behavior in everyday life settings. Data are collected on both the individual student's functioning and the ecological variables within the environment that the student interacts with that affect how the student thinks and behaves (Merrell, 2003).

Direct observations could be formal and systematic collection of data to develop hypotheses regarding a student's behavior that can guide the development of interventions. Observations could also be more informal and part of other assessments such as interviews or rating scales. Direct observation is a key means of monitoring students' responsiveness to interventions as well.

TYPES OF OBSERVATION

Naturalistic Observation. This type of observation requires directly observing the student in the natural setting at different times of the day so as to obtain authentic data on the target behavior as and when it occurs. A student would be observed during both structured times (e.g., language arts, math) and unstructured times (e.g., recess, before and after school) within the school day. Conducting observations of the student with his or her family in the home is also extremely valuable as it provides information on interaction styles within the family.

Analogue Observation. Analogue observations involve observing the individual in a simulated environment, often from behind a one-way mirror. Generally used in therapeutic settings, analogue observations allow for more controlled settings within which the target behavior may be stimulated to occur through role play, playing games, or participating in certain activities. Using analogue observation saves time and allows for data collection of low-frequency behaviors; however, the validity of the behavior itself may be compromised because it is not naturally occurring.

Self-Monitoring. Self-monitoring is an observation technique in which the target student is trained to identify and monitor his or her own behavior. Although the accuracy of self-monitoring data often is questionable, it is a time- and cost-effective technique and can also be used to monitor social and emotional variables that are not overt and observable.

RECORDING OBSERVATION DATA

Anecdotal Notes. This technique requires the observer to write down in detail all the events that occur as they unfold during the observation. In essence, the anecdotal notes could be considered to be the written transcription of all that occurred during the observation. Anecdotal records could be employed to explore reasons for certain outcomes, such as failure to complete work, or they may focus on predetermined target behaviors.

Anecdotal notes could be used to analyze the antecedents and consequences of the target behavior. A form with three columns could be employed in which the observer lists events under each of three columns as they occur: antecedent, behavior, and consequence. See Table 8.2. On the basis of these records, an analysis can be conducted

TABLE 8.2	Structure of an A-B-C Analysis Using Anecdotal Records		
Time and Setting	**Antecedent**	**Behavior**	**Consequence**
11:00 A.M.—during whole-group independent work in math. Unit on multiplication.		1. Sara works quietly at her desk.	
	2. Michele pokes her pencil into Sara's face.		
		3. Sara screams loudly and hits Michele on the arm.	
			4. Teacher says, "Sara can't you be quiet for even 5 minutes?"

of the pattern of occurrence of the inappropriate behavior, its frequency, intensity, antecedents, and consequences (Alberto & Troutman, 1995).

Systematic Observation Techniques.   Systematic direct observation involves the operational definition of the target behavior in observable and measurable terms, selection of a data-recording system that is appropriate for the target behavior, and a mechanism to share the observational data with others, usually in the form of charts or graphs (L. K. Elksnin & N. Elksnin, 2006). This last step is particularly important in an RTI approach in which the goal is to determine the student's responsiveness to a particular intervention and to share information about student progress with the student, parents, teachers, and other school personnel.

The following observational recording systems may be employed when collecting systematic observation data:

1. *Event recording*—Event recording is used to record the number of times a target behavior is observed at different times in the school day. A notation is made on a chart each time the behavior occurs, thereby yielding a precise record of the frequency of the behavior. Event recording can be used to monitor the frequency and rate of occurrence of a behavior in either a single student or a group of students. Digital counting devices are available to make the work of record keeping a little easier, but event recording is very time consuming and it is difficult for a teacher who is unassisted in the classroom to accomplish it, as he or she is often busy with the other demands of the job.

Figure 8.1 shows an event-recording data sheet that could be used to determine the frequency of target behaviors such as the number of times Gillian gets out of her seat during a 30-minute math class, or the number of times in the day that Henry hits his peers. Event recording is best suited for discrete behaviors that have a clear beginning and end.

2. *Duration recording*—Duration recording is used to monitor the occurrence of behaviors such as temper tantrums or epileptic seizures that have a clear beginning and

Student _____

Observer _____

Setting _____

Discrete Target Behavior (operationally define the behavior)

_____

_____

_____

Date	Time		Frequency of Target Behavior	Narrative Comments (Setting, activity, context, other)
	Begin	End		

FIGURE 8.1 Event-Recording Data Sheet

end. It provides a measure of the length or duration of a target behavior and allows the computation of the average duration of the target behavior over the course of the school day. Figure 8.2 shows a sample duration-recording data sheet.

  3. *Interval Recording*—Interval recording uses short observation periods that are divided into intervals, typically about 30 seconds in length. The observer records whether or not the target behavior occurred during each interval. Both discrete and continuous behaviors can be recorded using this technique, which provides a snapshot of a student's behavior during different times in the day. If the behavior occurs repeatedly during an interval, it is counted as having occurred only once. Also, if a behavior such as a temper tantrum starts in one interval and continues through the next two intervals, the behavior is recorded as having occurred three times.

  One could use either partial or whole interval criteria to record behavior using an interval recording system. During partial interval recording, an occurrence of the behavior is noted if the behavior occurs at any point during the interval. During whole interval recording, the behavior must last for the entire interval in order for it to be recorded as having occurred. It is generally difficult for a teacher to accurately complete

Student _____

Observer _____

Setting _____

Discrete Target Behavior (operationally define the behavior)

_____

_____

_____

Date	Behavior*		Duration	Narrative Comments (Setting, activity, context, other)
	Begin	End		
			Average duration per day	

FIGURE 8.2 Duration-Recording Data Sheet

*Record time of onset and termination of each occurrence of the behavior.

interval recording while he or she is fulfilling other teaching responsibilities, and having another observer in the room is usually beneficial.

4. *Time sampling*—In time sampling, the observation period is divided into equal intervals, each usually lasting about 1–5 minutes, although intervals of 30 minutes or more could be used. A behavior is recorded as having occurred if it is observed at the end of the interval. This technique is more feasible for use in a classroom than interval recording because it does not require continuous observation of the target behavior. A kitchen timer or prerecorded beeps on a CD or audiocassette can prompt the teacher to collect data. Alberto and Troutman (1995) suggest varying the length of the intervals so that students are not able to predict when the next beep will sound and modify their behavior accordingly. Figure 8.3 shows a sample time-sampling data recording sheet.

CHALLENGES OF USING OBSERVATION TECHNIQUES Systematic observation has been considered to be the "gold standard" for assessing the social-emotional-behavioral domain because it provides the most reliable and authentic picture of behavior as it occurs (Riley-Tillman et al., 2005). However, several challenges are associated with

Student _____

Observer _____

Setting _____

Target Behavior (operationally define the behavior)

_____

_____

_____

Interval (describe length of interval) _____

Date	Time Begin	End	1	2	3	4	5	6	7	8	9	10	Narrative Comments (Activity, context, other)

FIGURE 8.3 Time-Sampling Data Sheet

X = occurrence of target behavior during the interval

O = non-occurrence of target behavior during the interval

this type of data collection when it is used for ongoing progress monitoring, such as in an RTI model:

1. There is a *reactivity effect* due to the obtrusive nature of collecting data in the presence of those being observed. In other words, the individual is likely to change his or her behavior as a result of being watched, often attempting to present himself or herself in the best light. On occasion, youngsters may "act up" for the observer, demonstrating behaviors that are more aberrant or exaggerated than their typical behavior. Use of recording devices such as audiotapes and videotapes often increase obtrusiveness, so they need to be used judiciously.

2. A second challenge with observational techniques is the need to *operationally define the target behavior* in order to collect reliable and valid data. It can be difficult to pin down the precise variables of interest and also ensure that the definition is broad enough to allow for a range of subtleties that are part of the target behavior.

3. A third challenge is the need for *ongoing training of the observers* to ensure that they are accurately assessing the target behavior. When more than one observer is involved, it is even more important to ensure that all observers are trained in order to provide interobserver reliability. An additional concern is that of *observer drift*, a tendency for observers to move away from the original coding and definition system over time as they gain familiarity with the task and start imposing their own nuances on the coding of the observation data. Ongoing reliability checks and retraining of observers can prevent them from drifting away from the original recording system.

4. Yet another limitation of observation techniques occurs due to the *situational specificity of the target behavior*. It is a well-known fact that humans behave differently in different settings and that behaviors are not always consistent from day to day. For example, when Ravi is anxious about an upcoming math test he appears more restless and agitated in language arts class, whereas on another day he appears focused and attentive during a hands-on science activity. It is difficult to make generalizations of a student's behavior unless he or she has been observed on multiple occasions, by multiple observers, and in multiple settings. Misleading assumptions may be made about a student's preferences and behaviors if observations are limited to particular settings.

5. Finally, conducting systematic observations is extremely *resource intensive* in terms of time and personnel. This drain on resources limits the feasibility of observation in schools, particularly when it is used for ongoing progress monitoring purposes (Riley-Tillman et al., 2005).

Permanent Products

Any social-emotional-behavioral data that already exist are considered to be permanent products. Alberto and Troutman (1995) define a permanent product as "tangible items or environmental effects that result from a behavior" (p. 108). Attendance records, notes sent home, office discipline referrals, school suspensions, slips granted for good behavior, or data collected from existing behavior plans are examples of permanent products. It is time and cost effective to use data in the form of permanent products because they usually have been collected already and are accessible as needed. Permanent products provide a general sense of a student's responsiveness to a particular intervention (e.g., attendance records and discipline referrals provide an index of improved behaviors for a student who is on a behavior plan for physical aggression), but these data do not allow for an in-depth examination that would determine which specific intervention resulted in the desired behavior change and at what point during the intervention the change occurred. Riley-Tillman et al. (2005) point out that permanent products is a viable screening tool that assists in the identification of students who are at risk for behavioral problems, but additional sources of data usually are needed to supplement permanent products in order to get a clearer picture of the effectiveness of different interventions.

Interviews

Interviews are a useful assessment tool, particularly when the goal is to learn more about a child's or adolescent's social and emotional functioning. Interviews nicely supplement data obtained from observation and rating scales and provide insights into the way that students think and how they perceive themselves. Interviews may be informal and spontaneous, semistructured, or structured. Structured interviews use standard scripts, such as the Diagnostic Interview for Children and Adolescents (Reich, 2000), which is used by psychologists and clinicians to assist in making diagnoses for children and adolescents per the *Diagnostic and Statistical Manual of Mental Disorders* (DSM-IV) of the American Psychiatric Association. Interviews are an effective way for school personnel to learn more about a student's preferences, beliefs, and circumstances.

Several considerations will assist the practitioner to become more skilled in interviewing a student, thereby allowing him or her to obtain more meaningful information to guide in the development of interventions.

CONSIDERATIONS FOR EFFECTIVE INTERVIEWING

1. It is important to *consider the developmental level of the child*, specifically the child's cognitive, social-emotional, and language development. For instance, preschool-aged children or those with developmental disabilities may have limited verbal abilities, and their reasoning and concept formation is often difficult for an adult to follow, making it challenging to interview these youngsters. Interviewers of preschoolers and elementary school-aged children are advised to use both open questions (which prompt open-ended answers) and closed questions (which prompt "yes" and "no" responses), ask simply worded questions, and use toys and props to solicit responses. In contrast, adolescents may enjoy the one-on-one attention afforded in an interview and may be fairly communicative and cooperative. However, it is recommended that the interviewer be cautious in interpreting the results of the interview and look for additional evidence to support information obtained through the interview (Merrell, 2003). It is also advisable to frame questions in a manner that does not lead to guided responses; in other words, interviewers should avoid questions that cause students to feel obliged to provide the response that they believe the interviewer expects to hear.
2. It is critical to *build rapport with the student* being interviewed. Demonstrating genuine interest and positive regard for the student helps to lay the foundations for a trusting relationship, thereby building rapport.
3. It is important to pay attention to the *differences in interpersonal and cross-cultural communication styles* when interviewing youngsters. Some of these factors include rate and volume of speech, use of eye contact, conventions related to taking turns and interrupting when someone is talking, and manner of expression (Merrell, 2003).

AREAS OF QUESTIONING   First, an interviewer should collect background information about the student from the student and his or her parents and teachers. Next, the interviewer frames interview questions to inquire into the following five areas of adjustment (Merrell, 2003):

1. *Intrapersonal functioning*—Eating and sleeping habits, feelings about oneself, and the student's emotional status (e.g., depression, anxiety, anger, clarity of thought).
2. *Family relationships*—Relationships with siblings, parents, extended family members, family routines and responsibilities, and perceived support or conflict within family.

3. *Peer relationships*—The number of close friends, preferred activities, feelings of loneliness or peer rejection, and perceived conflicts.
4. *School adjustment*—Current school status and feelings about school, teachers, subjects, academic performance, extracurricular activities, attendance, and perceived conflicts at school.
5. *Community involvement*—Participation in clubs, organizations, and community activities; mobility in the community; part-time jobs; and relationships with others in the community.

BEHAVIORS TO OBSERVE DURING THE INTERVIEW   In addition to gathering data from the content of the interview itself, an interviewer can learn a lot by observing the student's appearance, behavior, and thinking and responding style during the interview. Merrell (2003) suggests observing characteristics in the following four areas:

1. *Physical characteristics*—Attire, physical problems, height and weight, motor coordination.
2. *Overt behavior*—Activity level, attention span, impulsivity, distractibility, and anxiety.
3. *Social-emotional functioning*—Range and appropriateness of affect, mood, reaction to praise or frustration, anxiety, and social skills.
4. *Cognitive functioning*—Communication skills, logical reasoning, and organization of thoughts as shown in the response.

LIMITATIONS OF INTERVIEWS   Although interviews are a valuable source of information about the thoughts, feelings, and attributions of children and adolescents, they have some limitations. First, the data obtained from the interview are only *credible if both the interviewer and interviewee are vested in participating* in this process. It is not atypical for youngsters to provide responses that they think the interviewer would like to hear. Other children and adolescents enjoy making outrageous comments and responses in an attempt to test the interviewer, thereby limiting the credibility of their responses. The subjective response of the interviewer is a variable that can influence how the interview is conducted and how the student is perceived. The interviewer needs to be aware of any biases that he or she brings to the interview situation. In addition, conducting interviews is extremely *time consuming*. It may take several interview sessions to build rapport so that the student will trust the interviewer and open up to him or her. Finally, *reliability of data* obtained across different interviewers often tends to be low. Youngsters tend to vary their responses on the basis of their current frame of mind or emotional experience, and they may respond in different ways to different interviewers with whom they share varying levels of rapport and trust.

Behavior Rating Scales

Behavior rating scales are questionnaires, either standardized and norm-referenced or informal, that are administered to the student, teacher, and/or parent and that rate the student on certain key behaviors. The rater should be familiar with the target student and should have experience working with him or her, ideally over a substantial period of time. Behavior rating scales may be limited in focus (e.g., targeting attention deficit hyperactivity disorder) or comprehensive, assessing across multiple dimensions, such as externalizing and internalizing problems, adaptive behavior, social skills, academic performance, and attention problems.

Behavior rating scales usually require minimal training of the rater, are cost effective, and do not require direct observation of the target behavior. This makes rating scales particularly attractive when the goal is to collect data on low-frequency behaviors. They are a useful tool to conduct initial screenings and can be followed up with more in-depth and comprehensive assessment approaches, such as observations and interviews, as needed. In addition, many behavior rating scales have strong technical adequacy and provide useful global information on a target student. Another strength of this technique is the fact that data are collected from respondents who are "experts" on the target student, typically students' teachers and parents. The following box presents key information about some of the widely used behavior rating scales: the Behavior Assessment System for Children, Second Edition (BASC-2; Reynolds & Kamphaus, 2004), Conners Comprehensive Behavior Rating Scale (CBRS; Conners, 2008), the Vineland Adaptive Behavior Scales, Second Edition (Vineland-II; Sparrow, Cicchetti, & Balls, 2005), and the Social Skills Rating System (SSRS; Gresham & Elliott, 1990).

Behavior Rating Scales

Behavior Assessment System for Children (BASC-2, Reynolds & Kamphaus, 2004) is widely used to assess the behavior of children and adolescents. This assessment system is appropriate for use with students aged 2 through 21 years. It includes Teacher Rating Scales, Parent Rating Scales, a Self-Report of Personality, a Student Observation System, and a Structured Developmental History component to provide a multidimensional and comprehensive profile of the student's behavior across multiple settings. The teacher, parent, and student self-report scales of the BASC-2 have adequate reliability and validity and the scale's norm sample is representative of the U.S. Census. Fewer data are available on the technical qualities of the observation and development history scales.

Conners Comprehensive Behavior Rating Scales (CBRS; Conners, 2008) is used with youngsters aged 6 to 18 years to assess emotional, behavioral, social, and academic functioning. This comprehensive assessment measure is used for clinical, research, and school purposes and features over 40 scales, including content, DSM symptom, validity, and clinical index scales. Parent, teacher, and adolescent self-report scales are available in both short and long forms. The scales have strong psychometric qualities and appropriate normative data are available.

Vineland Adaptive Behavior Scales, Second Edition (Vineland-II; Sparrow, Cicchetti, & Balls, 2005) assess adaptive behavior in individuals from birth to 90 years of age in the following domains: communication, daily living skills, socialization, motor skills, and maladaptive behaviors. The Vineland-II includes a survey interview, a parent/caregiver rating scale, a teacher rating scale, and an expanded interview. This test has solid technical qualities and clear guidelines for administration, scoring, and interpretation. A weakness is low interrater reliability on this measure compared with other measures, particularly on the teacher rating and maladaptive behavior scales.

Social Skills Rating System (Gresham & Elliott, 1990) is appropriate for use in students from preschool to grade 12. It provides information about a student's social behavior from the perspective of the teacher, parent, and student. It includes data on three scales: the Social Skills Scale, which includes behaviors such as cooperation, empathy, assertion, self-control, and responsibility; the Problem Behaviors Scale, which looks at internalizing, externalizing, and hyperactivity behaviors; and the Academic Competence Scale, which reviews the student's academic functioning. A unique feature of the SSRS is that it is accompanied by the Assessment Intervention Record, a guide that assists with developing appropriate interventions for students on the basis of the data collected.

Behavior rating scales can be used routinely to conduct universal screenings of youngsters who are at risk for social-emotional-behavior problems and to identify children who need selected or targeted interventions (Merrell, 2003). Despite the advantages of behavior rating scales, they have several limitations, particularly as progress monitoring tools in an RTI approach. First, rating scales are *designed to provide a single rating* of the student's behavior across several dimensions rather than multiple indexes of a student's behavior over a relatively shorter period of time. The latter is the type of data that is required in order to determine whether a student has made progress in response to an intervention (Riley-Tillman et al., 2005). Hence, behavior rating scales are not sensitive to student growth and have limited utility in determining the effectiveness of an intervention. A second limitation is that the *rater must have sufficient familiarity* with the student across all the dimensions assessed on the rating scale. A new teacher or one with a large caseload who is less familiar with the student may not provide accurate ratings, thereby limiting the usefulness and accuracy of the data obtained. In addition, positive or negative *respondent bias* may affect the ratings of the student. Finally, raters may be *unduly influenced by a few instances of unusual behavior* and may give them more weight than everyday behavior when they rate the student (Merrell; Riley-Tillman et al.).

Functional Behavioral Assessment (FBA)

A functional assessment of behavior seeks to identify the "function" that the behavior serves for an individual. Because they are time-consuming tasks, generally functional behavioral assessments are only conducted in school settings when significant problem behaviors appear, usually during Tier 3 (targeted interventions) in an RTI model. The FBA explores the antecedent variables that cause the problem behavior and the consequences that maintain the behavior. The intent is to replace the inappropriate behavior with a more appropriate alternative that meets the same function.

Under the Individuals with Disabilities Education Improvement Act (IDEA, 2004), an FBA must be conducted in order to develop PBS plans for all students who exhibit problem behaviors. Furthermore, when a student with a disability experiences disciplinary action as a result of bringing drugs or weapons to school or to a school-sponsored event, or when the student inflicts bodily harm on himself or herself or others, as part of the manifestation determination process an FBA must be conducted within 10 days of the incident.

Generally the following strategies are used during an FBA (Cohen & Spenciner, 2007; O'Neill, Horner, Albin, Storey, & Sprague, 1990):

1. *Operational definition of the problem behavior*—The target behavior is defined in observable and measurable terms so that data may be collected on it.
2. *Review of the student's records*—The goal is to get information on the background variables that may affect the behavior, such as attendance information, health history, discipline reports and referrals, previous individualized education programs or behavior intervention plans, etc.
3. *Functional interview*—Interviews with the student, parents, teachers, and others who have direct interactions with the student help to define the problem behavior, identify the environmental factors that could have an impact on the behavior, and determine the potential functions of the behavior.

4. *Behavioral observation*—A systematic observation of the target behavior can determine the antecedents and consequences of the target behavior.

5. *Identification of patterns*—Patterns in the student's behavior can determine the function of the behavior. For instance, it may be apparent that the student engages in head-banging behaviors each time he is asked to complete assigned work by his paraeducator, Mrs. G. His head-banging behavior upsets Mrs. G, and in an attempt to stop the undesired behavior, she does not insist that he complete the assigned task. Hence, the head banging seems to be a way to escape a task demand.

6. *Development, implementation, and monitoring of a PBS plan*—Using the FBA data, the antecedent variable or consequence of the behavior can be manipulated by enhancing needed supports or instituting necessary accommodations and modifications in order to encourage the child to use alternate replacement behaviors.

A functional analysis of behavior uses the data obtained from the FBA to manipulate the relevant variables in the child's environment to determine the impact of these variables on the target behavior. The goal of a functional analysis of behavior is to build a PBS plan (O'Neill et al., 1990).

Daily Behavior Report Cards (DBRCs)

One technique that is particularly relevant to an RTI approach, DBRCs are used by the student and teacher to monitor the effectiveness of an intervention applied toward a target behavior. A DBRC is similar to a home-school note or good note sent home. First, target behaviors are defined and a plan is developed to rate the student on these behaviors, usually several times daily. Positive and negative consequences for the behaviors may be identified and listed. Then a report card is designed, implemented, and shared between the teacher and student (Chafouleas, Riley-Tillman, Sassu, LaFrance, & Patwa, 2007; Riley-Tillman et al., 2005).

DBRCs may serve as the intervention itself or as the measure for monitoring student progress in response to an intervention. Studies indicate that DBRCs serve as an effective supplement to direct observation data. They also can substitute for direct observation when it is not possible to observe a target behavior (Chafouleas et al., 2007). Preliminary evidence suggests that DBRCs are appealing to teachers and easy to use, but additional empirical evidence is needed prior to putting them into widespread use as a monitoring tool.

Goal Attainment Scaling (GAS)

Another technique that has been widely used in the mental health and medical fields to monitor change toward a desired goal is GAS, which usually follows five steps (Roach & Elliott, 2005):

1. Selection of the target behavior.
2. Operational definition of the desired outcome for the target behavior.
3. Construction of the goal attainment scale, a 5-point scale in which 0 is the baseline behavior, +2 is the best possible outcome of the intervention, and −2 is the worst

possible outcome, and +1 and −1 describe intermediate outcomes. Variables that can be rated on this scale include frequency (−2 = never, 0 = often, 2 = always), accuracy (−2 = all incorrect, 0 = some incorrect, +2 = all correct), and effort (−2 = not attempted, 0 = some effort, +2 = excellent effort).

4. Implementation of the intervention and collection of data on student performance.
5. Graphing GAS ratings to evaluate effectiveness of the intervention.

For example, 6-year-old Marcus is extremely attached to his paraeducator and resists independently grooming and feeding himself and completing other tasks. The desired outcome is for Marcus to feed himself independently while he is at school. The following GAS was developed for him:

+2 = At snack time, Marcus will independently open his food, eat (taking appropriately sized mouthfuls), and clean up after himself with no assistance or prompts from his paraeducator.

+1 = At snack time, Marcus will open his food, eat (taking appropriately sized mouthfuls), and clean up after himself with verbal prompts but no physical assistance from his paraeducator.

0 = At snack time, Marcus will open his food, eat (taking appropriately sized mouthfuls), and clean up after himself with some verbal prompts and physical assistance from his paraeducator.

−1 = At snack time, Marcus will open his food, eat (taking appropriately sized mouthfuls), and clean up after himself with extensive physical assistance from his paraeducator.

−2 = At snack time, Marcus will open his mouth on cue, chew and swallow when his paraeducator feeds him appropriately sized mouthfuls, and allow his paraeducator to clean up after him.

GAS is an indirect measure of monitoring progress using observation data, permanent records, teacher or parent report, or other techniques. It is a nice supplement to direct data sources. Because it is an indirect measure, it tends to be subject to bias from the teacher or parent implementing the GAS. Yet it is appealing because it is simple to set up, is easy to implement in the schools, encourages joint setting of goals, and yields useful data on academic and behavioral progress in response to intervention.

Activity

Ari is depressed and unmotivated to come to school in the mornings. When he arrives at school, he finds it difficult to become engaged in academic work and rarely completes class assignments. Develop a GAS to monitor Ari's responsiveness to a behavior contract to increase the amount of effort he invests in completing his class assignments.

OTHER SOCIAL-EMOTIONAL-BEHAVIORAL ASSESSMENT TECHNIQUES

The techniques that follow are a useful way to learn about a student's social status and self-perceptions, although they are fairly time intensive and may not be suited to ongoing progress monitoring as required in an RTI approach. However, they are instructionally meaningful and contribute to a holistic assessment of a student's functioning.

Sociometric Assessments

Sociometric assessments provide a unique snapshot of the social dynamics within a social group such as a classroom or play group, providing an index of the social acceptance or rejection, likeability, and social status of an individual (Odom, Schertz, Munson, & Brown, 2004). Such assessments are unique among social-emotional-behavioral assessments because persons within a particular social group provide information on the social status of their members, rather than outside evaluators observing or rating children's relationships. The rigor of these measures has been investigated in several research studies and they have been found to have adequate technical qualities.

Gathering sociometric data allows the teacher to obtain a social map of the classroom that identifies students who are popular and well liked by peers, those who share reciprocal friendships, and those who are social isolates with few or no friendships. A sociogram is a graphical representation of these sociometric data. See Figure 8.4 for a sample sociogram.

Sociometric data can be used to develop seating charts, pair peer buddies, and strategically group children for activities such as fieldtrips or cooperative learning activities. These data are particularly useful when the social dynamics within a classroom are fraught with teasing, bullying, excessive competition, and other kinds of tension that adversely affect the classroom climate and community.

Free web-based software for developing sociograms for classroom use is available at http://www.phenotyping.com/sociogram/.

SPECIFIC SOCIOMETRIC PROCEDURES

1. *Peer nomination*—Peer nomination is the most commonly used sociometric technique. All students in a classroom nominate individuals from the class who meet certain criteria (e.g., those whom they like the most, like the least, are best friends with, would invite to a party, would work with on a class project). Behavioral criteria that indicate positive or negative characteristics are sometimes provided and children asked to nominate peers who meet these criteria (e.g., which 3 students in class have strong leadership skills? Which 3 students get angry a lot?) Alternately, nonbehavioral descriptions are provided (e.g., which 3 students in class would you most like to work with on a class project? Which 3 students would you least like to invite to your birthday party?).

It has been common practice to limit peer nomination items to positive criteria (i.e., nominating students according to positive behavioral criteria or nominating those with whom the target child would like to interact) rather than negative criteria (i.e., nominating students according to negative behavioral criteria such as anger, fear, or

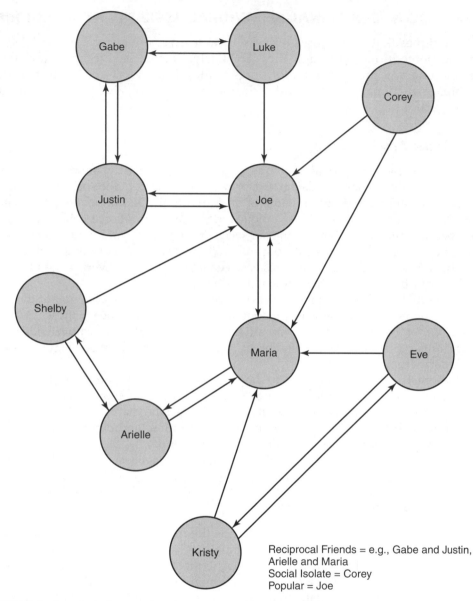

Reciprocal Friends = e.g., Gabe and Justin,
Arielle and Maria
Social Isolate = Corey
Popular = Joe

FIGURE 8.4 Sample Sociogram

aggression or nominating children with whom the target child would not like to interact). Occasionally, both positive and negative criteria are used to provide a complete
picture of the social relationships in a classroom (Merrell, 2003). A child's sociometric
status (popular, rejected, average, neglected, or controversial) is determined by calculating the proportion of positive and negative nominations that he or she receives.

   2. *Peer ratings*—Using the peer rating technique, students rate every other student in their class or play group according to provided preference criteria (e.g., rate on

a 3-point scale "how much you like to play with . . . ; talk to . . ." each other student). A score is then calculated for each student on the basis of the average rating that he or she receives from all their classmates. This score is the index of the average likeability of the student. The scores can rank individual students from highest to lowest rated. Peer ratings are relatively stable indicators of group dynamics, but they only provide a reliable and valid profile of the social group when at least 80% of the individuals in the group participate in the technique.

ADVANTAGES AND LIMITATIONS OF SOCIOMETRIC ASSESSMENTS   Sociometric assessments provide detailed information about the social status of students within a particular group and help identify students who are at risk for social-emotional-behavioral difficulties. Yet the use of negative nominations has been controversial and has raised ethical concerns that such nominations may have lasting negative impacts, such as further social isolation or rejection from peers. A few research studies have investigated these concerns and have not found any negative consequences for children participating in sociometric assessments (Hayvren & Hymel, 1984; A. M. Iverson & G. L. Iverson, 1996). Because children's peer relationships have changed over the years, more research investigating the lasting impact of sociometric techniques is warranted.

Projective Techniques

A detailed explanation of projective techniques is beyond the scope of this section, but this chapter would be incomplete if it did not mention these techniques. Projective assessments are based on the belief that the human "unconscious" projects itself on ambiguous stimuli such as pictures, incomplete sentences, ink blots, etc. Individuals are said to project onto these stimuli their innermost, possibly unconscious, thoughts and feelings. Projective techniques may be standardized, such as the Roberts Apperception Test for Children (McArthur & Roberts, 1982), or informal, such as the Draw a Person technique or the incomplete sentences activity presented in Figure 8.5. Generally, it requires great skill and advanced preparation to become qualified to appropriately use and interpret these assessments.

Complete the following sentences:

1. I am happy when . . .
2. My mother and father . . .
3. At home . . . .
4. My friend and I . . .
5. Sometimes I think . . .
6. I get very angry . . .
7. My mother . . .
8. When I grow up . . .
9. When I am at school, I . . .
10. I am afraid of . . .

FIGURE 8.5   Incomplete Sentences Activity

Assessing Affect and Attributions

Emotions and internal states are usually assessed using standardized and informal self-report techniques such as interviews and questionnaires. For instance, loneliness in youngsters can be assessed using direct naturalistic observation in varied settings; interviews with the student, peers, parents, and other adults; and self-report measures such as the UCLA Loneliness Scale (Russell, 1996) and the Children's Loneliness and Social Dissatisfaction Scale (Asher, Hymel, & Renshaw, 1984). The latter includes 24 items and uses a 5-point Likert scale; 16 items are related to loneliness, peer relationships, and social competence, and 8 are filler items such as "I like to read" that are related to interests and hobbies. The Children's Loneliness and Social Dissatisfaction Scale has been used widely with children with and without disabilities; in some cases, it has been administered with a few modifications such as reading items aloud to children.

It is not easy to assess attributions or beliefs accurately. Tur-Kaspa and Bryan (1993) developed the Social Attribution Questionnaire, which presents six social vignettes (e.g., "you ask your friend if you can borrow her bike and she says no") to youngsters in an interview format, followed by a list of causal statements (e.g., "her brother told her to say no"). Children are asked to weigh the relative importance of the causal statements for each vignette. The interviewer also inquires whether the child could do something to affect the outcome in each vignette in order to assess children's sense of control over different social outcomes.

Self esteem is defined as "one's overall sense of worth" (Cosden, Brown, & Elliott, 2002, p. 34). Self-concept is a related concept that has often been construed as being synonymous with self-esteem. Increasingly, self-concept is being considered to be multidimensional rather than global in nature; individuals' self-perceptions vary as they learn to understand themselves along different dimensions, such as physical appearance, athletic prowess, academic competence, and social competence (Bracken, 1996). Consequently, a child may have a positive self-concept in the areas of physical appearance and athletic skills, a negative academic self-concept, and fairly high overall self-esteem. Student's self-perceptions are assessed using self-report measures, interviews, or questionnaires.

The following box highlights two commonly used measures of self-concept, the Piers-Harris Children's Self-Concept Scale, Second Edition (Piers, Harris, & Herzberg, 2002) and the Culture-Free Self-Esteem Inventory, Third Edition (CFSEI-3; Battle, 2002).

CONCLUSIONS: SOCIAL, EMOTIONAL, AND BEHAVIORAL ASSESSMENTS IN AN RTI MODEL

Although the adoption of the RTI approach in the social-emotional-behavioral domain in school settings has been limited, this approach promises to be a viable model for preventing the escalation of behavioral needs in youngsters. RTI builds on the already established and empirically validated schoolwide PBS model. It is clear that interventions need to be implemented as soon as there is evidence of poor self-perception or behavioral difficulties, because such problems have far-reaching consequences on children's current and future adjustment. A problem-solving

Self-Concept Scales

Piers-Harris Children's Self-Concept Scale, Second Edition (The Way I Feel About Myself) (Piers et al., 2002), is used to assess self-concept in students who are 7 to 18 years of age. It provides domain scores for Behavioral Adjustment, Intellectual and School Status, Physical Appearance and Attributes, Freedom from Anxiety, Popularity, Happiness and Satisfaction, in addition to an overall Self-Concept Score. Students respond to a 60-item Likert-type questionnaire that asks whether an item is true or not true of them. This measure is easy to administer, score, and interpret, and computerized scoring is available. It has strong technical qualities and is best used as a screening measure. A Spanish version of the scale is also available.

Culture-Free Self-Esteem Inventory, Third Edition (CFSEI-3; Battle, 2002) is based on Harter's theoretical framework of self-esteem and is used to assess this construct in youngsters aged 6 to 18 years. There are Primary (ages 6–8), Intermediate (ages 9–12), and Adolescent (ages 13–18) versions. The Intermediate and Adolescent versions provide a global self-esteem score and subscores for academic, general, parental/home, social, and personal domains. A defensiveness score helps detect invalid results on the scale. The scale has strong technical qualities. Additional information about the culture fairness of this test would be beneficial.

model of RTI appears to be best suited for this domain, in which a school-based team works closely with the student and his or her family to develop appropriate interventions to address expressed needs. This chapter has provided an overview of the data collection techniques that could be used to monitor student behavior in response to interventions applied in the school setting.

End-of-Chapter Questions

1. Why is it important to learn about the social-emotional-behavioral adjustment of children and adolescents in school settings?
2. What are some of the areas of the social-emotional-behavioral domain that need to be assessed when a child evidences difficulties?
3. What are some reasons for the push to use an RTI approach in the area of social behavior difficulties?
4. Explain how each of the following techniques is used for ongoing progress monitoring to determine how a student is responding to interventions in the social-emotional-behavioral domain:
   1. Anecdotal notes
   2. Systematic observation
   3. Permanent products
   4. Interviews
   5. Behavior rating scales
   6. DBRC
   7. GAS
5. What is sociometric assessment? When and how can it be used?
6. Miranda is a 12-year-old sixth grader with mental retardation and cerebral palsy. She has recently started engaging in self-biting and self-scratching behavior that has resulted in long, deep marks on her arms and legs, some of which have become infected. Miranda's teachers have asked the psychologist to assist them to conduct an FBA in order to develop a behavior intervention plan for her. How will the team proceed with conducting this FBA? Discuss.
7. What techniques can be used to assess a child's self-perceptions? Discuss.

References

Alberto, P. A., & Troutman, A. C. (1995). *Applied behavior analysis for teachers* (4th ed.). Upper Saddle River, NJ: Merrill/Pearson Education.

Asher, S. R., Hymel, S., & Renshaw, P. D. (1984). Loneliness in children. *Child Development, 55,* 1456–1464.

Asher, S. R., & Rose, A. J. (1997). Promoting children's social-emotional development with peers. In P. Salovey & D. Sluyter (Eds.), *Emotional development and emotional intelligence* (pp. 196–224). New York: Basic Books.

Battle, J. (2002). *Culture-Free Self-Esteem Inventory* (3rd ed.). Austin, TX: ProEd.

Bracken, B. (1996). Clinical applications of a context-dependent, multidimensional model of self-concept. In B. A. Bracken (Ed.), *Handbook of self-concept: Developmental, social, and clinical considerations* (pp. 463–504). New York: Wiley.

Bryan, T. (1997). Assessing the personal and social status of students with learning disabilities. *Learning Disabilities Research and Practice, 12,* 63–76.

Bryan, T. (2005). Science-based advances in the social domain of learning disabilities. *Learning Disability Quarterly, 28,* 119–121.

Bullis, M., Nishioka-Evans, V., Fredericks, H. D. B., & Davis, C. (1993). Identifying and assessing the job-related social skills of adolescents and young adults with emotional and behavioral disorders. *Journal of Emotional and Behavioral Disorders, 1*(4), 236–50.

Caldarella, P., & Merrell, K. (1997). Common dimensions of social skills of children and adolescents: A taxonomy of positive behaviors. *School Psychology Review, 26,* 265–279.

Cartledge, G., & Milburn, J. F. (1996). *Cultural diversity and social skills instruction: Understanding ethnic and gender differences.* Champaign, IL: Research Press.

Chafouleas, S. M., Riley-Tillman, T. C., Sassu, K. A., LaFrance, M. J., & Patwa, S. (2007). Daily behavior report cards: An investigation of the consistency of on-task data across raters and methods. *Journal of Positive Behavior Interventions, 9*(1), 30–37.

Cohen, L. G., & Spenciner, L. J. (2007). *Assessment of children and youth with special needs.* Upper Saddle River, NJ: Allyn & Bacon/Pearson Education.

Conners, K. (1997). *Conners Rating Scales-Revised.* San Antonio, TX: Pearson.

Conners, K. (2008). *Conners Comprehensive Behavior Rating Scale.* North Tonawanda, NY: Multi Health Systems.

Cosden, M., Brown, C., & Elliott, K. (2002). Development of self-understanding and self-esteem in children and adults with learning disabilities. In B. Wong & M. Donahue (Eds.), *The social dimensions of learning disabilities: Essays in honor of Tanis Bryan* (pp. 33–52). Mahwah: New Jersey: Lawrence Erlbaum.

DiPerna, J. C., & Elliott, S. N. (1999). The development and validation of the Academic Competence Evaluation Scales. *Journal of Psychoeducational Assessment, 17,* 207–225.

Doll, B. (1996). Children without friends: Implications for practice and policy. *School Psychology Review, 25*(2), 165–183.

Drummond, T. (1993). *The Student Risk Screening Scale (SRSS).* Grants Pass, OR: Josephine County Mental Health Program.

Elksnin, L. K., & Elksnin, N. (2006). *Teaching social-emotional skills at school and home.* Denver, CO: Love Publishing.

Eyberg, S. M., & Pincus, D. (1999). *Eyberg Child Behavior Inventory and Sutter-Eyberg, Student Behavior Inventory: Professional manual.* Odessa, FL: Psychological Assessment Resources.

Eyberg, S. M., & Ross, A. W. (1978). Assessment of child behavior problems: The validation of a new inventory. *Journal of Clinical Child Psychology, 7*(2), 113–117.

Fairbanks, S., Sugai, G., Guardino, D., & Lathrop, M. (2007). Response to intervention: Examining classroom behavior support in second grade. *Exceptional Children, 73,* 288–310.

Gresham, F. (2004). Current status and future directions of school based behavioral interventions. *School Psychology Review, 33,* 326–343.

Gresham, F. (2005). Response to intervention: An alternative means of identifying students as emotionally disturbed. *Education and Treatment of Children, 28,* 328–344.

Gresham, F. M., & Elliott, S. R. (1990). *Social Skills Rating Scales.* Upper Saddle River, NJ: Pearson.

Harris-Murri, N., King, K., & Rostenberg, D. (2006). Reducing disproportionate minority representation in special education programs for students with emotional disturbances: Toward a culturally responsive response to intervention model. *Education and Treatment of Children, 29*(4), 779–799.

Harry, B., Klingner, J., Sturges, K., & Moore, R. (2002). Of rocks and soft places: Using qualitative methods to investigate disproportionality. In D. Losen & G. Orfield (Eds.) *Racial inequity in special education* (pp. 71–92). Cambridge, MA: Harvard Education Press.

Hayvren, M., & Hymel, S. (1984). Ethical issues in sociometric testing: Impact of sociometric measures on interaction behavior. *Developmental Psychology, 20,* 844–849.

Iverson, A. M., & Iverson, G. L. (1996). Children's long-term reactions to participating in sociometric assessment. *Psychology in the Schools, 33,* 103–112.

Kavale, K., & Mostert, M. (2004). Social skills interventions for individuals with learning disabilities. *Learning Disability Quarterly, 27,* 31–43.

Ladd, G. W., Kochenderfer, B. J., & Coleman, C. C. (1997). Classroom peer acceptance, friendship, and victimization: Distinct relational systems that contribute uniquely to children's school adjustment? *Child Development, 68,* 1181–1197.

Lane, K. L., & Menzies, H. M. (2003). A school-wide intervention with primary and secondary levels of support for elementary students: Outcomes and considerations. *Education and Treatment of Children, 26,* 431–451.

Leffert, J., Siperstein, G., & Millikan, E. (2000). Understanding social adaptation in children with mental retardation: A social-cognitive perspective. *Exceptional Children, 66,* 530–545.

Margalit, M., & Al-Yagon, M. (2002). The loneliness experience of children with learning disabilities. In B. Wong & M. Donahue (Eds.), *The social dimensions of learning disabilities: Essays in honor of Tanis Bryan* (pp. 53–75). Mahwah, NJ: Lawrence Erlbaum Associates.

McArthur, D. S., & Roberts, D. E. (1982). *Roberts Apperception Test for Children.* Los Angeles, CA: Western Psychological Services.

Merrell, K. W. (2003). *Behavioral, social, and emotional assessment of children and adolescents* (2nd ed.). Mahwah, NJ: Lawrence Erlbaum Associates.

Odom, S. L., Schertz, H., Munson, L., & Brown, W. H. (2004). Assessing social competence. In M. McLean, M. Wolery, & D. B. Bailey (Eds.), *Assessing infants and preschoolers with special needs* (3rd ed., pp. 412–450). Upper Saddle River, NJ: Merrill/Pearson Education.

O'Neill, R. E., Horner, R. H., Albin, R. W., Storey, K., & Sprague, J. (1990). *Functional analysis of problem behavior: A practical assessment guide.* Sycamore, IL: Sycamore Publishing Company.

Patton, J. (1998). The disproportionate representation of African Americans in special education: Looking behind the curtain for understanding and solutions. *The Journal of Special Education, 32,* 25–31.

Pavri, S., & Luftig, R. L. (2000). The social face of inclusive education: Are students with learning disabilities really included in the classroom? *Preventing School Failure, 45,* 8–14.

Pavri, S., & Monda-Amaya, L. (2000). Loneliness and students with learning disabilities in inclusive classrooms: Self-perceptions, coping strategies and preferred interventions. *Learning Disabilities Research and Practice, 15,* 23–34.

Pavri, S., & Monda-Amaya, L. (2001). Social support in inclusive schools: Student and teacher perspectives. *Exceptional Children, 63,* 391–411.

Pearl, R., Donahue, M., & Bryan, T. (1986). Social relationships of learning disabled children. In J. K. Torgesen & B. Y. L. Wong (Eds.), *Psychological and educational perspectives on learning* disabilities (pp. 193–224). Orlando, FL: Academic Press.

Piers, E. V., Harris, D. B., & Herzberg, D. S. (2002). *Piers-Harris Children's Self-Concept Scale* (2nd ed.). Los Angeles, CA: Western Psychological Services.

Quay, H. C., & Peterson, D. R. (1993). *The Revised Behavior Problem Checklist: Manual.* Odessa, FL: Psychological Assessment Resources.

Reich, W. (2000). Diagnostic Interview for Children and Adolescents (DICA). *Journal of the American Academy of Child and Adolescent Psychiatry, 39,* 59–66.

Reynolds, C. R., & Kamphaus, R. W. (2004). *The Behavior Assessment System for Children,* (2nd ed.). Upper Saddle River, NJ: Pearson.

Riley-Tillman, T. C., Kalberer, S. M., & Chafouleas, S. M. (2005). Selecting the right tool for the job: A review of behavior monitoring tools used to assess student response to intervention. *The California School Psychologist, 10,* 81–91.

Roach, A., & Elliott, S. (2005). Goal attainment scaling: An efficient and effective approach to monitoring student progress. *Teaching Exceptional Children, 37*(4), 8–17.

Russell, D. (1996). UCLA Loneliness Scale (Version 3): Reliability, validity, and factor structure. *Journal of Personality Assessment, 66*(1), 20–40.

Sandomierski, T., Kincaid, D., & Algozzine, B. (2008). Response to intervention and positive behavior support: Brothers from different mothers or sisters from different misters? *Positive Behavior*

Interventions and Supports Newsletter, 4 (2). Retrieved October 20, 2008, from http://flpbs.fmhi.usf.edu/FLPBS%20and%20RtI%20article.pdf

Severson, H. H., Walker, H. M., Hope-Doolittle, J., Kratochwill, T. R., & Gresham, F. M. (2007). Proactive, early screening to detect behaviorally at-risk students: Issues, approaches, emerging innovations, and professional practices. *Journal of School Psychology, 45,* 93–223.

Sparrow, S., Cicchetti, D. V., & Balls, D. A. (2005). *Vineland Adaptive Behavior Scales* (2nd ed.). Upper Saddle River, NJ: Pearson.

Sugai, G., Horner, R., & Gresham, F. (2002). Behaviorally effective school environments. In M. R. Shinn, H. M. Walker, & G. Stoner (Eds.), *Interventions for academic and behavior problems II: Preventative and remedial approaches* (pp. 315–350). Bethesda, MD: National Association of School Psychologists.

Tur-Kaspa, H., & Bryan, T. (1993). Social attributions of students with learning disabilities. *Exceptionality, 4,* 229–244.

Walker, H. M., & Severson, H. H. (1990). *Systematic Screening for Behavior Disorders (SSBD).* Longmont, CO: Sopris West.

Walker, H. M., & Shinn, M. R. (2002). Structuring school-based interventions to achieve integrated primary, secondary, and tertiary prevention goals for safe and effective schools. In M. R. Shinn, H. M. Walker, & G. Stoner (Eds.), *Interventions for academic and behavior problems II: Preventative and remedial approaches* (pp. 1–25). Bethesda, MD: National Association of School Psychologists.

Walker, H., & Sprague, J. (1999). The path to school failure, delinquency, and violence: Causal factors and some potential solutions. *Intervention in School and Clinic, 35,* 67–73.

Zins, J., Bloodworth, M., Weissberg, R., & Walberg, H. (2004). The scientific base linking social and emotional learning to school success. In J. Zins, R. Weissberg, M. Wang, & H. Walberg (Eds.), *Building academic success on social and emotional learning: What does the research say?* (pp. 3–22). New York: Teachers College Press.

CHAPTER 9

Assessment of Oral Language

Marisol is a first grader who has limited language skills and comprehension both in English and her native language, Spanish. Her teacher is frustrated by Marisol's apparent confusion when she is given verbal directions in English or Spanish. She is quiet and rarely speaks in class or on the playground. When she does speak, Marisol uses short utterances and limited vocabulary. She mimics gestures and body language and responds to overt physical cues. She is paired with a peer buddy who shows her how to complete class assignments. She seems to enjoy math and completes math problems with a higher level of accuracy and speed than some of her peers, but her reading, writing, and spelling skills are well below those of her peers. Marisol's teacher has found it difficult to reach her parents because they both work long hours and are not able to come in to see the teacher. Marisol's teacher has called a Student Study Team meeting to get some ideas about working with Marisol.

Reflections on the Scenario

1. What communication difficulties does Marisol seem to be experiencing?
2. How could her teacher obtain a better understanding of Marisol's receptive and expressive language skills in order to plan more effective instruction for her?
3. What language supports might Marisol need?
4. How could the Response to Intervention (RTI) model benefit Marisol? How might services be provided and by whom?

COUNCIL FOR EXCEPTIONAL CHILDREN (CEC) STANDARDS

This chapter addresses the following CEC standards (from Standard #8 Assessment):

ICC8K1—Basic terminology used in assessment.

ICC8K3—Screening, prereferral, referral, and classification procedures.

ICC8K4—Use and limitations of assessment instruments.

ICC8S2—Administer nonbiased formal and informal assessments.

ICC8S4—Develop or modify individualized assessment strategies.

ICC8S5—Interpret information from formal and informal assessments.

ICC8S6—Use assessment information in making eligibility, program, and placement decisions for individuals with exceptional learning needs, including those from culturally and/or linguistically diverse backgrounds.

GC8S2—Use exceptionality-specific assessment instruments with individuals with disabilities.

GC8S3—Select, adapt, and modify assessments to accommodate the unique abilities and needs of individuals with disabilities.

GC8S4—Assess reliable methods of response of individuals who lack typical communication and performance abilities.

LANGUAGE

"Language is the bridge by which a student and teacher interact. It is a vehicle for organizing and constructing the student's environment. . . Teacher language is present in all academic tasks even though the teacher language may be represented by written instructions and directions" (Carlson, Gruenewald, & Nyberg, 1980, p. 66). This quote emphasizes how language is inextricably linked to all teaching and learning. A student who has language difficulties is at a distinct disadvantage in the school system. A student who has communication disorders or language learning disabilities experiences difficulties in the areas of basic vocabulary, information processing, comprehension, conversation, and non-verbal communication. Difficulties may span the form, content, and use of language.

THE STRUCTURE AND COMPONENTS OF LANGUAGE

Speech is a verbal tool that is used to communicate or share meaning with others. Speech is composed of the following components, all of which require the use of neuro-muscular apparatus and coordination:

Articulation—How speech sounds are made and combined into language units (e.g., the "ch" sound, if produced correctly, will allow a student to say "teacher")

Voice—How an individual produces sound

Fluency—The rate and rhythm of speech

When speech sounds are combined in meaningful ways, they constitute language. Language has been defined as "a socially shared code or conventional system for representing concepts through the use of arbitrary symbols and rule-governed combinations of those symbols" (Owens, 1992, p. 4). Not all language requires the use of speech (e.g., American Sign Language uses gestures to communicate with others).

The language code is made up of five components:

1. *Phonemes*—Individual speech sounds that need to be recognized and produced accurately in order to articulate words (e.g., "c," "a," and "t" are individual phonemes that together make the word "cat").
2. *Morphemes*—The smallest units of language that have meaning. For example, prefixes (e.g., **un**kind) or suffixes (e.g., kind**ly**), verb tense (e.g., going vs. gone), and plurals (e.g., book vs. books) significantly change the meaning of words.
3. *Syntax*—The use of word order following the rules of the language in order to convey meaning. Syntax is similar to the grammatical structure of language.
4. *Semantics*—The comprehension and correct use of word meanings. Use of semantics is demonstrated through one's choice of vocabulary and understanding of the relationships between words (e.g., antonyms and synonyms).

5. *Pragmatics*—The social use of language in meaningful contexts. Pragmatics investigates how language is used for different purposes (e.g., to request vs. to demand), how it varies depending on the context or needs of the situation (e.g., language used at a ball game vs. language used at an official meeting), and the implicit rules of language (e.g., regarding physical proximity, eye contact, turn taking, appropriate nonverbal signals).

Speech and language, along with gestures, facial expressions, and other nonlinguistic codes, are used for the larger purpose of communicating with others. Effective communication skills allow individuals to interact and share ideas, thoughts, and feelings with one another, thereby satisfying their needs and wants.

TYPES OF SPEECH AND LANGUAGE DISORDERS

Individuals who experience difficulties in communication may have disorders in speech or language (American Speech-Language-Hearing Association, 2010). A person who has difficulty sharing his or her thoughts or feelings with others, either verbally or in writing, may have an *expressive language disorder*. A person who has difficulty understanding oral or written language may have a *receptive language disorder*. Such difficulties clearly affect a student's ability to comprehend and demonstrate mastery of academic content, in addition to influencing other life domains, such as communication, socialization, vocational, and personal functioning.

It is important to clarify that a difficulty should only be classified as a disorder when the student has received ample time and opportunities to acquire the skill that is lacking. For example, it is expected that a person who does not speak a foreign language will experience difficulty understanding or expressing himself or herself in a foreign country, and a child whose family has recently immigrated to the United States may not be proficient in English. A speech disorder may be present when an individual has difficulties in the areas of articulation (incorrect movement of lips, tongue, and mouth), voice (e.g., hoarseness, no voice), or fluency (e.g., stuttering).

LANGUAGE LEARNING IN AN RTI FRAMEWORK

RTI advocates a shift away from the individual pathology approach to diagnosing disabilities, calling instead for a contextual examination of the quality of instruction that is provided in the general education setting (Ehren, Montgomery, Rudebusch, & Whitmire, 2006). Adopting a preventative stance, school professionals work to ensure that all students achieve developmental competence in speech, language, and communication skills. Special steps are taken to reduce risk and stimulate speech and language development in students who need such assistance. Consequently, RTI requires schools to change the assessment and intervention models that they use. Service delivery is not limited to direct speech and language therapeutic services for individuals or small groups of students who have diagnosed language learning disorders. Instead, indirect supports and services are also provided through consultation and classroom-based interventions (Ehren et al., 2006). School support staff, including speech and language therapists and other related service providers, may contribute to problem solving when students demonstrate academic and behavioral difficulties related to language problems.

Language is the core of literacy learning. It is well documented that language delays that appear early in life indicate that further language-related problems are likely to develop later, often manifesting as reading and/or writing difficulties (Al Otaiba & Fuchs, 2006; Harlaar, Hayiou-Thomas, Dale, & Plomin, 2008; Vellutino, Tunmer, Jaccard, & Chen, 2007). For instance, Al Otaiba and Fuchs found that youngsters who were nonresponsive to early literacy interventions also had poor vocabulary and syntax skills. Vocabulary and syntactical awareness are closely related to the ability to comprehend text passages.

Consequently, the role of language in curriculum, assessment, instruction, and program design is highlighted in an RTI approach in which the focus often is to ensure literacy development in all students. The selection of evidence-based literacy interventions requires a close examination of the language demands of the intervention and the skills and competence of the students at the school. Language assessment techniques that are used in an RTI approach will need to incorporate curriculum-based techniques that directly inform classroom instruction and monitor student progress in skills learned, together with data from diagnostic and standardized tests.

TYPES OF SPEECH AND LANGUAGE ASSESSMENTS

This chapter highlights speech and language assessments that are frequently used in school settings and that can be applied to the RTI model. It is recommended that an audiologist or nurse conduct a hearing examination to screen for a possible hearing loss prior to proceeding with a speech and language assessment.

Language Sampling

Spontaneous language samples are naturally occurring speech samples that are recorded for later transcription and analysis. Spontaneous language samples provide the most authentic measure of the content, form, and use of language. Picture prompts, games, and other engaging activities may be used to stimulate language production in children. It is important not to pressure a child to speak because feeling compelled to talk often causes children to remain silent. The longer the language sample that is obtained, the greater the likelihood that it has reliability and validity and the lower the sample error rate. For instance, Muma (1998) found that sampling error rates for samples of 50 utterances were as high as 55%, but the error rate dropped to 15% among longer samples of 400 utterances.

Some guidelines for language sampling include 1) being sure to audiotape the sample to capture exactly what was said, 2) using open-ended prompts (e.g., "how did you make this model?", "can you tell me about your birthday?") to avoid generating yes/no or other very short responses from students, 3) taking turns as in a natural conversation to be a good conversation model for the child, and 4) considering the child's cognitive level and asking questions that are appropriate for the child (Haynes & Pindzola, 2008).

1. *Mean length of utterances*—The language sample may be reviewed for mean length of utterances (MLU). A speech and language pathologist usually determines MLU by collecting 50 to 100 consecutive utterances and dividing the number of morphemes by the number of utterances. For instance, if 3-year-old Reina said "mama come" (2 morphemes), "no go" (2 morphemes), "I jump" (2 morphemes), and "run fast" (2 morphemes), the total number of morphemes divided by the number of utterances would be 8/4 = 2. Because MLUs are time consuming to calculate, they are best used with children who have limited language skills, such as young children or those with significant language delays.

2. *Curriculum-based language assessment (CBLA)*—The curricular context provides particular information about the receptive or expressive language skills. CBLA is an assessment tool that is used to determine whether the student has the language skills and strategies that he or she needs in order to learn the curriculum. CBLA differs from curriculum-based measurement (CBM), which is focused on whether the student has indeed learned the curriculum. Generally conducted by the speech and language therapist, the CBLA involves identifying the curricular area (either social or academic) where the student has the greatest difficulties. The therapist examines the demands placed on a student when the student is required to complete a particular curricular task, the skills and strategies that the student uses to approach the task, what the student may learn to do differently, and how the task could be modified so that the student could complete it with greater success and efficiency (Nelson, 2005).

The therapist then interviews the student in order to obtain expository and narrative discourse samples that are associated with that curricular content. An expository sample would contain interview questions that ask the student about a topic of interest (e.g., "What do you like to read about?", "Which school subjects do you enjoy the most and which do you enjoy the least?") Such language samples provide information about the student's conceptualization, articulation, vocabulary, language use, and preferences. Narrative prompts are often situated in the curriculum (e.g., "what are the steps you must follow in order to solve a word problem?", "Retell the story that you just heard") and provide information on the student's ability to recall events in sequence. After the student's language needs are identified, instructional goals are developed to address these needs (Schoenbrodt, Kumin, & Sloan, 1997).

3. *Naturalistic observations*—Direct observations of a student's communication style and preferences can reveal whether the student's communication attempts effectively meet his or her goals and whether the student's use of communication is appropriate. Observing the social and functional use of language in natural settings over prolonged periods of time and across several social situations is recommended (Gomez, Lara-Alecio, Ochoa, & Gomez, 1996). Guided by checklists and rating scales, these observations could provide meaningful data to plan future instruction.

4. *Interviews*—Conducting interviews with the target student, his or her family, and school professionals who work closely with the student can provide information about the student's communication skills, both verbal and nonverbal. Interviews play a key role in speech and language assessment and interventions. They are a means to obtain information and gather data from the student and his or her family, a tool to give information, a way to build relationships between therapist and client, and a medium for implementing therapy (Haynes & Pindzola, 2008). The clinician collects data on verbal and nonverbal cues during an interview, studying body language, gestures, facial expressions, tone of voice, and level of animation in addition to the content of the communication.

5. *Norm-referenced tests (NRTs)*—Standardized tests are widely used to assess speech and language development and delays in children and youth. NRTs provide information about various components of speech and language. In an RTI framework, these NRTs may be used as part of the assessment process to rule out exclusionary factors such as a hearing loss or speech and language difficulties that could be causing academic difficulties.

Phonology

THE GOLDMAN-FRISTOE TEST OF ARTICULATION 2 (GOLDMAN & FRISTOE, 2000)   This test requires the examinee to produce consonant sounds and clusters, both spontaneous and imitative, in response to picture plates and verbal cues. The test is appropriate for individuals aged 2–21 years.

Morphology and Syntax

THE TEST FOR AUDITORY COMPREHENSION OF LANGUAGE, THIRD EDITION (CARROW-WOOLFOLK, 1999)   This test assesses the examinee's ability to comprehend oral language in three areas: vocabulary (word meaning), grammatical morphemes (e.g., prepositions, verb number and tense, noun–verb agreement, meaning of pronouns), and elaborated phrases and sentences (e.g., word relations, sentence construction). The examinee points to one picture out of three that best matches the prompt provided by the examiner. The test is appropriate for users between the ages of 3 and 9 years.

Semantics and Pragmatics

PEABODY PICTURE VOCABULARY TEST-IV (DUNN & DUNN, 2007)   This test is a popular measure of receptive vocabulary and is used as a general index of verbal ability. The test is normed on individuals aged 2–90 years. The examiner reads aloud a word and the examinee is required to indicate which of four pictures best represents that word. The test is easy to administer and score and can be adapted for use in individuals with a range of disabilities (e.g., a student who may not be able to verbalize a reply can use a pointer, eye gaze, or other means of expression).

Comprehensive Measures of Language

TEST OF LANGUAGE DEVELOPMENT-PRIMARY, FOURTH EDITION (NEWCOMER & HAMMILL, 2008)   This test assesses students aged 4–8 years, using nine subtests in the areas of picture vocabulary, relational vocabulary, oral vocabulary, syntactic understanding, sentence imitation, morphological completion, word discrimination, word analysis, and word articulation. The test yields composite scores for semantics and grammar, listening, organizing, and speaking, and an overall score for language ability.

TEST OF LANGUAGE DEVELOPMENT-INTERMEDIATE, FOURTH EDITION (HAMMILL & NEWCOMER, 2008)   Appropriate for use with youngsters aged 8–18 years, this test provides a measure of the following language domains: semantics and grammar, listening, organizing, and speaking. The TOLD-I includes six subtests in the areas of sentence combining, picture vocabulary, word ordering, relational vocabulary, morphological comprehension, and multiple meanings.

COMPREHENSIVE RECEPTIVE AND EXPRESSIVE VOCABULARY TEST- 2 (WALLACE & HAMMILL, 2002)   A comprehensive measure of receptive and expressive vocabulary, this test is appropriate for individuals aged 4–90 years (receptive) and 5–90 years (expressive). The test is easily administered and has good reliability and validity, but it does not have adequate numbers of difficult items to differentiate among individuals whose language abilities are significantly above or below the mean.

ASSESSING ORAL LANGUAGE IN ENGLISH LEARNERS (ELs)

For far too long, schools assessed students who were not proficient in English using tests that required English proficiency. It is no surprise that these English learners (ELs) did not perform well on measures that were administered in English. Unfortunately, these discriminatory and flawed assessment data were used to make important curricular and placement decisions that had far-reaching consequences for the students involved. For example, some of them were misidentified as having mental retardation and were placed in segregated and often substandard classrooms and programs.

Legislation and litigation drew public attention to the problem of discriminatory assessment of ELs, and steps were taken to prevent this situation from recurring. As a result of the *Lau v. Nichols* U.S. Supreme Court decision in 1974, schools were required to assess ELs to determine their English language proficiency so that they could receive instruction that is appropriate and meaningful to them. Language proficiency is assessed in order to identify and place students in programs where they will receive appropriate language instruction, the goal being to develop full English language proficiency (Atunez, 2003). Title I of the No Child Left Behind Act (NCLB) mandates an annual assessment of English language proficiency (i.e., oral language, reading, and writing skills) of all students in a given district. Furthermore, Title III of NCLB requires ongoing progress monitoring of English proficiency in the areas of comprehension, listening, reading, and writing.

The informal assessments that were described in the previous section could be used with EL students. In addition, the tests that follow are used commonly by school districts that have a large number of EL students to assess English language proficiency:

1. *The Language Assessment Scales (De Avila & Duncan, 2005)*—Assesses reading, writing, speaking, and listening in English and Spanish. Specific areas assessed include vocabulary, fluency, mechanics and usage, reading for information, finishing sentences, writing sentences, and writing a story or essay. The speaking and listening subtests are appropriate for students in prekindergarten through grade 12, and the reading and writing subtests are best suited for children in grades 2 through 12. Computerized scoring is available.

2. *IDEA Language Proficiency Test (Ballard, Tighe, & Dalton, 2005)*—Assesses reading, writing, speaking, and listening in students in prekindergarten through grade 12. The oral test measures syntax, morphological structure, lexical items, phonological structure, comprehension, and oral production. It may be administered on its own or in conjunction with the reading and writing tests. The reading test assesses vocabulary, vocabulary in context, reading and understanding, reading for life skills, and language usage. The writing test has three sections: conventions,

writing a story to describe a picture, and writing an original story with rubrics that are used to guide scoring. The test is available in English and Spanish, and computerized scoring software is available.

Differentiating Between Language Difference and Language Disorder

A language difference is apparent when the medium of instruction at school varies from a student's native language and the student receives instruction in a language in which he or she is less than proficient. Usually, the language spoken in the home differs from the school language. Such students need sheltered instruction in order to acquire and develop proficiency in English. The key issue is that these students do not have a language processing disability, and in most cases they acquire fluency in English over time with adequate instruction.

However, if the teacher suspects that a student has a language disability, the teacher would want to determine whether the language difficulties also occur in the child's native language. Interviewing the parents to determine whether the child shows language delays and other learning difficulties in the home language; finding out about the child's emotional adjustment, level of acculturation, and past educational history; and observing the child's use of language across multiple settings are recommended steps. In order to distinguish between language difference and language disability, it also is important to implement consistent and systematic language interventions and to monitor the student's responsiveness to these interventions over time prior to referring the student for special education.

ASSESSING ORAL LANGUAGE IN STUDENTS WITH SIGNIFICANT LANGUAGE DELAYS

Effective communication skills allow students to develop relationships and friendships. Youngsters with speech and language difficulties have a difficult time communicating with peers and adults in the environment. Communication difficulties make it difficult for teachers to assess the learning, cognitive skills, and academic achievement of youngsters who have severe communication disorders. It becomes necessary to use augmentative and alternative communication (AAC) systems to assess or instruct students who have minimal intelligible language skills or who are nonverbal. Such systems may include picture symbols, switches, and electronic voice output devices that allow the students to express themselves.

USE OF AUGMENTATIVE AND ALTERNATIVE COMMUNICATION SYSTEMS (AACs)

AACs are devices or procedures that are used to help an individual with disabilities communicate more effectively. AAC devices are used both for expressive communication and to better understand communication from an individual with a disability. Expressive communication may be facilitated by supplementing existing speech using gestures, picture communication books, or picture exchange communication systems and by replacing speech that is unintelligible or not functional (e.g., using a voice output communication aid). Receptive communication may be enhanced using visuals such as picture symbols, daily written or picture schedules, or social stories.

Developing an appropriate AAC system is an individualized and dynamic process that often involves trial and error before the most efficient and effective device is created. Several modifications may be required to make the system suitable for an individual. The following variables affect the selection of the appropriate AAC device (Kangas & Lloyd, 1998):

1. How will the symbols be represented (e.g., drawings, words, photographs, gestures)? The individual's cognitive, motor, and visual skills, and chronological age are important factors to consider.
2. How will the individual select the symbols (e.g., using a pointer, eye gaze)?
3. How will the message be transmitted (e.g., visual output in the form of text or pictures using a communication board or picture symbol system, auditory output in the form of speech in a text browser or voice output communication device)?

Individuals who use AACs to communicate should be assessed using AAC devices to learn more about their preferences, interests, learning styles, and academic achievements. There are two types of AAC devices: aided and unaided. Aided AAC devices require a special device to generate language through letters, words, or voice output. Such devices are typically electronic and are connected to a computer that generates a voice or to a screen that displays the message in written format. A voice output communication aid may have varied displays in the form of a computer keyboard that reads aloud words that the person types into the computer. Other AAC devices show symbols or pictures on the display; the user points to the one that he or she wants and the computer reads it aloud. Unaided AAC involves face-to-face communication with another person using sign language, gestures and body language, and communication boards. For instance, a picture board might be a sophisticated, commercially produced tool or it could be homemade with cut-outs of pictures that represent key activities and objects in an individual's life glued together on a hard board. The user may point to the relevant picture with a finger, use a "unicorn" pointer affixed to his or her head, or rely on eye gaze to look at the picture to indicate his or her wants and needs.

For resources on selecting appropriate AAC devices, visit the following websites:

Closing the Gap: *http://www.closingthegap.com/solutions/*

AbleData: *http://www.abledata.com/*

University of Washington Augmentative and Assistive Communication Resources: *http://depts.washington.edu/augcomm/00_general/resources.htm*

Center for Applied Special Technology: *http://www.cast.org/*

MONITORING LANGUAGE DEVELOPMENT IN AN RTI FRAMEWORK

As discussed throughout this chapter, RTI changes the focus of service delivery, targeting early identification and remediation of language differences and delays to prevent them from becoming chronic and further limiting academic progress. Language interventions are tailored to the needs shown by a student and the student's response to the interventions is closely monitored. The speech and language assessments used in an RTI approach must inform the school curriculum and instruction and must be sensitive to student growth and progress.

End-of-Chapter Questions

1. What is the role of language in classroom instruction?
2. Distinguish between speech and language.
3. What are the components of language? Explain each component and give an example of its use.
4. Explain the different types of speech and language disorders that children and adults may show.
5. How may the RTI approach be applied to assessments and interventions in the speech and language domain? Describe how RTI would change current practices in the domain.
6. What is language sampling? How may it be used to monitor student progress in the areas of language and literacy?
7. Why is the MLU measure useful? How is it calculated?
8. Explain what CBLA is and how it can be used. How does it differ from CBM?
9. What other techniques are used to assess students' speech and language skills? Discuss.
10. What precautions should you take when assessing English learners? What are some measures that you could use to assess this population of students?
11. How can one differentiate between a language disorder and a language difference? Explain.
12. What are some unique considerations that guide the assessment of students with severe language delays?
13. What is AAC? How can it assist with the assessment of students who have severe language delays?

References

Al Otaiba, S., & Fuchs, D. (2006). Who are the young children for whom best practices in reading are ineffective? An experimental and longitudinal study. *Journal of Learning Disabilities, 39,* 414–431.

American Speech-Language-Hearing Association. (2010). Typical speech and language development. Retrieved September 29, 2010, from http://www.asha.org/public/speech/development/

Atunez, B. (2003). Assessing English language learners in the great city schools. Washington, DC: Council of Great City Schools. Retrieved November 8, 2008, from http://www.cgcs.org/pdfs/AssessmentGuidance.pdf

Ballard, W. S., Tighe, P. L., & Dalton, E. F. (2005). *Idea Proficiency Test (IPT).* Brea, CA: Ballard & Tighe.

Carlson, J., Gruenewald, L. J., & Nyberg, B. (1980). Everyday math is a story problem: The language of the curriculum. *Topics in Language Disorders, 7*(1), 59–69.

Carrow-Woolfolk, E. (1999). *Test of Auditory Comprehension of Language* (3rd ed.). San Antonio, TX: Pearson.

De Avila, E., & Duncan, S. (2005). *Language assessment scales.* New York: McGraw-Hill.

Dunn, L., & Dunn, D. (2007). *Peabody Picture Vocabulary Test* (4th ed.). San Antonio, TX: PsychCorp.

Ehren, B. J., Montgomery, J., Rudebusch, J., & Whitmire, K. (2006). Responsiveness to intervention: New roles for speech-language pathologists. Retrieved October 10, 2008, from http://www.asha.org/slp/schools/prof-consult/NewRolesSLP.htm.

Goldman, R., & Fristoe, M. (2000). *Goldman Fristoe Test of Articulation* (2nd ed.). San Antonio, TX: Pearson.

Gomez, L., Lara-Alecio, R., Ochoa, S. H., & Gomez, R. (1996). Naturalistic language assessment of LEP students in classroom interactions. *The Bilingual Research Journal, 20*(1), 69–92.

Hammill, D., & Newcomer, P. (2008). *Test of Language Development: Intermediate* (4th ed.). Austin, TX: ProEd.

Harlaar, N., Hayiou-Thomas, M., Dale, P., & Plomin, R. (2008). Why do preschool language abilities correlate with later reading? A twin study. *Journal of Speech, Language, and Hearing Research, 51,* 688–705.

Haynes, W. O., & Pindzola, R. H. (2008). *Diagnosis and evaluation in speech pathology.* Upper Saddle River, NJ: Allyn & Bacon/Pearson Education.

Kangas, K. A., & Lloyd, L. L. (1998). Augmentative and alternative communication. In G. H. Shames, E. H. Wiig, & W. A. Secord (Eds.), *Human communication disorders: An introduction* (5th ed.). Upper Saddle River, NJ: Allyn & Bacon/Pearson Education.

Muma, J. (1998). *Effective speech-language pathology: A cognitive socialization approach.* Mahwah, NJ: Erlbaum.

Nelson, N. W. (2005). The context of discourse difficulty in classroom and clinic: An update. *Topics in Language Disorders, 25,* 322–331.

Newcomer, P., & Hammill, D. (2008). *Test of Language Development: Primary* (4th ed.). Austin, TX: ProEd.

Owens, R. E. (1992). *Language development: An introduction* (3rd ed.). New York: MacMillan.

Schoenbrodt, L., Kumin, L., & Sloan, J. M. (1997). Learning disabilities existing concomitantly with communication disorder. *Journal of Learning Disabilities, 30*(3), 264–281.

Vellutino, F. R., Tunmer, W. E., Jaccard, J. J., & Chen, R. (2007). Components of reading ability: Multivariate evidence for a convergent skills model of reading development. *Scientific Studies of Reading, 11,* 3–32.

Wallace, G., & Hammill, D. (2002) *Comprehensive Receptive and Expressive Vocabulary Test-2.* Austin, TX: ProEd.

CHAPTER 10

Career and Vocational Assessment

Quasim is a junior at Washington High School. He has cerebral palsy and has been included in the general education setting since early elementary school. In addition to fine and gross motor difficulties, Quasim also has had difficulties with reading, which affects his performance in content areas. He is prone to behavioral outbursts caused by frustration due to the difficulties he experiences when he is trying to complete a given task. Quasim loves fast cars and tinkering with all things mechanical. He hopes to be an auto mechanic, and his dream is to assist with NASCAR races when he has completed school. His uncle owns an auto body shop and has encouraged Quasim to work for him when he graduates. Quasim is enrolled in a remedial reading and writing course this year to prepare him for the high school exit exam that he did not pass last year. He also is enrolled in an auto mechanic training course that will assist with his career development.

Reflections on the Scenario

1. What are some considerations that will guide Quasim's academic programming during the remainder of his time in high school?
2. What are some legal mandates that must be considered in planning for postschool transitions?
3. Which stakeholders should be consulted to develop an individualized transition program (IEP) for Quasim?
4. What preventative approaches could have been taken early in Quasim's school career to ensure that he achieves academic, behavioral, independent living, and vocational success in postschool environments?

COUNCIL FOR EXCEPTIONAL CHILDREN (CEC) STANDARDS

This chapter addresses the following CEC standards (from Standard #8 Assessment):

ICC8K1—Basic terminology used in assessment.

ICC8K4—Use and limitations of assessment instruments.

GC8K1—Specialized terminology used in the assessment of individuals with disabilities.

GC8K3—Types and importance of information concerning individuals with disabilities available from families and public agencies.

ICC8S1—Gather relevant background information.

ICC8S2—Administer nonbiased formal and informal assessments.

ICC8S3—Use technology to conduct assessments.

ICC8S4—Develop or modify individualized assessment strategies.

ICC8S5—Interpret information from formal and informal assessments.

ICC8S7—Report assessment results to all stakeholders using effective communication skills.

ICC8S8—Evaluate instruction and monitor progress of individuals with exceptional learning needs.

THE IMPORTANCE OF TRANSITION PLANNING FOR STUDENTS WITH DISABILITIES

Data from the National Longitudinal Transition Study 2 (Wagner, Newman, Cameto, Levine, & Garza, 2006) that investigated the academic and functional performance and postschool outcomes for over 11,000 youth with disabilities reveal that in comparison with their peers who do not have disabilities, youth with disabilities are left behind on many key dimensions. On academic measures in language arts, math, science, and social studies, 77–86% of youth with disabilities had standard scores that were below the mean for their peers who did not have disabilities, and 14–27% of youth with disabilities scored more than two standard deviations below the mean across academic subtests. Passage comprehension emerged as the area of greatest difficulty, whereas vocabulary emerged as a relative strength for youngsters with disabilities. Clearly, there were vast individual differences in academic performance within the sample according to type of disability (e.g., students with higher cognitive skills performed higher on academic achievement measures). Generally, males outperformed females in the areas of math, science, and social studies. White youth with disabilities outperformed youth with disabilities from all other racial and ethnic backgrounds by 7–13 standard score points. Youth from higher socioeconomic backgrounds earned higher scores than youth from lower socioeconomic backgrounds regardless of race or ethnicity. Youth with learning disabilities, speech or other health impairments, emotional disturbances, or traumatic brain injuries scored higher on a measure of broad independence than did youth in other disability categories, such as autism, multiple disabilities, visual or orthopedic impairments, or deaf-blindness.

Seventy-two percent of youth with disabilities graduated from high school with a diploma or certificate of completion (Wagner et al., 2006). The remaining 28% dropped out of high school. The highest drop-out rate was for youth with emotional disturbances (44% drop-out rate). Up to 2 years after leaving school, 8 out of 10 youth with disabilities were engaged in postsecondary education, paid employment, or training to prepare for employment. Whereas 63% of youth in the general population were employed at the time of the study, only about 40% of youth with disabilities were employed. Approximately 75% of youth with disabilities were living at home with their parents up to 2 years after leaving high school. This figure is similar for youth in the general population.

Data for youth with disabilities who dropped out of high school are more troubling. These students were less likely to be engaged in school or work and less likely to possess a driver's license or a checking account, and a third of these students had spent a night in jail (Wagner et al., 2006).

Although the rate of successful transitions to postschool environments is slowly increasing for youth with disabilities, there is clearly a need to plan ahead to ensure more effective postschool outcomes for this population of citizens.

What Is Transition?

According to the Individuals with Disabilities Education Improvement Act (IDEA, 2004), "*transition services* means a coordinated set of activities for a child with a disability that—

1. Is designed to be within a results-oriented process, that is focused on improving the academic and functional achievement of the child with a disability to facilitate the child's movement from school to post-school activities, including postsecondary education, vocational education, integrated employment (including supported employment); continuing and adult education, adult services, independent living, or community participation;
2. Is based on the individual child's needs, taking into account the child's strengths, preferences, and interests; and includes—
   (i) Instruction;
   (ii) Related services;
   (iii) Community experiences;
   (iv) The development of employment and other post-school adult living objectives; and
   (v) If appropriate, acquisition of daily living skills and functional vocational evaluation." [34 CFR 300.43 (a)] [20 U.S.C. 1401(34)]

As is apparent from this definition, transition is a strengths-based process that is focused on positive postschool outcomes for youth with disabilities. The student is the center of transition planning, and the services that are provided are individualized to the student's strengths and preferences. The focus is on what students can do and how they can succeed.

Legal Requirements for Transition

Under IDEA, transition planning must begin no later than the student's 16th birthday. The IEP must include the following statements related to transition planning:

- "Appropriate measurable postsecondary goals based upon age-appropriate transition assessments related to training, education, employment and, where appropriate, independent living skills;
- The transition services (including courses of study) needed to assist the child in reaching those goals; and
- Beginning not later than one year before the child reaches the age of majority under State law, a statement that the child has been informed of the child's rights under Part B, if any, that will transfer to the child on reaching the age of majority under §300.520 " [see 20 U.S.C. 1415(m)].

[34 CFR 300.320(b) and (c)] [20 U.S.C. 1414 (d)(1)(A)(i)(VIII)]

IDEA is the major piece of federal legislation that mandates transition planning for school-aged students, but other pieces of federal legislation also call for equal access and early preparation of youth with disabilities for postsecondary education and training opportunities:

1. The Americans with Disabilities Act (1990) requires the provision of equal opportunity to individuals with disabilities, prohibits discrimination against them, and requires reasonable accommodations to be made for them in any facility or institution that receives federal financial aid.
2. Sections 503 and 504 of the Vocational Rehabilitation Act (1973) prohibit discrimination against individuals with disabilities in all areas, including employment, and promote hiring, training, advancement, and retention of qualified workers with disabilities.
3. The Carl D. Perkins Vocational–Technical Education Act (1998) calls for access to vocational and technical education and advising, tutoring, and training programs for special populations, including individuals with disabilities.
4. The School-to-Work Opportunities Act (1994) integrates both school-based and work-based learning experiences in providing special populations with equal access to activities and programs for high-wage and high-skill careers.

Why Transition Planning?

Students exit special education in the public schools either when they graduate from high school with a regular diploma or certificate of completion or when they reach their 22nd birthday, after which point they do not receive services from the school district. After school-based services are terminated, the student and his or her family often feel lost and unsure how to access services in postschool settings. Per IDEA (2004), schools must provide a "summary of performance" to students who exit special education. This summary must include the student's current academic achievement and performance and recommendations for assisting the student to reach stated postschool goals.

Under previous reauthorizations of IDEA, the age at which transition planning was required varied from 14 to 16 years. In the best of circumstances, the IEP team, in close collaboration with the student and his or her family, starts planning for transition while the student is in elementary school so that there is ample time to prepare for postschool environments. When the student reaches the age of majority (18 years), there is a transfer of responsibility for educational decision making from the parent or legal guardian to the student. Early preparation for self-determination and self-advocacy assists the student to effectively take over responsibility for his or her own educational planning.

Transition planning allows for ongoing supports to facilitate this transition from school to postschool environments. As discussed earlier in this chapter, the poor postsecondary education and vocational outcomes for students with disabilities highlight the need for early intervention and planning to assist with successful postschool transitions.

SELF-DETERMINATION, PERSON-CENTERED PLANNING, AND FAMILY INVOLVEMENT

Per IDEA, the student and parents are the core members of the transition planning team. The student must be invited to the IEP meetings at which postsecondary goals are set and when transition planning to meet those goals is underway. In order for the student to participate in a meaningful fashion, he or she must have early opportunities to develop self-determination skills. *Self-determination* has been defined as the "idea of being a causal agent in one's life" (Unok Marks, 2008; p. 56). For too long, individuals with disabilities have been treated as though they were incapable of making key decisions for themselves, and often have not even been consulted about major life decisions. The concept of self-determination, as applied to education, is the belief that all individuals are in a position to express their interests and preferences and that their input is a major consideration as decisions are being made about their future. Individuals who are self-determined are enabled to meet the roles and responsibilities that are typical of adulthood (Wehmeyer, 2001). Self-determination skills can be taught through direct instruction and varied practice opportunities in which individuals with disabilities are given the opportunity to make choices for themselves, participate in problem-solving and goal setting, and express their opinions on issues that are important to them.

Empirical support indicates that when self-determination skills are improved, other life outcomes also seem to improve. This effect is true for academic achievement, vocational success, participation in postsecondary education, and improvement in quality of life. Youth with disabilities who are self-determined are aware of their strengths and needs, participate in setting personally meaningful goals for themselves, and self-assess their progress toward meeting these goals, with necessary supports (Carter, Lane, Pierson, & Glaeser, 2006).

Person-centered planning is a process that is based on the principle of self-determination. This process involves the identification of the individual's personal and professional goals and close collaboration with the individual, his or her family, and support professionals to develop plans to achieve those goals. Person-centered planning for transition usually refers to assessment and planning activities that are conducted during high school. Person-centered planning strengthens family–school relationships, facilitates coordination of services across the agencies that support the student, allows the family to make connections with adult service agencies, ensures that services support the individual's goals, and builds natural support systems for the individual in the community (National Center on Secondary Education and Transition, 2004). A young adult with disabilities is an active participant in a person-centered planning approach and, with advanced preparation, may participate fully in the process.

Menchetti and Piland (2001) identify five salient elements of person-centered planning: group facilitation and support, strengths-based description, positive vision of the future, development of an action plan, and respect and empowerment of the target student. Some commonly used person-centered planning tools include Making Action Plans (MAPS), Personal Futures Planning (Mount & Zwernik, 1988), Essential Lifestyles Planning (Smull & Harrison, 1992), and Group Action Planning (A. P. Turnbull & H. R. Turnbull, 1993). MAPS, also called the McGill Action Planning System, is a popular person-centered planning process that was developed by Marsha Forest, Jack Pearpoint, Judith Snow, Evelyn Lusthaus, and their colleagues at the Center for Integrated Education in Canada (Forest & Pearpoint, 1992). Individuals such as the student, the student's parents, classroom teachers (both regular and special education), other school professionals, the school principal, and family members and friends meet for a couple of sessions to discuss the following questions about the target student:

1. What is the student's history?
2. What is your dream for the student?

3. What is your nightmare for the student?
4. Who is the student?
5. What are the student's gifts?
6. What are the student's needs?
7. What would an ideal day at school be like for the student?

Let us review the example of 20-year-old Katie, who participated in the MAPS process with her family, friends, and teachers to help plan for her transition from high school to postschool outcomes. The team got together at Katie's parents' home to discuss her history, dreams, fears, gifts, and needs in order to determine what needed to be done to make her goals come to fruition. Katie had always demonstrated a love for the arts, particularly fine arts, movies, and theater. As part of her action plan, the team decided that Katie would take community college courses in fine arts and seek a job at the local video store.

Parental involvement in the transition planning process is paramount. Generally the student's parents know him or her best and are key players at all stages of transition from assessment to planning to implementation. Parents' hopes, dreams, concerns, and aspirations related to their child must be solicited and supported. It is beneficial to review the steps in the assessment process with the parents so that they know what to expect and how to prepare to participate at each stage. Although parents from culturally and linguistically diverse backgrounds may not always offer their opinions in professional settings unless they are invited to do so, it is key to develop a transition planning process in which parental input and questions are welcomed and fully addressed.

In some instances, parents' wishes and desires for postschool transitions for their adolescent children may differ from the expectations of professionals, who often come from different cultural and educational backgrounds (Rueda, Monzo, Shapiro, Gomez, & Blacher, 2005). For example, not all parents may want their youngster to prepare to live independently from the family. As another example, requiring a male student to learn how to prepare a meal may not be a culturally appropriate goal in a particular family. It is important not to make assumptions about the future aspirations that parents may have for their children, but rather to provide opportunities for them to share their plans and expectations with professionals so that the team can work together toward these goals.

ASSESSING FUTURE PLANNING NEEDS

Transition Assessment

Transition assessment has been defined by the Council for Exceptional Children's Division on Career Development and Transition as the ". . . ongoing process of collecting data on the individual's needs, preferences, and interests as they relate to the demands of current and future working, educational, living, and personal and social environments. Assessment data serve as the common thread in the transition process and form the basis for defining goals and services to be included in the Individualized Education Program (IEP)" (Sitlington, Neubert, & Leconte, 1997, pp. 70–71).

The assessment tools that are selected for transition assessment may be formal or informal. Formal tools are standardized tests that allow the student's scores to be compared with the abilities of same-age peers. Typically, formal assessments cover the areas of adaptive behavior, daily living skills, achievement, employability, and aptitude.

Interest inventories are used to determine the student's preferences for particular careers or types of work. Self-determination assessments tap into the student's self-awareness and readiness to identify relative strengths and needs. Informal assessments are usually criterion-referenced and often use multiple measures and respondents. They include interviews and questionnaires, observations in the natural environment, environmental or ecological assessments, and curriculum-based assessments (CBAs).

In the course of a transition assessment, it makes sense to assess both the student and the potential environments within which the student will live, learn, work, and play. Assessing both the student and the environments will allow the transition team to determine the goodness of fit between the student and the selected environments, which will enable smoother and more successful transitions. Effective transition assessment mandates information gathering in authentic life settings such as postsecondary school or job sites, the student's home, and their community. On the basis of the assessment data, necessary supports and accommodations can be provided to assist the student to transition to the future work or living environment. Alternatively, additional efforts can be initiated to find alternate programs, work, or residential settings that better suit the student's strengths, needs, and preferences (Sitlington et al., 1997).

ASSESSING THE STUDENT

Interviews

Widely used to learn more about a student's preferences and interests, interviews may be conducted with the student, family members, friends, teachers, counselors, and other knowledgeable adults who work closely with the student. Interviews that are used for vocational purposes are often semistructured and developed by teachers. It is recommended that the interview questions be shared with the interviewee before the face-to-face interview so that the interviewee has some advance notice of the areas to be discussed. Some topics on which interviews may gather data include

- *Student background information*—Medical and health history, schooling experiences, and social and emotional adaptation.
- *Family and home situation*—Family composition and membership, living arrangement, language spoken in the home, relationships with family members, and responsibilities the individual assumes in the home.
- *Peer relationships*—Friendships, preferred activities with friends, and sources of conflict.
- *School progress*—Preferred academic areas, academic progress, and areas needing assistance.
- *Vocational interests*—Current and future jobs, job goals, student's and family's preferences for jobs and postsecondary education.
- *Community living*—Independence in transportation, mobility, independent living skills, and goals for future living situation.

Rating Scales

Commonly used to gather data from teachers, parents, and the target student, rating scales are a way to collect data on a student's transition skills, interests, preferences, needs, and challenges. Data may be triangulated by seeking *ratings* from more than one rater who knows the student well and across multiple settings and situations. As in all rating scales, responder bias can adversely affect the results.

A popular commercially produced inventory that gathers information about a student's strengths, needs, and preferences from the student, parent, and school personnel is the Transition Planning Inventory-Updated Version (TPI-UV, Clark & Patton, 2004). Appropriate for individuals with disabilities aged 14–22 years, the TPI-UV collects data in the areas of transition planning that are mandated by IDEA (2004). The inventory includes 46 items in the domains of Employment, Postsecondary Education/Training, Daily Living, Leisure Activities, Community Participation, Health, Self-Determination, Communication, and Interpersonal Relationships. The same items are administered using a Likert scale to the student, parent or primary caregiver, and teacher and/or other school personnel. The TPI-UV also includes a Profile and Further Recommendations form. The Home form is available in Spanish, Chinese, Japanese, and Korean.

Vocational Interest Inventories

Interest inventories allow for the assessment of an individual's job preferences on the basis of expressed areas of interest. Some experts suggest exercising caution when using a vocational interest inventory. They believe that it is a limited index of a student's future interests because it calls on the student's prior knowledge and familiarity with certain careers. Thus, although Sarom may have a potential flair for a career in fashion design, if she has not had any prior exposure to that career choice she may not indicate it as an interest when she completes the inventory and may instead only list careers with which she is already familiar, such as health aide or office receptionist. Vocational interest inventories may be made by a teacher or commercially produced. Several published inventories exist on the market, including some that are tailored to the needs of students with limited reading skills.

Recently, there has been a move to electronically publish and distribute vocational interest inventories. A simple web search generates several interest inventories. The reader is cautioned to review the technical adequacy of these measures prior to administering them.

Behavioral Observation

Observing the individual interacting in authentic vocational, educational, and community settings over a period of time provides important data to assist with planning for transitions. The student's strengths and areas of need may be assessed and appropriate interventions may be developed accordingly. Many behavioral observation methods, including anecdotal notes, event sampling, and time sampling, have been discussed in Chapter 8 of this text. It is beneficial for multiple team members to observe the student across settings in order to form a valid and reliable picture of the student (Sitlington, Neubert, Begun, Lombard, & LeConte, 1996).

Curriculum-Based Vocational Assessments

CBAs may be developed by the teacher or other school staff to assess the student's mastery of the content taught. CBAs include criterion-referenced tests and portfolios, both of which have been discussed at length in previous chapters in this text. Curriculum-based

Vocational Interest Inventories

The Career Ability Placement Survey (CAPS, Knapp, Knapp, & Knapp-Lee, 1992)—A comprehensive and multidimensional battery, CAPS lists eight ability dimensions that are required for a majority of the occupations in the 14 Career Occupation Preference System Career Clusters: Science (Professional and Skilled), Technology (Professional and Skilled), Consumer Economics, Outdoor, Business (Professional and Skilled), Clerical, Communication, Arts (Professional and Skilled), and Service (Professional and Skilled). Appropriate for use with individuals in seventh grade and higher, the CAPS takes 50 minutes to administer. Examinees score themselves and receive immediate feedback on the occupational clusters for which they are best suited.

The Reading Free Career Interest Inventory: 2 (Becker, 2000/2001) is designed to measure the vocational interests of people with disabilities aged 13 years and older. It uses 55 sets of pictures of people participating in career tasks and asks the testee to indicate which of the displayed career choices seem to be most interesting to him or her. The resulting scores are classified into 11 interest categories (automotive, building trades, clerical, animal care, food service, personal service, patient care, horticulture, housekeeping, laundry service, and materials handling), within five clusters (mechanical, outdoor, mechanical/outdoor, clerical/personal care, and food service/handling operations). The test is easy to administer and score, can be administered to individuals and groups in about 20 minutes, and has adequate technical qualities.

vocational assessments target a student's performance in a vocational education, career development, or transition-related setting (Sitlington & Clark, 2001). Data are collected on the student's performance in vocational settings in areas such as comprehending instructions, having the prior knowledge required, interacting with peers and supervisors, demonstrating on-task behaviors, and seeking help when needed. The intent is to provide the supports and instructional modifications that the student may need in order to be successful.

Student Self-Determination, Self-Monitoring, and Choice Making

Assessing student self-determination requires the input of multiple respondents who are very familiar with the student and who have the opportunity to see the student interact across multiple authentic settings (Wehmeyer, 2001). This process includes soliciting the student's self-evaluation of his or her interests and preferences. The information may be collected through informal means, such as observation over time of the objects toward which the student generally gravitates, the student's verbalizations and affect when given a choice of activities, the amount of time that he or she spends with a particular object, or the student's selection of a preferred item. If a student is verbal, interviews may be used. Norm-referenced measures are also available to assess self-determination. For instance, *Arc's Self-Determination Scale* (Wehmeyer, 1996) provides student self-report data in the areas of student autonomy (independence and acting on one's beliefs), self-regulation (problem solving, goal setting, and task performance), psychological empowerment, and self-realization. The results provide an indicator of later adult outcomes related to quality of life.

Another measure is the *AIR Self-Determination Scale* (Wolman, Campeau, DuBois, Mithaug, & Stolarski, 1994). This scale includes teacher, parent, and student rating forms that yield a profile of the student's level of self-determination.

Giving students the opportunity to make choices increases their personal satisfaction and quality of life, prepares them to be independent, and increases their motivation (Kleinert et al., 2001). Students might make choices between activities (e.g., choosing art or music as an elective) or within activities (e.g., whether to use a blue or a red marker), and choices may be assessed orally or in writing using open-ended or closed-ended questions.

In addition to being encouraged to make choices, students should be encouraged to monitor their own learning against identified learning goals. Giving students the opportunity to select the skills on which they will work and the strategies they will use to develop a skill assists them to learn how to manage their time and learning and also motivates them to accomplish their learning goals. Some students may be able to work independently, while others work with a buddy, use assistive devices, or use a computer. Figure 10.1 shows a sample form that a student may use to self-monitor his or her learning.

Student Name: Maria Nieves

Date: 10/3/2009

Class: Math- Word Problems

1. Today, I will focus on:

☑ Reading the question carefully ☐ Developing a number sentence

☐ Math facts ☑ Checking my work

2. Insert a tally mark each time I:

Target skill	Tally
Read question carefully	II
Check my work	IIII

3. How did I do today?

☐ I did better ☑ About the same ☐ I did worse

4. I still need to work on:

1) Reading the question carefully

2) Not talking to others

3)

Maria | Mrs. Gutierrez

Student Signature | Teacher Signature

FIGURE 10.1 Student Self-Monitoring Form

ASSESSING POTENTIAL ENVIRONMENTS

Work Sample Assessment

Students' interests and proficiencies may be assessed by observing them as they participate in simulated work settings, completing authentic job tasks in their vocational interest area. For example, a work sample for Freddy may be obtained by observing him type information into a database to determine his readiness for a clerical task in the area of data entry. The work sample would be evaluated in terms of Freddy's interest and engagement in the task, his speed, and his accuracy at entering data. Freddy's performance would be compared with entry-level skills for other incoming employees and he might receive additional training or accommodations such as assistive technology or coaching if necessary.

Commercially prepared work samples could be used to assess vocational readiness. Generally, such samples are expensive options and may lack authenticity because they are not tailored to specific work situations. However, they are quick and easy to use because they follow standardized procedures and scoring criteria. In contrast, teacher-created work samples are developed on the basis of local job analyses (Sitlington et al., 1996). Consequently, they are more specific to the task being assessed, but usually they have fewer formalized procedures and directions to follow.

Situational Assessments

The student is observed completing an authentic task in a controlled work environment. The task may be modeled for the student, after which he or she is given an opportunity to practice and execute the task in the presence of an observer. The student may receive some level of prompting or support as he or she completes the task that may be reduced gradually and eventually eliminated. Usually, situational assessments are conducted on the job by placing students in an internship, having them participate in job shadowing, or putting them in a community-based setting. Job skills, speed, accuracy, and work-related behaviors including social skills, persistence, and endurance are assessed over a period of time in a supported environment. The evaluator usually follows the target student for a certain time and determines

The Valpar Component Work Sample System (Brandon, Button, Rastatter, & Ross, 1974) is designed to assess vocational readiness in individuals with disabilities aged 14 years and older. The battery includes 24 hands-on work samples in four subtests: a developmental assessment (which assesses physical and perceptual abilities), workshop evaluation (which simulates an assembly workshop setting to observe the worker's interpersonal skills and productivity), interpersonal/social skills (observation of social and practical behaviors), and money-handling skills (observation of proficiency with money).

the student's competence across a variety of tasks in the natural job environment, including his or her ability to take public transportation to get to the workplace; greet peers and superiors on arrival at the workplace; clock in and get ready to start work; complete work-related tasks with precision, accuracy, and speed; receive constructive feedback and modify behavior accordingly; socialize with colleagues; and seek assistance as needed.

A *task analysis* is the process by which a complex task is broken down into its component steps (Snell & Brown, 2000). After mastering prerequisite job skills, an individual works on new and more complex skills until he or she is able to complete the entire task successfully. Using the process of *chaining,* each step taught is contingent on mastery of the previous step. Task analysis is a useful tool in the assessment and systematic instruction process to teach a new employee the subskills that comprise the major task (Schloss, 2001).

A *job analysis* is much like a task analysis, but it is specific to a job situation. A job analysis involves breaking down a job into its component steps and teaching the worker to complete these steps. In order to complete the job effectively, the worker must not only be proficient in completing the substeps that comprise the job but must be able to respond appropriately to environmental cues that prompt the performance of certain tasks or call for modifications to the sequence of steps. For instance, a job analysis for an assistant chef job will include following cues from the chef, which will vary depending on customer requests, the menu for the day, and the number of other assistants available in the kitchen. A job analysis serves a dual purpose: It assists with teaching a worker the job steps and skills, and it is a way to assess a worker to determine which skills have been mastered and with which ones the individual still needs assistance.

HOW TO ADOPT AN RTI APPROACH TO PLANNING FOR TRANSITION

Although there is no empirical research available that explores the application of the RTI model to transition, the RTI approach is promising in improving postschool outcomes for students. Transition planning in an RTI approach would support all students, not just those with identified disabilities. RTI is expected to enable early identification of students who are not ready to transition to life after school. The approach uses ongoing progress-monitoring data and the student's unique environment to develop approaches to intervene early on (Powers, Hagans, & Miller, 2007). Interventions are systematically applied to accomplish desired outcomes, which may include reintegration to general education.

If an RTI approach is used, struggling students need not wait until their 16th birthday to develop a transition plan; rather, their needs will be addressed as soon as they become apparent. Family and community partnerships are key for effective preparation of a student for life after school and will be facilitated in an RTI approach that focuses on problem solving to ensure effective outcomes. The student's preferences and interests serve as the starting point, and family input is sought for areas of focus and career development activities and ideas (Powers et al., 2007).

Unlike early intervention in the areas of reading and math, transition planning is complex and requires the team to identify needs and strengths across domains and skills. This multiskill, multidomain intervention planning poses a challenge to the current RTI models.

A Proposed Model of RTI for Transition Planning

TIER I   Tier I transition services include resources to get all students and their families ready for transition from school to postschool settings, including postsecondary education, career or vocational training, independent living, the workforce, and community activities. Career awareness and career exploration activities can expose students to a range of careers and give them opportunities to explore their interests and preferences (Sitlington et al., 1996). Some resources that are helpful at this stage include career interest inventories; career workshops and job fairs; college tours; opportunities where functional, vocational, and social skills are taught; opportunities to build self-determination skills; and family resource directories.

TIER II   Tier II transition services are designed to assist students who are at risk in skill development to become ready for postschool outcomes, including postsecondary education and employment settings. Career preparation activities may be used to prepare the student to identify and develop prerequisite job skills or prerequisite coursework for a chosen postsecondary education program (Sitlington et al., 1996). Specific interventions at this stage may include structured work experience, mentorships and internships, individual goal setting, community involvement, academic advising and counseling, self-management, and self-advocacy skills.

TIER III   Tier III transition services are reactive in nature and are designed to assist individuals who are having difficulties with postschool outcomes to get back on their feet. Strategies used at this stage include remedial education courses to pass a General Educational Development test, job coaching, supported living, and community mobility training.

Online Resources

Beach Center on Disability articles on Person-Centered Planning: *http://www.beachcenter.org/families/person-centered_planning.aspx*

Parent Advocacy Coalition for Educational Rights Center: *http://www.pacer.org/tatra/*

The National Center on Secondary Education and Transition: *http://www.ncset.org/*

National Collaborative on Workforce and Disability for Youth: *http://www.ncwd-youth.info/*

National Secondary Transition Technical Assistance Center: *http://www.nsttac.org/*

End-of-Chapter Questions

1. What do the data from the National Longitudinal Transition Study 2 indicate about the academic and postschool outcomes for students with disabilities?
2. Transition services are mandated under IDEA. What are the key components of transition? What do transition services include?
3. According to IDEA, in what ways must the lEP address transition planning for students aged 16 years and older?
4. Which pieces of legislation, besides IDEA, call for transition planning for youth with disabilities?
5. What is the practical significance of planning for transitions for youth with disabilities?
6. Define self-determination and discuss why it is important to build self-determination skills in youngsters with disabilities.
7. Of what does the person-centered planning process consist?
8. Describe the MAPS process. What is the value of using such a process to plan for a student's future?
9. How should parental involvement be encouraged in the transition planning process?
10. Sitlington and colleagues note the importance of assessing the student and the potential environment to effectively plan for transition. Discuss your understanding of their model.
11. What are some assessment tools that could be used to assess a student's interests, preferences, and skills? Discuss each.
12. What are some assessment tools that could be used in assessing potential environments? Discuss each.
13. In what ways could an RTI approach be applied to enhance transition assessment and planning?
14. Discuss possible transition planning activities at each of the three tiers in an RTI model.

References

Carter, E. W., Lane, K., L., Pierson, M. R., & Glaeser, B. (2006). Self-determination skills and opportunities of transition-age youth with emotional disturbance and learning disabilities. *Exceptional Children, 72,* 333–346.

Brandon, T. L., Button, W. L., Rastatter, C. J., & Ross, D. R. (1974). *Manual of the Valpar Component Work Samples.* Arizona: Valpar.

Clark, G., & Patton, J. (2004). *Transition Planning Inventory (Updated Version).* Upper Saddle River, NJ: Pearson.

Forest, M., & Pearpoint, J. (1992). Common sense tools: Maps and circles for inclusive education. In J. Pearpoint, M. Forest, & J. Snow (Eds.), *Inclusion papers: Strategies to make inclusion work* (pp. 40–56). Toronto, Ontario, Canada: Inclusion.

Kleinert, H. L., Denham, A., Burke Gronek, V., Clayton, J., Burdge, M., Kearns, J. F., et al. (2001). Systematically teaching the components of self-determination. In H. Kleinert & J. Farmer Kearns (Eds.), *Alternate assessment: Measuring outcomes and supports for students with disabilities* (pp. 93–134). Baltimore: Paul H. Brookes Co.

Menchetti, B. M., & Piland, V. C. (2001). Transition assessment and evaluation: Current methods and emerging alternatives. In S. Alper, D. L. Ryndak, and C. Schloss (Eds.), *Alternate assessment of students with disabilities in inclusive settings* (pp. 220–248). Needham Heights, MA: Allyn & Bacon.

Mount, B., & Zwernik, K. (1988). *It's never too early, it's never too late: A booklet about personal futures planning.* St. Paul, MN: Minnesota Governor's Planning Council on Developmental Disabilities.

National Center on Secondary Education and Transition. (2004). *Person-centered planning: A tool for transition. Parent Brief.* Minneapolis, MN.

Powers, K., Hagans, K., & Miller, M. (2007). Using Response to Intervention to promote transition from special education services. In S. Jimerson, M. Burns, & A. VanDerHeyden (Eds.), *Handbook of response to intervention: The science and practice of assessment and intervention.* New York: Springer Science.

Rueda, R., Monzo, L., Shapiro, J., Gomez, J., & Blacher, J. (2005). Cultural models of transition: Latina mothers of young adults with developmental disabilities. *Exceptional Children, 71,* 401–414.

Schloss, C. N. (2001). Measuring responses through direct observation. In S. Alper, D. L. Ryndak, & C. Schloss (Eds.), *Alternate assessment of students with disabilities in inclusive settings* (pp. 171–182). Needham Heights, MA: Allyn & Bacon.

Sitlington. P. L., & Clark, G. M. (2001). Career /vocational assessment: A critical component of transition planning. *Assessment for Effective Intervention, 26*(4), 5-22.

Sitlington, P. L., Neubert, D. A., Begun, W., Lombard, R. C., & Leconte, P. J. (1996). *Assess for success: Handbook on transition assessment*. Reston, VA: Council for Exceptional Children.

Sitlington, P. L., Neubert, D. A., & Leconte, P. J. (1997). Transition assessment: The position of the Division on Career Development and Transition. *Career Development for Exceptional Individuals, 20,* 69–79.

Smull, M., & Harrison, S. (1992). *Supporting people with severe reputations in the community*. Alexandria, VA: National Association of State Directors of Developmental Disabilities Services, Inc.

Snell, M., & Brown, L. (2000). *Instruction of students with severe disabilities* (5th ed.). Upper Saddle River, NJ: Merrill/Pearson Education.

Turnbull, A. P., & Turnbull, H. R. (1993). Empowerment and decision making through group action planning. In *Life-long transitions: Proceedings of the third annual parent/family conference* (pp. 39–45). Washington, D.C.: U.S. Department of Education.

Unok Marks, S. (2008). Self-determination for students with intellectual disabilities and why I want educators to know what it means. *Phi Delta Kappan, 90*(1), 55–58.

Wagner, M., Newman, L., Cameto, R., Levine, P., & Garza, N. (2006). An overview of findings from Wave 2 of the National Longitudinal Transition Study-2 (NLTS2). Menlo Park, CA: SRI International. Retrieved on November 23, 2008, from http://www.nlts2.org/reports/2006_08/nlts2_report_2006_08_complete.pdf.

Wehmeyer, M. (1996). A self-report measure of self-determination for adolescents with cognitive disabilities. *Education and Training in Mental Retardation and Developmental Disabilities, 31,* 282–293.

Wehmeyer, M. (2001). Assessment in self-determination: Guiding instruction and transition planning. *Assessment for Effective Intervention, 26,* 41–49.

Wolman, J. M., Campeau, P. L., DuBois, P. A., Mithaug, D. E., & Stolarski, V. S. (1994). *AIR self-determination scale and user guide*. Stanford, CA: American Institute on Research.

Assessment of Reading

Lisa is a happy 10-year-old with an outgoing attitude and a strong sense of fun. She gets along well with her teachers and peers and has lots of friends. Lisa is a gifted gymnast. She is strong in math but struggles with reading. Her parents are very supportive of Lisa's schooling and ensure that she completes her homework and reads with them every night. She has attended afterschool tutoring programs since first grade. Her vision and hearing screenings do not indicate any sensory problems. Lisa reads haltingly and without the correct intonation. She slowly sounds out individual words and comprehends little of what she reads, although her listening comprehension is commensurate with her age peers. Her fourth-grade teacher is frustrated with Lisa's limited responsiveness to the teacher's efforts to enhance reading fluency and comprehension.

Reflections on the Scenario

1. What are some ways in which Lisa's teacher can assess her reading skills in order to plan appropriate interventions?
2. What are some of the reading skills on which Lisa's teacher would want to focus?
3. What are some strategies she could use to build Lisa's reading proficiency?
4. What ongoing assessment techniques would the teacher employ to monitor Lisa's reading progress?
5. What may be some additional supports and services that Lisa may need in order to learn to read well?

COUNCIL FOR EXCEPTIONAL CHILDREN (CEC) STANDARDS

This chapter addresses the following CEC standards:

ICC8K1—Basic terminology used in assessment.

ICC8K4—Use and limitations of assessment instruments.

ICC8S2—Administer nonbiased formal and informal assessments.

ICC8S3—Use technology to conduct assessments.

ICC8S5—Interpret information from formal and informal assessments.

ICC8S6—Use assessment information in making eligibility, program, and placement decisions for individuals with exceptional learning needs, including those from culturally and/or linguistically diverse backgrounds.

ICC8S8—Evaluate instruction and monitor progress of individuals with exceptional learning needs.

ICC8S9—Develop or modify individualized assessment strategies.

ICC8S10—Create and maintain records.

GC8S3—Select, adapt, and modify assessments to accommodate the unique abilities and needs of individuals with disabilities.

READING

Reading skills are required across most life domains. Many everyday life tasks, such as reading labels on products that are used regularly, reading maps and signs, playing board or video games, following recipes, and using the Internet to look up information or get the news call for a certain level of reading proficiency. Academic learning requires a student to read text and express his or her learning in writing. There is a general consensus that effective reading skills are essential for school success. A majority of students who have difficulties at school have been found to exhibit difficulties in the area of reading. Similarly, most careers require that the prospective employee be literate and able to make meaning from written text.

FIVE ESSENTIAL COMPONENTS OF READING

The National Reading Panel (National Institute of Child Health and Human Development, 2000) reviewed the scientific research and published a report that identifies five essential components of reading which are incorporated into the No Child Left Behind (NCLB) legislation. These five essential components of reading are

1. *Phonemic awareness*—Identifying and correctly using phonemes, the smallest units of sounds that make up speech (International Reading Association, 1998). This skill includes correctly hearing sounds, segmenting, blending, and recognizing similarities and differences in word sounds. A student who demonstrates phonemic awareness has a basic understanding that words are made of individual phonemes that can be put together in various combinations to create new words (e.g., Suzy knows that m-a-p makes "map," and when her teacher replaces the initial sound with "c," Suzy knows that it makes c-a-p, or "cap").

There is an essential distinction between phonological and phonemic awareness, terms that are often used synonymously. Phonological awareness is a broader term that refers to a youngster's understanding of how language is structured (Haager, Dimino, & Windmueller, 2007). Phonological awareness includes skills such as phonemic awareness, rhyming, segmenting and blending of syllables in a word, and putting words together to form sentences (Chard & Dickson, 1999). When phonological awareness activities are arranged along a continuum from simple to complex, the simplest activities include rhyming songs and segmenting sentences into words, and later activities include segmenting words into syllables and blending syllables into words. A more complex activity would be segmenting words into onset and rimes. For example, frog = fr (onset) and og (rime), and run = r (onset) and un (rime). Another complex activity would be blending onset-rimes into words (e.g., k-ing = king). Phonemic awareness is the most complex type of phonological awareness skill that specifically deals with the manipulation (understanding, blending, and segmenting) of phonemes in the spoken word (Haager et al., 2007).

2. *Phonics* —Also called alphabetic principle or symbol-sound correspondence, this skill requires the reader to recognize and use a set of rules that clarify the relationship between word sounds and symbols (i.e., letters or a combination of letters). Phonics allows the reader to sound out written symbols and to hear speech sounds and write the symbols accordingly.

3. *Reading fluency* —This skill calls for accuracy and speed in reading text using appropriate expression to indicate meaning. Meyer and Felton define reading fluency as "the ability to read connected text rapidly, smoothly, effortlessly, and automatically with little conscious attention to the mechanics of reading, such as decoding" (1999, p. 284). A fluent reader reads automatically, expending few cognitive resources on the reading process itself and thereby being able to comprehend the text that is being read.

The research literature points to a close relationship between oral reading fluency and reading comprehension (Hosp & Fuchs, 2005; Kranzler, Brownell, & Miller, 1998). Lisa, the student presented in the vignette at the start of this chapter, demonstrates difficulties in word recognition and fluency. She struggles with decoding words, which hinders her ability to read for meaning.

4. *Vocabulary development* —This ability calls for understanding the meaning of words that are encountered orally and in written format. A child's vocabulary helps the child with word recognition and reading comprehension. Early readers call on their receptive vocabulary to make sense of new words that they encounter as they read. More sophisticated readers build their oral vocabulary by learning the meanings of new and unknown words as they read more advanced text. Vocabulary development involves using a host of strategies to help students make meaning of the words they encounter in text.

5. *Reading comprehension* —Comprehension calls for using various strategies to understand and make meaning of the text and communicate coherently about what was read. Effective comprehension strategies require the reader to make connections between new text and what the reader already knows. Fluent readers read for meaning and regulate their use of reading strategies so that they may comprehend the text they read.

As is evident from these brief descriptions, a fluent reader develops complementary skills across these five essential components. It is essential that reading instruction be systematic and explicit, targeting each of these skills in a logical sequence.

RESPONSE TO INTERVENTION AND READING: A BRIEF SUMMARY OF THE RESEARCH

More than 80% of students who have been identified with special education needs have difficulties with literacy (E. Mesmer & H. Mesmer, 2008). Given the importance of reading in formal education and the magnitude of reading difficulties that are experienced by youngsters in our schools, much of the research literature supporting the Response to Intervention (RTI) approach stems from the reading domain. Over 30 years of reading research suggest that when students who are at risk for reading difficulties are diagnosed early and receive appropriate interventions, many of these students acquire the skills they need to be successful readers (Foorman, Francis, Fletcher, Schatschneider, &

Mehta, 1998; Vellutino, Scanlon, & Lyon, 2000). Providing explicit instruction in the essential components of reading is salient in helping build the literacy skills that are required to be a successful reader and reduce the risk for further reading difficulties (National Institute of Child Health and Human Development, 2000).

In an RTI approach, universal literacy practices are established in the classroom and students are screened several times each year to determine their progress in mastering essential literacy skills (E. Mesmer & H. Mesmer, 2008). Gersten and colleagues (2009) recommend that all students be screened for potential reading difficulties at the start of and in the middle of the school year. Differentiated reading instruction should be provided to all students in Tier I, and students who are at risk for potential reading disabilities should be monitored frequently. Although essential reading instruction is provided, some students, reportedly 8–80% of the class, are likely to continue to struggle (Al Otaiba & Fuchs, 2002). These students are identified early using reliable and valid screening measures and are provided with supplemental instruction in small group settings. Gersten and colleagues recommend intensive small-group instruction, three to five times a week for 20–40 minutes, to target up to three foundational reading skills. Ongoing progress monitoring systems should be administered at least monthly to determine whether the students are responding to the interventions implemented. Although most students will attain reading proficiency as measured by established criterion benchmarks, nonresponders should receive individualized and more intensive interventions and their progress should continue to be monitored, usually weekly. Intensive interventions are found to be most effective when groups contain three or fewer students and when interventions are provided daily for up to 20 weeks. Students who respond to intervention maintain the resulting gains in reading proficiency for several years after the intervention has been terminated. If a student continues not to respond to the interventions, a team of school professionals reviews whether the student is eligible for special education.

TECHNIQUES FOR READING ASSESSMENT AND PROGRESS MONITORING

Early assessment of reading difficulties will assist in developing an appropriate curriculum and instruction to foster skill development in areas that are lacking. Reading assessments are used for many different purposes. Students are assessed to determine whether they meet grade-level benchmarks, guide instructional planning, screen for potential reading difficulties, and monitor student progress over time. Reading assessments may be used to identify whether a student is eligible for special education services. Diagnostic reading assessments help identify specific skills and difficulties that a student demonstrates and can assist with planning interventions. Reading assessments are also conducted for accountability purposes. Under NCLB legislation, all schools are required to assess students' reading skills to determine the effectiveness of the school's programs. Various formal and informal reading assessments are reviewed in the next section.

COMPREHENSIVE LITERACY MEASURES

Several screening measures are empirically validated for use within an RTI approach. The following measures are among the highly rated and empirically sound *criterion-based comprehensive screening measures* that were reviewed by the National Center on

Response to Intervention (2010): Dynamic Indicators of Basic Early Literacy Skills (DIBELS), AIMSweb, STAR Reading, and the System to Enhance Educational Performance Oral Reading Fluency (STEEP ORF). These measures are amenable to individual and group administration and can be used as screening tools to identify students who may be at risk for reading difficulties. They also can be used as progress-monitoring measures to monitor growth in essential reading components in response to interventions that are applied.

DIBELS (Kaminski & Good, 1998) is a technically sound measure of early literacy and reading fluency skills that focuses on the assessment of phonological awareness, alphabetic principle, nonsense word fluency, and fluency with connected text. The DIBELS measure is widely used for screening and progress monitoring purposes for youngsters from preschool to sixth grade. This measure is described more fully in Chapter 5.

AIMSweb (http://www.aimsweb.com) is a commercially produced progress-monitoring system that consists of curriculum-based measurement (CBM) probes in reading and math for students in kindergarten through eighth grade. It is available in both English and Spanish. AIMSweb Oral Reading CBM is appropriate for youngsters in grades 1–8. AIMSweb includes oral reading fluency passages and maze passages to monitor progress in the area of reading comprehension. This system also includes measures of early literacy, including letter-naming fluency, letter-sound fluency, phoneme segmentation fluency, and nonsense word fluency.

STAR Reading (Renaissance Learning, http://www.renlearn.com/sr/) is a commercially produced computer-administered measure of early literacy, reading fluency, and comprehension skills. The STAR Early Literacy Test is most applicable for students in prekindergarten through third grade and is administered individually or to groups of students. It lasts about 10 minutes. The test items are generated on the basis of the student's response to earlier items, so each test is tailored to the individual student. The test assesses a student in the areas of general reading readiness, phonemic awareness, phonics, graphophonemic knowledge, structural analysis, vocabulary, and reading and listening comprehension. The measure has strong technical qualities.

The STAR Reading Test is appropriate for individuals or groups in grades 1–12. Like the STAR Early Literacy Test, it is individually tailored to the student; items are generated on the basis of students' responses to earlier items. The test may be used by students with disabilities who need accommodations for their physical and/or sensory disabilities (e.g., voice output, screen color and resolution, use of a scribe). The measure is rated as having strong technical qualities and is applicable for screening and progress monitoring purposes in an RTI model.

STEEP ORF (iSTEEP; http://www.isteep.com) was developed as a method of implementing RTI using a standard protocol. The STEEP ORF is a computer-administered, commercially produced measure of oral reading fluency. A standard protocol model of specific interventions is generated on the basis of student performance on the ORF measure and two additional brief assessments, together with ongoing progress monitoring probes. This model is well suited to assessing an entire class and even an entire school. Norms for a particular school and district may be generated and built into the STEEP system to tailor it for that school or district.

For additional details on each of the screening measures described here, visit the National Center on Response to Intervention Website: http://www.rti4success.org/chart/screeningTools/screeningtoolschart. html

ASSESSING THE FIVE KEY ELEMENTS OF READING

Assessing Phonemic Awareness

Phonemic awareness has received increasing research attention over the past several years due to its critical connections with student's language and literacy development (Chard & Dickson, 1999; Flax, Realpe-Bonilla, Roesler, Choudhury, & Benasich, 2009; National Institute of Child Health and Human Development, 2000). Good screening measures help the teacher predict later reading ability and identify students who are at risk for future reading difficulties. Some measures of phonemic awareness are described in the following section.

TEST OF PHONOLOGICAL AWARENESS   The Test of Phonological Awareness (Chard & Dickson, 1999; Torgesen & Davis, 1996) includes 20 items. Each of the first 10 items depicts a target word followed by three words each represented by a picture. The student must state which pictures have the same initial sound as the target word. The remaining 10 items each consist of four words depicted by pictures and the student is asked which word begins with an initial sound that is different from that of the other three words. This measure can be administered in small groups and is appropriate for the second half of kindergarten.

YOPP-SINGER TEST OF PHONEME SEGMENTATION   The Yopp-Singer Test (Yopp, 1995) is individually administered and consists of 22 items. The examiner reads a word aloud to the student, who must state each of the phonemes in the word. Students receive credit for each item only if they correctly state all the sounds in the word in the correct sequence. The examiner may give the student immediate corrective feedback and may tell him or her the correct sounds if the student makes an error. All errors are recorded to assist with instructional planning. A free, reproducible version of this test is available at http://teams.lacoe.edu/reading/assessments/yopp.html.

Assessing Phonics

The following measures are used specifically to assess a student's symbol-sound correspondence or phonics:

NONWORD SPELLING (CHARD & DICKSON, 1999)   Students are given five nonwords to spell, each containing three phonemes (e.g., feg, rit, mub, gof, pid). Students earn a point for each phoneme they spell correctly in each of the five words for a total possible score of 15 points. This measure is most appropriate for use with children in the second half of kindergarten and for older students who experience difficulties in phonological and phonemic skills.

MAKING WORDS (CUNNINGHAM, 1991)   This word study pattern-recognition activity also can be used for assessment purposes. Students are given a set of letters and a series of instructions and modeling from the teacher that guides them through the development of a sequence of words, starting from smaller, simpler words and proceeding to more complex, longer words (e.g., pass + ages makes "passages"). Students learn how manipulating individual letters in a word can change the entire word. Observing the student's proficiency with forming words per the directions provided and his or her proficiency with identifying underlying patterns provides data to plan appropriate interventions.

SCHOLASTIC PHONICS INVENTORY (SPI, HTTP://TEACHER.SCHOLASTIC.COM/PRODUCTS/ READINGASSESSMENT_SPI/INDEX.HTM)   This is a measure of letter recognition, high-frequency sight words, and decoding skills using nonwords. The SPI can be administered by computer to individuals or groups of students in grades 3–12. Recommendations for an appropriate curriculum (e.g., Reading 180, System 44) are made on the basis of a student's reading proficiency levels. The test may accommodate students who have difficulties using a mouse, and the measure can be administered in English or Spanish.

Assessing Reading Fluency

In order to be a fluent reader, the student must have letter-sound correspondence, proficiency with phonics, and decoding skills. Fluency is essential for reading accurately and with comprehension. Techniques used to assess reading fluency are presented in the next section.

CBM-ORF   CBM is an assessment technique that has been used successfully to assess students' reading skills for over 30 years. CBM is particularly suited to an RTI approach. This technique has strong technical adequacy and is a sensitive and accurate tool to identify students who are experiencing difficulties in reading, determine students' current reading levels, monitor students' ongoing reading progress on a regular basis, and determine a student's responsiveness to interventions (Hosp, Hosp, & Howell, 2007; Shapiro, 2004; Shinn, 1989). CBM probes are quick and easy to administer, score, and graph, and they yield meaningful data that allow teachers to make data-based instructional decisions.

CBM-ORF adopts standardized procedures for assessing students' reading skills by having them read aloud for 1 minute from assigned passages that may be commercially developed or randomly selected from the student's local school curriculum. The number of words read correctly in a minute by the student is monitored, typically three times a year, to determine progress over time. In an RTI model, students' responsiveness to instruction may be assessed biweekly by using CBM probes. The student's performance also is compared with national normative or benchmark data to determine the student's reading proficiency and risk status for reading difficulties. Generally validated as screening and progress monitoring measures, CBM-ORF probes provide only preliminary diagnostic data to guide reading intervention. CBM

Some web resources:

> ChartDog is an application that helps with developing charts to graph student progress. *http://www.jimwrightonline.com/php/chartdog_2_0/chartdog.php*

> Cool Tools: Reading Informal Assessments, developed by Project Central in the Florida Department of Education, provides sample informal assessments in the five elements of reading. *http://www. paec.org/itrk3/files/pdfs/readingpdfs/cooltoolsall.pdf*

> Intervention Central is an excellent resource for CBM probes, graphs, and other resources. *http://www.interventioncentral.org/*

> OKAPI! is an application that helps develop CBM reading probes in a usable format. *http:// www.interventioncentral.org/htmdocs/tools/okapi/okapi.php*

> Progress Monitoring Tools have been reviewed by the National Center on Response to Intervention. *http://www.rti4success.org/chart/progressMonitoring/ progressmonitoringtoolschart.htm*

> Reading screening measures is a review of screening tools conducted by the National Center on Response to Intervention. *http://www.rti4success.org/index.php?option=com_ content&task=view&id=1091*

is best used in conjunction with other measures to diagnose a student's strengths and difficulties in reading. Chapter 5 describes CBM more fully and also provides a description of how to develop reading probes, administer and score a reading CBM, plot the data on a graph, and use these data to plan instruction.

RUNNING RECORDS   Originating in the work of Goodman (1969) and Clay (1985), running records are a very popular reading assessment that is used both for diagnostic and progress-monitoring purposes. The student reads aloud from leveled reading passages while the teacher observes the student's behaviors and marks the errors that the student makes. The teacher sits next to the student and is able to see the passage that the student is reading. Using a copy of the text being read or a blank scoring sheet, the teacher places a checkmark above each word that is read correctly and writes the misread word above any words that are read incorrectly. Although the assessment is not traditionally timed, timing is recommended to determine the student's rate of reading fluency.

Running records are used to determine a student's reading level: independent (greater than 95% accuracy), instructional (90–95% accuracy), and frustration (less than 90% accuracy). Conducting a miscue analysis after administering a running record helps the teacher plan instruction to remedy the student's errors. Running records also allow the teacher to observe the reading behaviors of student, thereby facilitating instructional decision making (Fawson, Ludlow, Reutzel, Sudweeks, & Smith, 2006).

This measure is popular because it is authentic and closely aligned to everyday classroom practice, but additional data are needed about the technical qualities of running records (Fawson et al., 2006; Paris & Hoffman, 2004). If a student is assessed using a single passage at each testing period, the variability in the passages read by the student over several testing periods could reduce the reliability of the scores. Fawson and colleagues recommend that a minimum of three passages of a similar difficulty level be read at each administration period in order to get reliable results, with the teacher recording either the median or mean score as the obtained score to eliminate variability in passage difficulty levels, unfamiliar words, etc. Paris and Hoffman caution that teachers need ongoing professional development training in using the data obtained from running records in a consistent and instructionally meaningful fashion.

Technological innovations have made it a lot easier to conduct classroom assessments. Teachers in schools today increasingly rely on computerized administration and the use of personal digital assistants (e.g., palm pilots), digital pens, and other devices to administer and score running records.

MISCUE ANALYSES   Miscue analysis is a technique that is commonly used to assess word recognition and errors. It is based on the premise that by examining the types of errors a student makes, the teacher can gain insights into how the student processes written text (McKenna & Picard, 2006). A reader generally relies on three types of cues to assist with reading: V—visual or graphophonic cues (i.e., the visual similarity in the letters within a word as indicated when a child misreads "pride" for "price"), M—the meaning of the word (i.e., the semantic cues indicated when the reader reads "puppy" as "doggy"), and S—structural cues in the structure and syntax of language used by the reader to determine whether what he or she read sounds correct (e.g., a reader might correct "the boy go home" to "the boy goes home"). By evaluating the miscues that a student makes, a teacher can ascertain the extent to which the student uses each of the three cuing systems while reading.

Miscue analyses often follow the administration of running records. A student reads aloud from a passage at the appropriate instructional level and the teacher systematically records the errors that the student makes while reading. The teacher then analyzes the errors to determine error trends that provide feedback for instruction. The errors also assist in identifying the student's appropriate instructional level and provide insights on the cuing system used by the student to help decode text (McKenna & Picard, 2006).

An accuracy and error rate can be calculated easily using the following formulas:

$$\text{Accuracy Rate} = \frac{\text{Number of words read correctly}}{\text{Total number of words read}} \times 100$$

$$\text{Error Rate} = \frac{\text{Number of errors}}{\text{Total number of words read}} \times 100$$

Gains in reading may be examined over time by graphing a student's accuracy and miscue rates over the course of the grading period or the school year. Instructional level passages have an accuracy rate of 92–95% and an error rate of no more than 10%. If a student has an error rate that is higher than 10%, it is recommended that the student be reassessed using an easier passage. Box 11.1 describes common errors that students make while reading and clarifies which dysfluencies are not considered to be reading errors.

Additional research is required on the psychometric qualities of miscue analysis. The technique is most effective when passages of equivalent difficulty levels are used so

BOX 11.1

Common Errors Made While Reading

Passage: "The big dog jumped on the little boy. He was scared and ran to his mother. She gave him a hug and took him to pet the dog."

Substitution—The student reads a different word in the place of the misread word (e.g., Joe reads, "The big *doll* jumped on the little boy.").

Omission—The student leaves out a word from the sentence being read (e.g., Mark reads, "The dog jumped on the little boy.").

Insertion—The student adds an extra word that is not included in the original sentence (e.g., Zoe reads, "He was *very* scared and ran to his mother.").

Reversal—The student reverses the order of the words in the sentence or the order of the letters in a word (e.g., Auguste reads, "The big *god* jumped on the little boy." Mistral reads, "He *ran to his mother, and he was scared.*").

Repetition—The student repeats some of the sounds in the word, the entire word, or a string of words in a sentence (e.g., Luis reads, "She *g-g-g-g-*gave him a hug-*hug* and *t-t-*took him to pet the dog-*pet the dog.*").

Hesitation—The student takes longer than 2 seconds to read a word and the teacher says the word for the student.

Some dysfluencies are not marked as errors. Be sure to review the rules for what is marked as an error on a particular reading measure. The following dysfluency indicators are generally not considered errors, although they are still counted as errors on some reading measures.

Self-correction—The student first reads the word incorrectly but then proceeds to correct himself or herself and read it correctly.

Mispronunciation—A student inaccurately pronounces the word or words being read, but the degree of mispronunciation is not so severe that the listener cannot comprehend the meaning of the word that has been mispronounced. This mispronunciation could be due to dialect or accent differences.

that student scores are not influenced by the student's opportunity to make certain kinds of errors on a given passage. Teacher-selected passages may have more or fewer high-frequency error types, thereby inadvertently resulting in more or fewer reported miscues that can be misinterpreted to indicate that a student is gaining or lacking fluency. Passages developed for Informal Reading Inventories (discussed later in this chapter) generally control for variability in high-frequency error types.

Word Sorts

Word sorts are a fairly simple technique that can be used to assess various reading skills, including phonemic awareness, phonics, vocabulary, word recognition, and reading comprehension (Gillet & Temple, 1990; Lipson & Wixson, 1997). Students are given flashcards with different words written on them. They are asked to sort these flashcards according to instructions provided by the teacher. When using *closed word sorts,* the teacher provides the student with clear criteria for sorting the flashcards. For example, the teacher may ask the student to sort the cards into two piles, one in which all the words have short vowel sounds (cat, hut, red, sock, sun, fish, bus) and one in which all the words have long vowel sounds (tape, cake, feet, rope, kite, cute, toad). Alternately, teachers could ask students to sort words according to their meanings (e.g., objects you would find in the home and objects you would find outdoors). Another way to sort flashcards is using an *open sort.* Using this technique, students are not given any guidelines about sorting the cards. They are asked to sort the cards and explain their rationale for sorting them the way that they did, and the teacher's observations of the student's sorting techniques provides insights about student's thinking patterns.

Some questions that are relevant to the review of a student's performance on a word sort include

1. What reading skills is the student demonstrating when he or she is asked to sort words?
2. What are common error patterns that the student displays?
3. On what types of cues is the student relying to sort word cards?

E-sorts or electronic word sorts have been used to increase student motivation among struggling or reluctant learners to participate in word sorts. Zucker and Invernizzi (2008) reported on their experience with My e-Sorts, an electronic word sort that asks students to develop their own digital sorts and share them with their peers. A tutor assisted the students to select words from stories that the students had authored which met certain spelling patterns. The use of this digital extension of the word sorts was found to improve students' attitudes toward reading and spelling.

A useful website that includes sample word sort activities amongst other literacy activities and lesson plans is http://readwritethink.org/. The resources on this site are aligned to the International Reading Association and National Council of Teachers of English standards for English Language Arts.

Assessing Vocabulary and Prior Knowledge

Vocabulary serves as a critical link between decoding and comprehension. Youngsters who have limited vocabularies have been found to experience difficulties in comprehending text. These difficulties worsen as children go on to middle and high school and are evident even when students have mastered decoding skills (Joshi, 2005). Vocabulary development is greatly influenced by a student's prior knowledge and life experiences; children who have early exposure to language-rich environments and books have higher vocabularies.

Vocabulary development occurs both purposefully and incidentally each day of a child's life. Elementary school children have been reported to build their vocabulary by an average of 7 new words per day (Beck, McKeown, & Kucan, 2002). Anderson and Nagy (1992) found that students' reading vocabularies grow by 2000 to 3000 words per year. Exposure to books and to a text- and language-rich environment enhances the rate of vocabulary development.

The need to build vocabulary to promote reading in English learners is even more important. English learners generally pick up conversational fluency well before they gain academic fluency in English. The limited academic fluency often also indicates limited vocabulary and comprehension of written text.

It is relatively difficult to assess vocabulary accurately. Informal measures of vocabulary include free recall or word-association activities in which the teacher asks the student to tell everything that he or she knows about a particular word or topic (Lipson & Wixson, 1997). English learners or students with disabilities may be given alternative response modes to demonstrate their understanding of vocabulary, including drawing or acting out their responses. Teachers often ask preparatory questions to tap into their students' background knowledge about a particular topic and use techniques such as the K-W-L charts to identify what students know about a topic, what they want to know about the topic, and, after the lesson is completed, what was learned.

Word study is another tool that is used to assess a student's vocabulary. Students learn that adding a common prefix or suffix to a root word changes the meaning and grammatical structure of the word in consistent ways. For instance, an assessment task may involve presenting a word bank that is composed of common prefixes such as "un, in, dis, mis" or suffixes such as "ly, ness, ful." The student is given sentences that include a root word (e.g., "shy") followed by a blank, and the student appends the correct suffix to make the sentence syntactically and semantically accurate.

Several norm-referenced measures provide valid assessments of a student's listening and/or reading vocabularies:

The Peabody Picture Vocabulary Test (L. M. Dunn & D. M. Dunn, 2007)—This test is an individually administered measure of listening vocabulary that may be administered to individuals 2.5 years and older. The examinee is presented with a page containing four color pictures and is expected to point to the picture of the word that was said by the examiner. This test is quick and easy to administer and is amenable to different response modes for assessing individuals with physical disabilities (e.g., pointing, nodding or blinking when the examiner points to the correct picture). Individuals with a range of speech, language, physical, cognitive, and emotional disabilities were included in the norm sample for this test. The test manual provides evidence of the reliability and validity of this measure.

Expressive Vocabulary Test (Williams, 2007)—This test is conormed with the Peabody Picture Vocabulary Test. It is an individually administered measure of expressive vocabulary and word retrieval that is normed for students aged 2.6 years to adulthood. Examinees are shown a picture and asked to provide a word that describes what they see. The test has been found to have acceptable technical qualities and takes less than 20 minutes to administer.

Comprehensive Receptive and Expressive Vocabulary Test (Wallace & Hammill, 2002)—Appropriate for children and adults aged 4–90 years, this test is used to gather information about a student's receptive and expressive vocabulary. The test is easy to administer and score and yields reliable data. The measure has limited items at higher difficulty levels and consequently does not distinguish among students with a range of language abilities.

Assessing Reading Comprehension

Comprehension is the ultimate purpose for all reading. A skilled reader who comprehends what he or she is reading interacts with the text, monitors understanding of the material that is being read, clarifies parts that were confusing, connects what is read to his or her prior knowledge, and makes predictions about events that are likely to occur in the text. The research literature points to a close relationship between oral reading fluency and reading comprehension (Hosp & Fuchs, 2005; Kranzler et al., 1998).

Salvia, Ysseldyke, and Bolt (2007) identify five types of reading comprehension that characterize the reading of successful readers. Effective assessments of reading comprehension involve each of these five types:

1. Literal comprehension requires the student to rely on the factual information that is explicitly presented in the text (e.g., main events, plot, characters).
2. Inferential comprehension calls for the student to interpret the material presented in the text (e.g., the student identifies common themes in the events that occurred).
3. Critical comprehension requires the student to make critical judgments and take a stand using the information that is provided (e.g., developing a position statement on the advantages of renewable energy sources after reading several articles on the topic).
4. Affective comprehension calls for the student to reflect on his or her emotional response to the reading (e.g., the student expresses how he or she feels about the author's arguments or notes the emotions that an article evoked).
5. Lexical comprehension requires the student to be able to comprehend key vocabulary words to make meaning of the reading (e.g., comprehending technical terms in a paper describing a physics experiment on force).

Several measures are used specifically to assess reading comprehension. These measures may ask a student to paraphrase what was read, answer questions about a passage, respond to multiple-choice items that are based on reading comprehension, demonstrate story recall or retell the story, and complete cloze procedures and maze passages. Question-and-answer is probably the most frequently used comprehension tool and involves the teacher posing questions on content that was read and the student answering these questions with correct responses which indicate that the student comprehended what was read.

CLOZE PROCEDURE AND MAZE PASSAGES   Maze passages have been used to measure reading comprehension since the 1970s (Guthrie, 1973). A short passage of about 250–300 words that is at the student's reading level but is unfamiliar to the student is selected. Every fifth word in the passage is replaced with a blank, for a total of about 50 blanks. The first and last sentences are left intact. In a cloze passage, the reader reads the passage aloud and recalls the missing words in the passage, as illustrated in Sample I. In a maze passage, the student is provided with a word bank of possible choices and selects the missing word from the menu of word choices, as depicted in Sample II. The number of correctly generated words for each blank is the student's score on the passage. An administrator may also calculate the percentage of correct words.

Sample I: "The clouds looked like fluffy balls of cotton in the blue sky. The sun shone brightly _____ the afternoon sky and _____ birds chirped loudly in the _____. It was a perfect _____ to go sailing. My _____ had just bought a new _____. Mom and dad loaded the car and we drove to the ocean.

Sample II: "The clouds looked like fluffy balls of cotton in the blue sky. The sun shone brightly _____ (of/in/as) the afternoon sky and _____ (he/her/the) birds chirped loudly in the _____ (trees/flowers/animals). It was a perfect _____ (sun/day/moon) to go sailing. My _____ (dad/dog/house) had just bought a new _____ (flower/boat/bike). Mom and dad loaded the car and we drove to the ocean.

Originally used as untimed tests of reading comprehension, maze passages are becoming increasingly popular as quick timed measures of reading comprehension. CBM progress-monitoring systems such as AIMSweb use maze passages as a progress-monitoring measure for reading fluency and comprehension. AIMSweb Maze CBM passages are appropriate for students in grades 1–8. The student silently reads 3-minute timed passages from which some of the words are missing and selects one of three options for each word that is deleted from the passage. This measure has been rated by the National Center on Student Progress Monitoring as an empirically supported measure of reading comprehension.

Maze passages are considered to be appropriate measures of reading comprehension. Some of the advantages of using a maze passage include its face validity as a test of reading comprehension, appropriateness for group administration, and applicability to computerized administration and scoring (Wayman, Wallace, Wiley, Ticha, & Espin, 2007).

Comprehension Retell

Using retellings, students are asked to orally recall the plot, characters, and main events of a narrative text after they have completed reading it. If the passage is expository, the student is asked to recall the main ideas of the text and the supporting details. When a teacher asks a student to retell a story, the directions should be open-ended and not leading (e.g., "Tell me what you just read about," "What is the story about?"). The student is given ample time to recall what he or she read and is not interrupted or prompted by the teacher. Retellings provide insights about the student's reading comprehension and their organization of the information that was read.

The student's response is recorded and analyzed for accuracy and detail (e.g., theme, setting, character, plot, solutions). The retell may be scored by giving points for recalling the main ideas in the story, providing supporting details, going beyond materials provided in the text, being organized in the retelling, and being coherent. A checklist or rubric may be used to score the retell. Some CBM measures such as the DIBELS have a retell that follows the oral reading fluency probe, in which the student is asked to retell the story that he or she just read and is scored on the basis of the number of words generated that demonstrate comprehension of the passage within 1 minute.

If the teacher wants to probe understanding of particular parts of the text or feels that the student needs additional prompts to respond, structured questions may be used to elicit responses after the child's initial recall of the main ideas of the text. For young children who are gaining familiarity with narrative and expository texts, prompts for retelling the text could be printed and laminated on index cards and possibly put together as a little book. The student then knows to narrate what happened first in the story, with some supporting details; what happened next, with details; and what happened at the end of the story, with supporting details. Alternately, the student can discuss the main idea of the text, supporting details, and some key connections that he or she made with the text. To modify the strategy for use with English learners, the teacher may ask targeted questions that reduce the language demand on the student. The teacher may encourage the student to respond using his or her native language, visuals, gestures, or other forms of demonstrating understanding of the material read.

Graphic Organizers

Another comprehension strategy that could be used both as a study skill and as an assessment measure uses graphic organizers or semantic webs to organize the information about which a student may have read. Tree maps may be used to classify information about concepts that have a hierarchical relationship. For example, a science lesson on living organisms classifies them according to whether they are plants or animals. Animals in turn are classified as mammals, fish, birds, insects, amphibians, and reptiles. Story maps could be used to track a sequence of events in a story (e.g., providing a linear sequence of events that occurred first, next, and last in the story). Circle maps are used to generate ideas about a topic. For example, students might read an "All About Whales" book and generate ideas from the structure of the book (e.g., where whales live, what they eat, what they do) to write their own book titled "All About Insects" that follows the same basic structure. Analyzing the visual representation of the text provides insights into students' comprehension of the text and their organization of the information.

Metacognitive Reading Strategies

Metacognitive strategies require the reader to stop reading at regular intervals and think about what he or she is reading and about the strategies that he or she is using to read. One such metacognitive strategy is called a think aloud. The student is presented with a brief passage on a familiar topic at the appropriate instructional level. Usually the passage is untitled. The student reads a segment of the story aloud and is asked to stop at a certain point to tell what is happening in the story. A list of think-aloud questions could be generated in advance of having the student read, and the student stops to answer these questions as he or she reads. Alternately, a teacher may ask the student questions that are related to the reading process. Sample questions might be "How did you know what the story is about?" "What clues helped you?" "What is happening in the story?" and "How do you know what is happening in the story?"

Having the teacher model how to do a think aloud is valuable. If a student's response is incorrect, it is very meaningful for him or her to explain the response. A student's comments are recorded for later analysis to find common patterns in the thinking strategies that the student used when reading a passage. The student's responses are analyzed for the hypotheses that he or she generated while reading, the types of information that he or she used to arrive at these hypotheses and to support or change the hypotheses, the strategies that he or she used to read unfamiliar words, and so on. This information helps provide feedback for ongoing instruction.

INFORMAL READING INVENTORIES (IRIs)

IRIs are diagnostic assessments of reading that usually consist of graded word lists and reading passages that vary in difficulty level. Comprehension questions generally follow each reading passage. Passages may be narrative, expository, or both. Some IRIs also assess vocabulary or word meaning. Most IRIs are timed and provide a reading fluency (speed and accuracy) and comprehension score.

On the basis of the IRI score, a student is found to read at an independent, instructional, or frustration level at the particular grade level. An IRI is used to determine a student's reading level, to place students in appropriate reading groups, and to design appropriate instruction. The reader is referred to Nillson (2008) for an analysis of eight commonly used IRIs that have been published since 2002, with a description of the strengths and unique features and applicability of each IRI for different audiences.

ASSESSING READING INTEREST, MOTIVATION, AND ATTITUDES

Clinical Observation of Reading

A clinical observation is a systematic observation of the student's behaviors during reading (e.g., behaviors indicative of motivation to read, attention toward the reading activity, emotion displayed while reading). A teacher can learn a lot about the student's affect associated with reading and his or her reading skills by spending a few minutes each week observing the student engaged in reading aloud or during silent sustained reading. It is challenging to observe all the students at the same time, so the teacher may want to observe separate groups of students on different days.

There are various ways to record the teacher's observations of the student's reading. The teacher could maintain a reading log to note observations of each student's reading on a regular basis. Boyd-Batstone (2004) recommends maintaining anecdotal records using address mailing labels that have the target students' names and the date preprinted on them. Only observable data should be recorded on the labels, and the observation should be guided by the state standards for the content area in which the student is being observed. A sample observation might be "Miguel blends initial and medial sounds when reading 3–4 letter words, but often leaves out the final sound (e.g., bla for black and fru for fruit)." It helps to note examples of miscues made by the student. Anecdotal notes are taken in shorthand using abbreviations and past tense. After the record has been made, the adhesive label is affixed to the student's progress monitoring record. The notes taken on a student are then analyzed every 6–8 weeks to identify relative strengths and need areas and to determine what progress the students have made.

Diagnostic Reading Checklists

A diagnostic reading checklist may be adopted to guide the teacher's observation of a student's reading behaviors at different times in the school year. A checklist helps focus the observation and often provides a continuum of response options along which to rate the student's demonstration of the targeted reading behaviors.

Student Interviews

Students' attitudes toward reading also can be ascertained by asking them questions about their reading preferences and habits and the availability of books in their home environment. Teachers might ask about the types of books and reading genres they enjoy, whether they read at home during their leisure time, what their favorite book is and why, whether others in the home enjoy reading, whether adults read to them, and so on. This information provides insights into whether students like to read and what types of books they prefer.

NORM-REFERENCED READING TESTS
AND THEIR ROLE IN AN RTI MODEL

As is described throughout this chapter, effective reading assessments provide information on the five elements of reading using authentic reading materials across multiple contexts. In an RTI approach, universal screenings are conducted three to four times a year to identify children with potential reading difficulties early. The National Center on Response to Intervention (2010) conducted a review of reading measures for screening purposes to identify students who were at risk for academic failure and who need supplemental instruction in reading. The universal screening measures that were rated as having empirical support include the DIBELS, AIMSweb, STAR, STEEP, and SPI, all of which were described in this chapter.

The progress made by youngsters who continue to struggle is monitored on a regular basis. Several of the measures discussed in the chapter that are used for screening purposes also have been identified as effective progress-monitoring measures (National Center on Response to Intervention, 2010). Ongoing informal teacher-made assessments and diagnostic checklists can provide supplementary data about the skills that a student has mastered and areas that continue to need work.

While norm-referenced tests of reading play only a limited role in an RTI approach, they may be adopted as a screening measure to identify students who are at risk for reading delays, or as a diagnostic measure to explore a student's reading difficulties when the student is nonresponsive to supplemental and/or intensive interventions. The next part of this chapter presents a brief discussion of some common norm-referenced tests of early literacy skills and reading competency.

1. *The Test of Early Reading Ability–Third Edition (TERA 3; Reid, Hresko, & Hammill, 2001)* is designed to assess young children's mastery of early developing reading skills. The test is appropriate for children aged 3–6 through 8–6. The TERA is composed of three subtests that assess knowledge of the alphabet, conventions of print, and making meaning from print. Colored pictures of everyday objects make the test materials more appealing to children.

2. *The Phonological Awareness Test – 2 (Robertson & Salter, 2007)* is an individually administered test that is used with youngsters aged 5–9 years in kindergarten through fourth grade. The test is designed to identify a student's phonological awareness and knowledge of correspondence between phonemes and graphemes (the relationship between sounds and letters) and has solid technical qualities. The test includes subtests that assess a student's skills in the following areas: rhyming,

segmentation, isolation of phonemes by their position in the word (initial, medial, final), deletion of phonemes in a word, substitution of phonemes in a word, blending of phonemes to form words, graphemes, decoding, and invented spelling. The results of this test provide diagnostic information that is very useful in remedial reading programs.

3. *The Comprehensive Test of Phonological Processing (CTOPP; Wagner, Torgesen, & Rashotte, 1999)* is used to measure phonological awareness, phonological short-term memory, and rapid naming or retrieval of objects from long-term memory in children and young adults. There are two versions of the measure, one appropriate for children aged 5 and 6 who are enrolled in kindergarten and first grade, and one for students in third grade and above (i.e., aged 7–24). The CTOPP has been found to be a technically sound test that is grounded in the theory of phonological processing (Wagner et al., 1997).

4. *Gates-MacGinitie Reading Tests (GRMT–4; MacGinitie, MacGinitie, Maria, & Dreyer, 2000)* is a group-administered measure of reading achievement that is used for children in kindergarten through adulthood. The subtests vary slightly by the grade level of the student being assessed; the prereading level includes subtests for literacy, oral language, letter–sound correspondence, and listening comprehension. The beginning reading level includes subtests for consonants and consonant clusters, vowels, and basic story words. Decoding and comprehension items are included for older students.

5. *Woodcock Reading Mastery Test, Revised–Normative Update (WRMT–R/NU; Woodcock, 1998)* is an individually administered test that measures reading fluency and comprehension in individuals from kindergarten through age 75. The test is made up of six subtests and three clusters: Visual–auditory learning and letter identification make up the Readiness cluster, word identification and word attack subtests comprise the Basic Skills cluster, and word comprehension and passage comprehension tests make up the Reading Comprehension cluster. The WRMT–R/NU is a normative update and not a complete revision of the test. Details about the norming sample are sketchy, reliability data are provided only for every other grade level of students for whom the test is applicable, and there is only limited support for the validity of the clusters in the test, so this measure should be used with caution.

6. *Gray Oral Reading Tests–4 (Wiederholt & Bryant, 2001)* is an individually administered test of reading fluency and comprehension for youngsters aged 6–18 years. Students are presented with reading passages that are arranged in order of difficulty, followed by multiple-choice comprehension questions, yielding scores on reading rate, accuracy, fluency, and comprehension. Although the test has adequate reliability and validity, appropriate administration and scoring of the test calls for an examiner with advanced experience and skill levels.

7. *Test of Reading Comprehension, Third Edition (Brown, Hammill, & Wiederholt, 1995)* measures vocabulary and silent reading comprehension in students aged 7–17 years. This test may be administered individually or to small groups of students and includes eight subtests that assess general vocabulary, syntactic similarities, paragraph reading, sentence sequencing, mathematics vocabulary, social studies vocabulary, science vocabulary, and reading directions of schoolwork. This test is found to have adequate technical qualities,

though teachers are cautioned to review the test to see how well it is aligned to the local school curriculum and instruction. The test is found to be more appropriate as a screening device than as a diagnostic tool. It has also been found to be more effective in assessing students in middle school or older than in primary-school–aged children.

End-of-Chapter Questions

1. In what ways is reading critical to school success?
2. Describe the five elements of reading and explain each one.
3. What is known in the research literature about the application of the RTI model to students who are exhibiting difficulties with reading?
4. Distinguish between phonological awareness and phonemic awareness. Provide an example of each type of understanding.
5. Discuss two techniques that you would use to assess phonemic awareness in young children.
6. What are some empirically validated universal literacy screening measures that can be used in an RTI model?
7. How does one assess reading fluency?
8. Explain what a miscue analysis is and why this technique assists with planning instruction.
9. What is a word sort? How can word sorts be used to assess word recognition?
10. Describe some techniques that are used to assess a student's vocabulary and prior knowledge.
11. What are the different types of reading comprehension? Discuss some techniques that are used to assess reading comprehension.
12. How are Informal Reading Inventories used to assess a student's reading skills?
13. Why is it important to tap into a student's attitudes toward reading and motivation to read?
14. What role do norm-referenced tests play in an RTI approach to literacy assessment and instruction?

References

Al Otaiba, S., & Fuchs, D. (2002). Characteristics of children who are unresponsive to early literacy intervention: A review of the literature. *Remedial and Special Education, 23*, 300–316.

Anderson, R. C., & Nagy, W. E. (1992). The vocabulary conundrum. *American Educator, (16)*, 14–18, 44–46.

Beck, I. L., McKeown, M. G., & Kucan, L. (2002). *Bring words to life: Robust vocabulary instruction.* New York: The Guilford Press.

Boyd-Batstone, P. (2004). Focused anecdotal records assessment: A tool for standards-based authentic assessment. *The Reading Teacher, 58,* 230–239.

Brown, V. L., Hammill, D. D., & Weiderholt, J. L. (1995). *Tests of reading comprehension* (3rd ed.). Austin, TX: Pro-Ed.

Chard, D. J., & Dickson, S. V. (1999). Phonological awareness: Instructional and assessment guidelines. *Intervention in School and Clinic, 34*(5), 261–270.

Clay, M. (1985). *The early detection of reading difficulties* (3rd ed.). Auckland, New Zealand: Heinemann.

Cunningham, P. M. (1991). *Phonics they use: Words for reading and writing.* New York: HarperCollins.

Dunn, L. M., & Dunn, D. M. (2007). *The Peabody Picture Vocabulary Test–IV.* Bloomington, MN: Pearson.

Fawson, P. C., Ludlow, B. C., Reutzel, D. R., Sudweeks, R., & Smith, J. A. (2006). Examining the reliability of running records: Attaining generalizable results. *The Journal of Educational Research, 100*(2), 113–126.

Flax, J. F., Realpe-Bonilla, T., Roesler, C., Choudhury, N., & Benasich, A. (2009). Using early standardized language measures to predict later language and early reading outcomes in children at high risk for language learning impairments. *Journal of Learning Disabilities, 42*, 61–75.

Foorman, B. R., Francis, D. J., Fletcher, J. M., Schatschneider, C., & Mehta, P. (1998). The role of instruction in learning to read: Preventing reading failure in at-risk children. *Journal of Educational Psychology, 90*, 37–55.

Gersten, R., Compton, D., Connor, C. M., Dimino, J., Santoro, L., Linan-Thompson, S., et al. (2009). *Assisting students struggling with reading: Response to Intervention and multi-tier intervention in the primary grades. A practice guide.* (NCEE 2009-4045). Washington, D.C.: National Center for Education Evaluation and Regional Assistance, Institute of Education Sciences, U.S. Department of Education. Retrieved October 3, 2010, from http://ies.ed.gov/ncee/wwc/pdf/practiceguides/rti_reading_pg_021809.pdf.

Gillet, J., & Temple, C. (1990). *Understanding reading problems* (3rd ed.). Glenview, IL: Scott Foresman.

Goodman, K. S. (1969). Analysis of oral reading miscues: Applied psycholinguistics. *Reading Research Quarterly, 5,* 9–30.

Guthrie, J. T. (1973). Reading comprehension and syntactical responses in good and poor readers. *Journal of Educational Psychology, 65,* 294–299.

Haager, D., Dimino, J., & Windmueller, M. (2007). *Interventions for reading success.* Baltimore: Paul H. Brookes Co.

Hosp, M. K., & Fuchs, L. S. (2005). Using CBM as an indicator of decoding, word reading, and comprehension: Do the relations change with grade? *School Psychology Review, 34,* 9–26.

Hosp, M. K., Hosp, J. L., & Howell, K. W. (2007). *The ABCs of CBM: A practical guide to curriculum-based measurement.* New York: Guilford Press.

International Reading Association. (1998). *Phonemic awareness and the teaching of reading: A position statement from the Board of Directors of the International Reading Association.* Retrieved October 3, 2010, from http://www.reading.org/downloads/positions/ps1025_phonemic.pdf.

Joshi, R. M. (2005). Vocabulary: A critical component of comprehension. *Reading and Writing Quarterly, 21,* 209–219.

Kaminski, R. A., & Good, R. H., III. (1998). Assessing early literacy skills in a problem solving model: Dynamic Indicators of Basic Early Literacy Skills. In M. Shinn (Ed.), *Advanced applications of curriculum-based measurement* (pp. 113–142). New York: Guilford Press.

Kranzler, J. H., Brownell, M. T., & Miller, M. D. (1998). The construct validity of curriculum based measurement of reading: An empirical test of a plausible rival hypothesis. *Journal of School Psychology, 36,* 399–415.

Lipson, M. Y., & Wixson, K. K. (1997). *Assessment and instruction of reading and writing disability: An interactive approach* (2nd ed.). Boston: Addison Wesley Publications.

MacGinitie, W., MacGinitie R., Maria, K., & Dreyer, L. G. (2000). *Gates-MacGinitie Reading Tests* (4th ed.). Itasca, IL: Riverside Publishing Company.

McKenna, M. C., & Picard, M. C. (2006). Revisiting the role of miscue analysis in effective teaching. *The Reading Teacher, 60*(4), 378–380.

Mesmer, E., & Mesmer, H. (2008). Response to intervention (RTI): What teachers of reading need to know. *The Reading Teacher, 62*(4), 280–290.

Meyer, M. S. & Felton, R. H. (1999). Repeated reading to enhance fluency: Old approaches and new directions. *Annals of Dyslexia, 49,* 283–306.

National Center on Response to Intervention. (2010). *Screening Tools Chart.* Retrieved October 3, 2010, from http://www.rti4success.org/chart/screeningTools/screeningtoolschart.html

National Institute of Child Health and Human Development. (2000). *Report of the National Reading Panel. Teaching children to read: An evidence-based assessment of the scientific research literature on reading and its implications for reading instruction.* NIH Publication No. 00-4769. Washington, D.C.: U.S. Government Printing Office.

Nillson, N. L. (2008). A critical analysis of eight informal reading inventories. *The Reading Teacher, 61*(7), 526–536.

Paris, S. G., & Hoffman, J. V. (2004). Reading assessments in kindergarten through third grade: Findings from the Center for the Improvement of Early Reading Achievement. *The Elementary School Journal, 105*(2), 199–217.

Reid, D., Hresko, W., & Hammill, D. (2001). *Test of Early Reading Ability* (3rd ed.).Austin, TX: Pro-Ed.

Robertson, C., & Salter, W. (2007). *Phonological Awareness Test.* East Moline, IL: LinguiSystems.

Salvia, J., Ysseldyke, J., & Bolt, S. (2007). *Assessment in special and inclusive education* (10th ed.). Boston: Houghton Mifflin.

Shapiro, E. (2004). *Academic skills problems: Direct assessment and intervention* (3rd ed.). New York: Guilford Press.

Shinn, M. (1989). *Curriculum based measurement: Assessing special children.* New York: Guilford Press.

Torgesen, J. K., & Davis, C. (1996). Individual difference variables that predict response to training in phonological awareness. *Journal of Experimental Child Psychology, 63,* 1–21.

Vellutino, F. R., Scanlon, D. M., & Lyon, G. R. (2000). Differentiating between difficult-to-remediate and readily remediated poor readers: More evidence against the IQ-discrepancy definition of reading disability. *Journal of Learning Disabilities, 33*(3), 223–238.

Wagner, R. K., Torgesen, J. K., Rashotte, C. A., Hecht, S. A., Barker, T. A., Burgess, S. R., et al. (1997). Changing relations between phonological processing abilities and word-level reading as children develop from beginning to skilled readers: A 5-year longitudinal study. *Developmental Psychology, 33,* 468–479.

Wagner, R. K., Torgesen, J. K., & Rashotte, C. A. (1999). *Comprehensive test of phonological processing.* Austin, TX: Pro-Ed.

Wallace, G., & Hammill, D. (2002). Comprehensive receptive and expressive vocabulary test (2nd ed.). Austin, TX: Pro-Ed.

Wayman, M. M., Wallace, T., Wiley, H. I., Ticha, R., & Espin, C. (2007). Literature synthesis on curriculum-based measurement in reading. *The Journal of Special Education, 41,* 85–120.

Weiderholt, L., & Bryant, B. (2001). *Gray oral reading test* (4th ed.). Austin, TX: Pro-Ed.

Williams, K. (2007). *Expressive vocabulary test* (2nd ed.). Bloomington, MN: Pearson.

Woodcock, R. (1998). *Woodcock reading mastery test–revised/normative update.* Circle Pines, MN: American Guidance Service.

Yopp, H. K. (1995). The Yopp-Singer test of phonemic segmentation. *The Reading Teacher, 49*(1), 20–29.

Zucker, T. A., & Invernizzi, M. (2008). My eSorts and digital extensions of word study. *The Reading Teacher, 61*(8), 654–658.

CHAPTER 12

Assessment of Written Language and Spelling

Ms. Juanita Gonzales is a second-year teacher who is teaching first grade this year. She taught middle school last year. Juanita is concerned about Setharin, a young boy in her class. Setharin is a talkative 6-year-old with a ready smile and a keen sense of fun. He loves coming to school and says that science and music are his favorite subjects. Setharin is a halting reader but struggles even more in the area of writing. His handwriting is illegible, and even he has difficulty reading what he has written. Setharin has difficulty forming most letters. He often reverses letters and he rarely leaves space between words. He finds it difficult to segment and spell words correctly. Setharin's kindergarten teacher allowed him to draw instead of writing in his journal, and he often dictated his responses to a parent volunteer. Juanita thinks that he should be forced to write now that he is in first grade and is not sure how far she should push him.

Reflections on the Scenario

1. What is your initial impression of Setharin's writing proficiency?
2. How would you assess his writing and spelling skills?
3. What types of writing activities and accommodations would you suggest Juanita use with Setharin?
4. What are some interventions that could help him enhance his writing skills?
5. How should Juanita monitor Setharin's writing progress?

COUNCIL FOR EXCEPTIONAL CHILDREN (CEC) STANDARDS

This chapter addresses the following CEC standards:

ICC8K1—Basic terminology used in assessment.

ICC8K4—Use and limitations of assessment instruments.

ICC8S2—Administer nonbiased formal and informal assessments.

ICC8S6—Use assessment information in making eligibility, program, and placement decisions for individuals with exceptional learning needs, including those from culturally and/or linguistically diverse backgrounds.

ICC8S8—Evaluate instruction and monitor progress of individuals with exceptional learning needs.

ICC8S9—Develop or modify individualized assessment strategies.

GC8S3—Select, adapt, and modify assessments to accommodate the unique abilities and needs of individuals with disabilities.

WRITING

Writing is a critically important vehicle for effective communication. However, writing often gets short shrift in schools as attention is focused on competing curricular demands. Although all states have standards related to writing, building reading skills often takes precedence over other content areas. Consequently, writing is not always taught effectively in elementary and secondary schools.

Students with and without disabilities often have difficulties with writing. For instance, data from the National Assessment of Educational Progress (as cited in Troia, 2005) indicate that although 67% of fourth graders and 51% of eighth graders believed that they were good writers, their performance on standardized writing tests revealed that only 27% of fourth graders and 23% of eighth graders performed at or above writing proficiency grade levels.

Extensive study of the writing skills of students with learning disabilities has revealed that these students know less than other students about the purpose of writing, the writing genres, and the elements of good writing (Graham, 2006). De La Paz (2007) notes that students with learning disabilities have difficulties identifying text structure and providing supporting details. They generate less writing than typically developing peers and exhibit poor planning and organization in their writing. In addition, students with learning disabilities make more mechanical errors (spelling, punctuation, and capitalization), have poor handwriting, and often take longer to put their thoughts on paper. These difficulties further hinder their ability to plan and generate written content and their motivation to write. Direct teaching of planning strategies and practice with writing strategies have proven to assist students with learning disabilities to learn to write better (Graham). The process of writing skill development has not been studied as extensively with students with other types of disabilities, but there is general acknowledgment that many students with disabilities have ongoing difficulties in this content area.

AREAS OF WRITTEN LANGUAGE

Writing calls for the mastery and simultaneous application of several subskills, which makes it challenging to assess. Effective writers usually also have strong vocabularies and the ability to generate important points to share with others, organize their thoughts effectively, demonstrate strong mechanics and conventions of writing, and evaluate and edit their written product in a constant process of refinement.

Various researchers have identified models that make up the multidimensional writing domain. One such model is the 6 + 1 Trait Writing analytical model for assessing and instructing students in writing (Northwest Regional Educational Laboratory, 2009). The model includes seven traits:

1. *Ideas*—The content or essential message of the writing, including the main message and the supporting details.

2. *Organization*—The structure, logic, or connections between points presented or chronological sequence of events. The organization assists the reader to follow along with the writer's message.

3. *Voice*—The writer's thoughts are expressed through words, and the voice adds flavor to the words that indicates feeling, humor, annoyance, passion, or other emotions, thereby bringing the writing to life.

4. *Word choice*—The selection of words includes considerations such as a rich vocabulary, persuasive word choice, and the use of metaphors or similies that increase writing effectiveness and thereby enhance the readers' interest and engagement with the text.

5. *Sentence fluency*—The flow of language such that when read aloud, the writing sounds fluent and smooth. Awkward sentence patterns and extremely long sentences reduce the fluency of writing.

6. *Conventions*—The mechanics of writing consisting of proper spelling, grammar, and punctuation.

7. *Presentation*—The visual appeal of writing, including handwriting, spacing, color of font and background, graphics, etc.

The Northwest Regional Educational Laboratory has developed a 5-point scoring rubric for each of the traits on the 6 + 1 Trait Writing system, with 5 = strong, 3 = developing, and 1 = not yet evident.

Best practices in writing assessment suggest that a student should be asked to complete an authentic writing task with a clearly defined target audience and reason for writing (Calfee & Miller, 2007). It is recommended that the student receive immediate corrective feedback.

A RESPONSE TO INTERVENTION (RTI) APPROACH TO WRITING AND SPELLING ASSESSMENT

Given the No Child Left Behind mandate to raise test performance for all subgroups of students in the public schools and the consequent pressure on schools to raise test scores, the RTI model is being used widely to monitor skill acquisition in reading, writing, and spelling. Curriculum-based measures (CBM) are quick and easy to administer, sensitive to student improvement, and have sound technical qualities, particularly for elementary and middle school students with and without disabilities. These measures provide an objective index of student performance that is not biased with regard to the child's gender or racial, ethnic, or language background. CBM is widely used in an RTI model to assist teachers with data-based decision making. The following section describes some of the assessments that are commonly used to assess writing and spelling within an RTI framework.

CBM in Writing and Spelling

CBM writing probes are short writing prompts that are administered to weekly or biweekly to monitor progress in written language. Students are given a story starter and asked to think about the story for 1 minute, then to write about the prompt for 3 minutes. The writing CBM may be administered individually or to a group of students. Students do not receive any assistance from the teacher in completing this writing task. Students' writing responses are scored using one of a range of criteria including total words written, words spelled correctly, correct writing sequence, and total correct punctuation. Detailed descriptions of how to administer, score, and interpret CBMs in spelling and writing are presented in Chapter 5 of this book.

It is recommended that students write their responses to CBM prompts in a spiral-bound notebook, starting at the beginning of the school year so that progress over time can be monitored easily (Hosp, Hosp, & Howell, 2007). In addition, it is recommended that students respond by writing on lined rather than blank paper. Instructional goals could be tailored to the CBM assessment and could be based on expected rates of increase in academic fluency (e.g., a goal after 16 weeks of intervention might be for Setharin to write 10 total correct words in 3 minutes with 90% accuracy when he is provided a story starter at the first-grade level).

It is important to note that although CBM probes monitor writing progress in terms of the number of words generated, they do not provide information on the content or organization of the student's writing. Those important features must be assessed using other assessment tools such as writing rubrics or portfolios.

Spelling CBMs require a teacher to develop alternate forms of grade-level spelling lists that sample the year-long curriculum, each of which serves as a probe. First-grade and second-grade probes have 12 words, and probes for third grade and above have 17 words (Hosp et al., 2007). Words on the list are dictated to the student, who gets 7 seconds to write the spelling of the word on a lined sheet of paper before the teacher moves on to dictating the next word. Each probe takes about 2 minutes and can be administered individually or to a group. Scoring generally involves computing the total number of correct letter sequences, as described in Chapter 5. This is a time-consuming process, but it is sensitive to student growth over time and provides a fine-grained analysis of the types of spelling errors that a child makes. Some spelling programs use a general measure of spelling ability, the total number of words spelled correctly, as the index to measure a student's spelling ability. The student receives a score of 1 if the word is spelled correctly and 0 if the word is spelled incorrectly. The first spelling assessment consists of administering three probes and using the median score. On subsequent assessments, a single probe is given. The student's total score is graphed and progress is determined in relation to the benchmark goal line. Fuchs and colleagues (1993) computed weekly growth rates on spelling CBMs using correct letter sequences, as displayed in Table 12.1.

TABLE 12.1	Weekly Growth Rates on Spelling CBM
Grade	**Growth Per Week (Correct Letter Sequences)**
2nd	1–1.5
3rd	0.65–1
4th	0.45–0.85
5th	0.3–0.65
6th	0.3–0.65

WRITING SAMPLES

A writing sample is a piece of student writing that is analyzed to determine the student's strength and needs and to monitor his or her progress in writing skills over time. There are a few ways to generate writing samples from students:

1. *Spontaneous written response*—The student writes for an authentic purpose and the resulting writing sample is analyzed for style and mechanics. The sample may be an open-ended journal entry, a letter to a friend or relative, or another type of writing.
2. *Elicited written response*—The student provides a written response to a prompt. The sample may be a writing assignment, a persuasive essay on a given topic, a letter to the editor of the local newspaper, or another type of writing.
3. *Dictated writing sample*—This form is used with young children or students with significant disabilities. The student draws a picture to depict his or her thoughts and then dictates an oral response to an adult who writes down exactly what the student says. Such dictated writing samples yield information about the child's oral language, vocabulary, ability to organize thoughts, knowledge of conventions of print, and more. The adult can ask the child to find particular words in the sample, indicate words starting with particular letters, point to words they can read, etc.

A writing sample is a permanent product that can be evaluated and rated and stored in a portfolio to determine ongoing progress. It is a good idea to collect writing samples from students that span different subject areas and are different types of written assignments (e.g., in-class essays, short answer responses, homework samples) to get an overall picture of the students' writing skills.

Spinelli (2006) suggests that the teacher look for responses to the following questions when he or she is analyzing written samples:

- *Handwriting*—Is the student consistently using cursive or print? Is the writing legible? Are there any consistent difficulties with letter or number formation? Does the student write consistently from left to right?
- *Spelling*—Does the student spell phonetically regular words correctly? Does the student spell phonetically irregular words correctly? Does the student confuse the spelling of common synonyms or homonyms?
- *Word use and sentence structure*—Does the student use grammatically correct sentences? Does the student use age-appropriate vocabulary? Does the student make consistent errors in punctuation?

Error Analyses of Writing Samples

It is useful to evaluate writing proficiency on the basis of the extent to which the student has difficulties at each of the five stages of the writing process (Spinelli, 2006):

1. *Prewriting or planning*—Did the student write for an identified purpose, select an appropriate topic, identify the target audience, and use strategies such as graphic organizer or story outline to assist with planning for writing?
2. *Writing or drafting*—Can the student generate a rough draft of the planned writing project? Mechanical errors and spelling need not be a focus at this stage, but the student should be able to transfer his or her thoughts into complete sentences.

3. *Revising or editing*—Can the student read through his or her writing and make necessary revisions to enhance content and meaning? Peer review or teacher conferences may be conducted at this stage to share feedback with the student.

4. *Proofreading*—Can the student proof his or her writing to correct grammatical, spelling, and other mechanical errors as appropriate for his or her grade level?

5. *Publishing or sharing*—Can the student share his or her writing by reading it to others, talking about it, or publishing it in a book format?

Common patterns of errors made by students in their writing are analyzed to determine the cause for the errors, thereby providing information to assist with ongoing instruction. The teacher would record the number of words generated in the writing sample, the number of words spelled correctly, the types of sentences that were written, whether they were simple or complex sentences, the types of errors made in the sentence, etc. Each type of error is counted only once (e.g., if the student misspells a particular word or neglects to use capitalization for a proper noun, the error is counted only once).

Writing Portfolios and Rubrics

Writing samples often are assessed using rubrics, which serve several purposes: to clarify the teacher's expectations and evaluation criteria for the student, to assess the extent to which the student has met these criteria, and to determine variations in the quality and completeness of the response (De La Paz, 2009). Portfolios are a useful way to monitor student progress and skill development. Some writing artifacts that could be included in the portfolio include writing samples of rough drafts and finished versions of the same piece, journal entries, self-evaluation checklists, and teacher evaluation checklists. Artifacts included in the portfolio could be scored using either a holistic rubric in which a single overall score is assigned to the writing sample or an analytic rubric in which each writing sample is scored using a list of predetermined scoring criteria. Portfolios and rubrics are discussed further in Chapter 5.

Think Alouds

Teachers can invite students to think aloud when the students are approaching a writing task to learn more about the way in which they generate ideas, plan, structure and organize their writing, think through spelling words, prepare a draft of their writing, and then edit their written product. Teachers also can use think-aloud techniques to model effective writing strategies for students.

Clinical Observation and Interview of Writing

Observing a student during writing and spelling is informative because it supplements the data that are collected from the written product. The teacher can observe the student in several areas:

- *Posture and positioning while writing.* Good posture involves sitting erect at a desk with the head at the appropriate distance from the paper, and proper positioning involves holding the paper at a slant on the desk, holding the pencil firmly using the thumb and first two fingers, and writing from left to right.

- *Handwriting.* Indicators of good handwriting include writing in cursive rather than printing, staying within line boundaries, copying easily from the board or book to paper, and producing legible writing.
- *Strategy use during the writing task.* The student may use self-talk or mnemonics, develop an outline prior to writing, and edit writing for errors that are then corrected.
- *Affect.* Frustration as indicated by constant erasing of work, tearing up the paper, crumpling and throwing the paper away; enjoyment of writing is shown by behaviors such as whistling or looking happy while writing or appearing completely absorbed in the task.
- *Effort.* A student displaying positive effort starts the task right away, follows the teacher's directions, and stays engaged with the task, whereas one who does not show good effort appears distracted and off-task, engages in other activities, and looks bored or fatigued.

A clinical interview often follows a clinical observation. In such an interview the student is asked about his or her approach to the writing task, how he or she selected a topic, how the student organized his or her thoughts, how the student came up with the title and developed the plot, what strategies the student used to spell certain words, and so on. The student's response to these questions sheds light on the student's thought process, the metacognitive strategies that he or she uses when writing, his or her interest and motivation, and his or her affect associated with writing tasks. This information is informative in planning further instruction.

TECHNIQUES FOR SPELLING ASSESSMENT

Children develop spelling skills in a sequential fashion. Starting at the prephonetic and phonetic stages, children use inventive spelling to string together consonant or vowel sounds. Qualitative changes in spelling skills occur as children are exposed to written and spoken language, orthographic systems, and different spelling patterns.

Error Analysis in Spelling

Gentry (2004) presents a five-stage system of developmental spelling errors that is useful to review in analyzing the types of errors made by youngsters:

1. *Precommunicative spelling*—Randomly stringing together letters to form words. No patterns are evident in these letter strings (e.g., efena for mama, lamo for dog).
2. *Semiphonetic spelling*—Some evidence of emerging symbol-sound correspondence is apparent (e.g., f = fish, r = road).
3. *Phonetic spelling*—All the phonemes in a word are spelled out (e.g., wud for would).
4. *Transitional spelling*—Spelling of words represents a knowledge of orthographic systems, conventions of English spelling, and visual memory of common spelling patterns (e.g., tought for tough, rode for road).
5. *Conventional spelling*—No errors in words spelled.

Beirne-Smith and Riley (2009) explain that children rarely make random errors in spelling. Error patterns in spelling tend to be consistent across writing samples, word lists, and other written products. A vast majority of spelling errors are omission or substitution errors or incorrect vowel use in words that could be spelled using different patterns. In order to conduct an error analysis, the teacher collects a large number of writing samples and reviews the spelling errors made by a student. This review allows the teacher to get a sense for the student's developmental spelling level and his or her conceptual understanding and use of spelling patterns.

Here are some common spelling errors (Spache, 1940):

1. Omission of a silent letter (e.g., peple for people, frend for friend).
2. Omission of a sounded letter (e.g., presdent for president, Satrday for Saturday).
3. Omission of a doubled letter (e.g., huged for hugged, swiming for swimming).
4. Doubling of letters (e.g., dogg for dog, affter for after).
5. Addition of a single letter (e.g., hee for he, parck for park).
6. Transposition or partial reversal (e.g., was for saw, no for on).
7. Phonetic substitution for a vowel (e.g., dus for does, tot for taught).
8. Phonetic substitution for a consonant (e.g., gug for jug, kat for cat).
9. Phonetic substitution for a syllable (e.g., knoct for knocked, wodint for wouldn't).
10. Phonetic substitution for a word (e.g., than for then, hare for hair).
11. Nonphonetic substitution for a vowel (e.g., ploy for play, fame for farm).
12. Nonphonetic substitution for a consonant (e.g., rog for rock, feel for field).

Informal Spelling Inventory (ISI)

An ISI is a teacher-made spelling test that is used as a diagnostic tool to determine mastery of spelling subskills (e.g., spelling words with short vowel sounds, spelling words with long vowel sounds, spelling words from a certain word family) or integration of different patterns in spelling words (e.g., spelling words with vowel diphthongs and short vowel sounds). ISIs are useful tools for determining the grade level at which a student is currently spelling (Spinelli, 2006). An ISI for the first-grade level usually includes 15 words randomly selected from across the curriculum, and ISIs for grades 2–8 usually have 20 such words. It is important to include words of varying levels of difficulty from across the grade-level curriculum in developing each grade-level spelling list.

To test students using an ISI, the teacher usually starts by administering a spelling list that is about two grades below the student's current grade level and continuing upward until the child spells six consecutive words incorrectly. The teacher dictates the first word on the list, uses it in a sentence, and then calls out the word again. The student has 7 seconds to write the word, after which the teacher dictates the next word on the list. The student's performance on the ISI is determined by adding up the total number of words spelled correctly at each grade-level list administered and computing an accuracy rate (Spinelli, 2006) such that

- the mastery level is the highest level at which a student responds with 90–100% accuracy,
- the instructional level is the highest level at which a student responds with 75–89% accuracy, and
- the frustration level is the level at which a student responds with less than 74% accuracy.

Some resources for developing informal spelling inventories:

> Directions for Administering the Primary & Elementary Spelling Inventories—Los Angeles County Office of Education Assessment Tools: *http://teams.lacoe.edu/documentation/ classrooms/patti/k-1/teacher/assessment/spelling.html*
>
> *Everyday Spelling*—Scott Foresman Publishers: *http://pearsonschool.com/*

NORM-REFERENCED TESTS OF WRITTEN LANGUAGE AND SPELLING AND THEIR ROLE IN AN RTI MODEL

Some norm-referenced tests that specifically assess writing and spelling skills are featured in this section. These tests are best suited to diagnosing student learning needs in writing and spelling and to monitoring progress over time.

1. *The Test of Written Language, 3rd edition (TOWL–3; Hammill & Larsen, 1996)—* A widely administered test of writing skills, the TOWL can be used with students aged 7–18 to assess vocabulary, spelling, style, logical sentences, sentence combining, contextual conversations, contextual language, and story construction. The test yields composite scores for each of three areas: Contrived Writing, Spontaneous Writing, and Overall Writing. The TOWL is based on a strong conceptual model and has good reliability and validity, but it is very time consuming and complicated to score. There also are some limitations in the norming sample that limit its representativeness for all populations of students.

2. *The Test of Written Expression (TOWE; McGhee, Bryant, Larsen, & Rivera, 1995)—* The TOWE is designed to diagnose strengths and weaknesses, document student progress, and assist with research in the area of writing (Murray-Ward, 2004). The test is appropriate for children aged 6.5–15 years and can be administered individually or to a group. The TOWE has two parts: a "contrived" writing section in which the student produces a letter, word, or sentence in response to the examiner, and an "on demand" section in which the student completes a story that was read aloud by the examiner. The test measures vocabulary, capitalization, punctuation, spelling, ideation, semantics, and syntax. Test administration and scoring is fairly complicated. The test is correlated with other achievement tests and with tests of intelligence. The TOWE has a limited normative sample and does not provide any data on inclusion of English learners or special-needs populations in the normative group. It is recommended that scores on this test be reviewed in conjunction with other evidence, including authentic writing samples and observations (Murray-Ward).

3. *Oral and Written Language Scales (OWLS; Carrow-Woolfolk, 1995)—*The test battery is made up of three scales: Written Expression, Oral Expression, and Language Comprehension. The Listening Comprehension and Oral Expression scales may be used with children aged 3–21 years, and the Written Expression scale may be used alone or may be individually or group administered to children and adults ages 5–21 years. It measures a broad array of writing skills, including conventions, syntactic forms, and the ability to communicate meaningfully using tasks such as dictated

writing, writing notes and questions, completing stories, retelling stories, and using brief descriptive writing and expository writing. The OWLS is a reliable and valid measure that is relatively easy to administer. It is a little complicated to score correctly, particularly for novices, although the manual provides detailed instructions.

4. *The Test of Written Spelling (TWS–4; Larsen, Hammill, & Moats, 1999)*—Normed for use with children aged 6–18 years, the TWS–4 is a 50-item test of spelling abilities that provides information about a student's need for intervention in spelling and may be used to determine progress made in this area over time. Two parallel forms of the test are available. The test has adequate technical qualities. The TWS has been criticized (DeMauro, 2004) for not being better integrated with the underlying theory on which it was based.

End-of-Chapter Questions

1. What are some common difficulties that students with disabilities face in the area of writing?
2. Describe the areas of writing that may be assessed using the 6 + 1 Trait Writing analytical model.
3. How would you go about using CBM to assess a student's writing and spelling skills? What do you see as potential advantages and limitations of this approach?
4. Describe some ways in which a teacher could analyze students' writing samples to learn more about their strengths and limitations in writing?
5. What are the five stages of the writing process? What common errors do students make at each stage?
6. Explain the process of conducting a think aloud in writing.
7. What are some types of data that one could gather by observing a student write?
8. What is a clinical interview? How might it be used to assess writing proficiency?
9. Describe the five steps in which spelling skills develop. What types of errors are typically made at each of these stages?
10. How does one develop and use an ISI?
11. What are the potential uses of norm referenced tests in the assessment of writing and spelling proficiency?

References

Beirne-Smith, M., & Riley, T. (2009). Spelling assessment of students with disabilities: Formal and informal procedures. *Assessment for Effective Intervention, 34*(3), 170–177.

Calfee, R. C., & Miller, R. G. (2007). Best practices in writing assessment. In S. Graham, C. MacArthur, & J. Fitzgerald (Eds.), *Best practices in writing instruction* (pp. 265–286). New York: Guilford Press.

Carrow-Woolfolk, E. (1995). *Oral and Written Language Scales*. Austin, TX: Pro-Ed.

De La Paz, S. (2007). Best practices in teaching writing to students with special needs. In S. Graham, C. MacArthur, & J. Fitzgerald (Eds.), *Best practices in writing instruction* (pp. 308–328). New York: Guilford Press.

De La Paz, S. (2009). Rubrics: Heuristics for developing writing strategies. *Assessment for Effective Intervention, 34*(3), 134–146.

DeMauro, G. (2004). Review of the test of written spelling. *Mental Measurement Yearbook*. Lincoln, NE: Buros Institute of Mental Measurements and University of Nebraska.

Fuchs, L., Fuchs, D., Hamlett, C., Walz, L., & Germann, G. (1993). Formative evaluation of academic progress: How much growth can we expect? *School Psychology Review, 22*, 27–49.

Gentry, J. R. (2004). *The science of spelling: The explicit specifics that make great readers and writers (and spellers!)*. Portsmouth, NH: Heinemann.

Graham, S. (2006). Writing. In P. A. Alexander & P. H. Winne (Eds.), *Handbook of educational psychology* (pp. 457–478). Mahwah, NJ: Erlbaum.

Hammill, D. D., & Larsen, S. C. (1996). *Test of written language* (3rd ed.). Austin, TX: Pro-Ed.

Hosp, M. K., Hosp, J. L., & Howell, K. W. (2007). *The ABCs of CBM: A practical guide to curriculum-based measurement*. New York: Guilford Press.

Larsen, S., Hammill, D., & Moats, L. (1999). *Test of written spelling* (4th ed.).Austin, TX: Pro-Ed.

McGhee, R., Bryant, B., Larsen, S., & Rivera, D. M. (1995). *Test of written expression*. Austin, TX: Pro-Ed.

Murray-Ward, M. (2004). Review of test of written expression. *Mental Measurement Yearbook*. Lincoln, NE: Buros Institute of Mental Measurements and University of Nebraska.

Northwest Regional Educational Laboratory. (2009). *6 + 1 trait writing*. Retrieved on May 7, 2009, from http://www.thetraits.org/about.php.

Spache, G. (1940). A critical analysis of various methods of classifying spelling errors. *Journal of Educational Psychology, 31*, 111–134.

Spinelli, C. (2006). *Classroom assessment for students in special and general education* (2nd ed.). Upper Saddle River, NJ: Merrill/Pearson.

Troia, G. A. (2005, October). *The writing instructional research we have, the writing instruction research we need*. Paper presented at the Literacy Achievement Research Center Symposium on Literacy Achievement, Michigan State University, East Lansing.

CHAPTER 13

Assessment of Mathematics

Joel is an avid soccer player who plays on his middle-school soccer team. Although he has always struggled academically, Joel is now working particularly hard to keep up his grades so that he can continue to play soccer. Math is his weakest subject and he finds geometry and algebra especially puzzling. Joel can complete basic math operations with limited fluency, but he often is stumped by word problems and finds it difficult to apply the correct operation to a problem. He understands place value and integers, but he frequently makes errors when he encounters fractions, decimals, exponents, and percentages. He is learning to read and draw simple graphs and to read basic frequency distributions with prompts from his teachers. He thinks math is a waste of time and is not convinced that he needs to succeed in math in order to make it in the real world.

Reflections on the Scenario

1. What are your initial impressions about Joel's attitude and skills in math?
2. How would you learn more about Joel's math attitudes and skills?
3. What common math assessments might you use to assess Joel?
4. What approaches could you adopt to make math meaningful and relevant for Joel?

COUNCIL FOR EXCEPTIONAL CHILDREN (CEC) STANDARDS

ICC8K1—Basic terminology used in assessment.

ICC8K4—Use and limitations of assessment instruments.

ICC8S2—Administer nonbiased formal and informal assessments.

ICC8S3—Use technology to conduct assessments.

ICC8S5—Interpret information from formal and informal assessments.

ICC8S6—Use assessment information in making eligibility, program, and placement decisions for individuals with exceptional learning needs, including those from culturally and/or linguistically diverse backgrounds.

ICC8S8—Evaluate instruction and monitor progress of individuals with exceptional learning needs.

ICC8S9—Develop or modify individualized assessment strategies.

ICC8S10—Create and maintain records.

GC8S3—Select, adapt, and modify assessments to accommodate the unique abilities and needs of individuals with disabilities.

WRITING

Mathematical knowledge and skills are of great importance for effective life functioning. Life skills such as budgeting, telling time, and making purchases and daily tasks such as cooking and cleaning require basic conceptual understanding and application of mathematical concepts. Most jobs call for essential mathematical foundations and skills. Certain fields such as engineering and technology require advanced mathematical expertise and problem-solving skills.

Recent federal and state mandates call for enhancing student achievement across content areas. Increasingly, there has been a focus on mathematics achievement. Only 35% of the nation's fourth graders were minimally proficient in math according to data from the 2005 National Assessment of Educational Progress (Lembke, Foegen, Whittaker, & Hampton, 2008). In order to advance to the next grade level, a student often must demonstrate proficiency in district and state math benchmarks.

MATHEMATICAL KNOWLEDGE, SKILLS, AND DISPOSITIONS

The National Council of Teachers of Mathematics (NCTM, 2000) has called for pedagogical and curricular reform in math that emphasizes problem-based learning. The National Mathematics Advisory Panel (2008) concluded on the basis of strong research evidence that the teacher is a critical variable who contributes to student achievement gains in mathematics. Many teachers at both the elementary-school and secondary-school level, particularly those who teach multiple subjects, have reported that they need additional content and pedagogical preparation in order to effectively teach math.

The NCTM identifies several key skill areas in math that should be fostered in students. These skills include mathematical problem solving, mathematical reasoning and seeking proof that is based on exploration and validation of ideas, communicating mathematical thinking and reasoning with others, making connections among different mathematical concepts and ideas, and achieving conceptual understanding of math. Certain mathematical content areas should be incorporated in all school curriculum: 1) numbers and operations, including number value, computation, basic operations, mental math, and use of estimation; 2) algebra, including the use of algebraic expressions to express mathematical relationships, 3) geometry, spatial reasoning, and measurement; and 4) data analysis, statistics, and probability, which include skills associated with designing a research question, collecting data, and analyzing and interpreting these data (National Council of Teachers of Mathematics, 2009).

The NCTM assessment principle calls for gathering important assessment data that are instructionally meaningful to teachers and students. The NCTM recommends that assessment data be gathered using multiple methods that assess both math skills and procedural knowledge and that all assessment activities be tied to instructional decisions to enhance students' math learning.

An important consideration when teaching and assessing mathematics is understanding the foundational role of language in learning math and in performing well on measures of math proficiency. Although it is often overlooked, language proficiency is key to grasping math concepts. The "language of mathematics" relates to the linguistic and symbolic features of math (e.g., technical math vocabulary; mathematical sentences, such as those used in writing algorithms and equations; understanding relational concepts to solve word problems). Students who come from culturally and linguistically diverse backgrounds, particularly those who are English learners, may have difficulty comprehending and appropriately using mathematical language. In addition, students with disabilities often have language-processing problems that make it more difficult for them to acquire mathematical knowledge and skills. As teachers plan to instruct and assess their students in mathematics, they need to be aware of these variances in student learning and provide appropriate scaffolds and supports for all students to acquire, master, and apply mathematical concepts to everyday life situations.

A RESPONSE TO INTERVENTION (RTI) APPROACH TO MATH ASSESSMENT

Given the procedural and spiraling nature of mathematical learning, in which each concept builds on previously learned concepts, early intervention and prevention of future deficits is critical (VanDerHayden, 2009). Generally speaking, there has been less research on the RTI model in math than on the model for developing literacy skills, but increasingly researchers have turned their attention to achieving mathematical effectiveness by using an RTI approach (Bryant et al., 2008; Fuchs, Fuchs, & Hollenbeck, 2007; Gersten et al., 2009). In such a model, the Tier I math instruction is received by all students in the general education classroom. Tier II math instruction includes small-group interventions to develop specific math skills. Tier III math interventions are provided by specialized personnel and may include one-on-one tutoring. Teachers use assessment data to monitor students' growth and progress in mathematics at each tier. Teachers make decisions about the effectiveness of their instruction using these data and make modifications to their instruction, pacing, learning strategies, and teaching methods to better meet student needs.

Students who struggle with math learning often assume passive roles, use ineffective strategies, experience difficulties with the cognitive load of the curriculum and activities, and consequently demonstrate lower achievement gains in math. Gersten and colleagues (2009) published a What Works Clearinghouse practice guide that offers eight recommendations for using an RTI model in math that address the needs of struggling learners:

1. Screen all students to determine which students are at risk for mathematics difficulties and ensure early interventions for those students.
2. Ensure that intervention curricula focus on foundational concepts and skills such as whole numbers in early elementary grades and rational numbers in upper elementary and middle school grades.
3. Provide both explicit and systematic instruction. Effective intervention strategies include providing opportunities for students to participate in large- and

small-group problem solving and to communicate their thought processes with their peers, providing guided practice and corrective feedback, and providing a cumulative review at the end of each session.

4. Ensure that students receive instruction to solve word problems and that this instruction focuses on analyzing the common underlying structures of various problem types and operations.

5. Allow students to translate abstract mathematical symbols into visual representations of mathematical ideas (e.g., number lines, diagrams, charts). Concrete materials including manipulatives may be needed for students who are not yet ready for visual representations.

6. Build fluency with basic math facts. Interventions at all grade levels should incorporate a 10-minute time block per intervention session for the student to practice math facts, possibly using flash cards or computerized practice activities.

7. Monitor the progress of at-risk students who are receiving support in an RTI model at least monthly using curriculum-based assessments. These data can guide student groupings, instructional pacing, and other instructional decisions.

8. Focus on strategies to enhance the motivation of struggling students, particularly those who are receiving Tier 2 and Tier 3 interventions. These strategies include encouraging students to set goals for themselves and chart their own progress and providing praise and rewards for their accomplishments.

TECHNIQUES FOR MATH ASSESSMENT

As with other content areas, there is controversy associated with the measures that are considered to be effective for assessing math. The NCTM calls for measurements that result in holistic rather than skill-specific data and that build conceptual understanding and problem solving (Fuchs, Fuchs, Karns, Hamlett, & Katzaroff, 1999; Kelley, Hosp, & Howell, 2009). Sample holistic assessments include portfolios and rubrics, observation protocols, journals, and student self-assessments. Such holistic tools are informative about overall math learning and contribute to the richness of assessment data collected by teachers to make instructional decisions about their students' progress. However, they are not very sensitive to student progress, generally lack reliability and validity, and are time intensive to administer, score, and interpret (Kelley et al., 2009). Curriculum-based measurement (CBM), on the other hand, is most widely used in an RTI approach for screening and progress monitoring of single and multiple math skills.

CBM for Math Skills

CBM probes in math are cost effective and quick to administer, are sensitive to student growth, and provide instructionally meaningful data. CBM provides a reliable and valid measure to assess mathematical proficiency in students. Using CBM, students can be assessed both individually and in groups. Commercially available computer adaptive assessment tools can be purchased at low cost to administer CBM probes, thereby not occupying the teacher's valuable instructional time.

Directions for administering and scoring a math CBM are provided in Chapter 5 of this text. A salient feature about CBM in math, compared with CBM in reading, writing, and early literacy, is that math CBM assesses a student's proficiency in specific skill areas that the student is expected to master during that school year. A single math probe cannot successfully assess the student's mastery of all the subskills that are taught at a particular grade level. For instance, the eighth-grade math curriculum on which Joel's teacher is monitoring his progress includes numbers and operations (rational numbers, fractions, decimals, exponents, ratios, powers and roots, etc.), algebra (equations, linear relationships, quadratic functions, etc.), geometry (properties of geometric figures, spatial relations, transformation and symmetry, etc.), measurement (perimeter and area, volume, etc.), and data analysis and probability (data collection, reading and interpreting data, probability concepts, etc.). Therefore, teachers need to develop probes (or select commercially produced probes) which include a wide range of items that tap into multiple skills that the students are expected to master over the course of the school year. Many alternate forms of the probes are needed, all of equivalent difficulty and containing items that tap into the various skill areas that are part of the math curriculum for that particular year.

Math CBM generally assesses students in three broad areas: early numeracy, computation, and concepts and application. CBM probes have traditionally only assessed computation fluency and most of the research literature in this area has been associated with computation skills (Hosp, Hosp, & Howell, 2007), although recent research is investigating the effectiveness of other types of math probes. Similarly, there is very limited research on the application of math CBM in the secondary grades (Foegen, 2000; Foegen & Deno, 2001).

The National Center on Response to Intervention (2009) describes the skill areas in which mathematical progress is monitored for students in kindergarten through sixth grade. Kindergarten students and first graders typically are administered early numeracy probes in the areas of number identification, quantity discrimination (e.g., identifying the bigger number in a pair of numbers) and missing number (e.g., identifying a missing number in a sequence of numbers). Early numeracy probes are individually administered, although probes may be group administered for students in advanced grades. Students in grades 1–6 are assessed in the area of math computation, an important early mathematics skill. Students in grades 2–6 are also assessed on concepts and applications, the application of mathematical skills to everyday experiences.

The length of CBM probes vary by grade level. Probes typically last 2 minutes for first and second graders, 3 minutes for third- and fourth-grade students, 5 minutes for fifth graders, and 6 minutes for sixth graders. These probes are scored on the basis of the number of digits a student got correct, and a digits correct per minute index typically is used to track student progress.

General Math CBM Resources

National Center on Response to Intervention: *http://www.rti4success.org*

Research Institute on Progress Monitoring: *http://www.progressmonitoring.net/*

Error Analyses of Math Work Samples

An error analysis of work samples provides information about the common error patterns that a student makes, which provide direct feedback for areas that need further

Resources for CBM Probes in Mathematics

1. Accelerated Math (Renaissance Learning)
   Accelerated Math is a commercially available and empirically validated resource that is available for a fee. Accelerated Math generates probes for math practice and progress monitoring for students in grades 1–12. Probes are automatically scored and students receive immediate feedback.

   http://www.renlearn.com/am/

   http://www.interventioncentral.org/

2. AIMSweb (Pearson)
   This commercially available and empirically validated resource is available for a fee. AIMSweb has two separate resources for monitoring progress in mathematics:
   i) AIMSweb Test of Early Numeracy (TEN)
   AIMSweb TEN is appropriate for students in kindergarten and first grade and has four measures for oral counting, number identification, quantity discrimination, and missing number. Each of the 4 TEN measures includes 33 forms that are available for purchase.
   ii) AIMSweb Math (Pearson)
   This product is most appropriate for universal screening and progress monitoring of students who have skill deficits in grades 1–8. It takes 2–4 minutes to administer each test. There are 50 alternate forms available in the areas of computation and math fact.

   http://www.AIMSweb.com/

3. Intervention Central
   Free math fluency probes, a math worksheet generator, and the ChartDog program to create CBM charts are available.

   http://www.interventioncentral.org/

4. Monitoring Basic Skills Progress (Fuchs, Hamlett, & Fuchs, 1999)
   Applicable for students in the secondary grades, this commercially available computerized software distributed by ProEd includes features for graphing data and conducting error analyses and instructional recommendations. Administration of the test takes between 1–10 minutes depending on the grade level and whether the student is being assessed using the computation probe, concepts and applications probes, or both. The software has adequate technical qualities.

   http://www.proedinc.com

5. Schoolhouse Technologies
   Free resources for developing math probes, tests, and worksheets can be downloaded and run on your own computer.

   http://www.schoolhousetech.com/

6. Yearly Progress Pro (McGraw-Hill)
   This computer-administered progress-monitoring tool is appropriate for students in grades 1–8. Test administration takes 15 minutes, and the probe is automatically scored by the computer and generates subscale scores and error analyses.

   http://www.ctb.com/ctb.com/control/productFamilyViewAction?productFamilyId=591&p=products

instruction. An error analysis complements the accuracy and fluency information that is obtained through CBM and other tests of math proficiency. In addition, an error analysis provides diagnostic information and insights on why the student is making certain errors. If the student fails to show his or her calculations, the teacher may interview the student and ask for an explanation of the mathematical reasoning that he or she followed to complete the problem.

Generally, students' mathematical errors fall into the following error pattern categories (Spinelli, 2006):

1. *Basic fact error*—The student performs the correct operation but uses an incorrect math fact (e.g., $5 + 6 = 10$).
2. *Regrouping*—The student makes an error related to a misunderstanding about place value. This type of mistake is common when a student has problems with carrying over or borrowing during arithmetic calculations (e.g., $49 + 33 = 712$ or $82 - 16 = 76$).
3. *Incorrect operation*—The student uses an incorrect operation to complete a mathematical problem (e.g., $13 \times 5 = 18$).
4. *Incorrect algorithm*—A student follows the wrong procedures to solve a problem, typically because he or she has not gained proficiency in the steps that are to be following in completing an operation (e.g., $32 - 19 = 27$).
5. *Direction*—The student completes the steps in the wrong direction or order, including using a left-to-right progression (e.g., $79 + 42 = 112$).
6. *Omission*—The student misses a step in the process or omits a part of the answer (e.g., $65 \times 22 = 130$).
7. *Placement*—The student mixes up the place value, writing a number in the wrong column (e.g., $65 \times 22 = 260$).
8. *Attention to sign*—The student confuses the operational sign or does not pay close attention to it (e.g., $19 - 6 = 25$).
9. *Random error*—The student makes careless errors caused by hurrying through the work or guessing the response when he or she does not understand what procedure and operation to perform (e.g., $18 \times 2 = 100$).

Student errors tend to reflect the error patterns described here; particular errors are typical at certain developmental and proficiency levels. Teachers at certain grade levels may be able to preempt these errors by drawing students' attention to them and teaching strategies to guide their accuracy and fluency.

Clinical Observation

Clinical observations in math require a teacher to observe the students as they are engaged in a mathematical task or activity. Elements that are observed include the students' attention to the task, ability to follow directions, organize themselves and get started without prompts or assistance, ask for assistance as needed, copy the numbers and letters (showing correct understanding of sequencing, letter/number formation, place value, etc.), use strategies including manipulatives and counting aids, and demonstrate good attitude and motivation to complete the task, among others. Observations will also reveal the learning environment and sources of distraction.

Think Alouds and Math Interviews

In a math think aloud, a student is presented with a problem and asked to talk through the steps that he or she should use to work out the problem and arrive at the answer. A think aloud may be followed with an oral math interview in which the student is asked to explain his or her reasoning as he or she worked through the math problem or activity. The student explains his or her comprehension of the task and the steps that he or she would follow to accomplish it. He or she may write a problem sentence and/or use graphics to explain the thinking behind the process. Instructional techniques such as Cognitively Guided Instruction (Carpenter, Fennema, & Franke, 1996) are based on teachers listening to how students think and using this information to guide instruction. Questions that are related to prior math instruction, math knowledge, and motivation also may be included in the math interview.

Student Self-Assessment

Students reflect on and then assess their own learning. They complete a checklist about their motivation, skills, and proficiency in different content related to mathematics. It is informative for a teacher to learn about a student's perceptions of his or her own math proficiency. The self-assessment also could include questions about math work habits and preferences.

Math Portfolios and Grading Rubrics

A math portfolio is a compendium of artifacts demonstrating the progress that a student has made in math during the course of the school year. A school may require specific items (e.g., initial assessments, quarterly tests, benchmark assignments, math facts tests) to be included in the portfolio. Alternately, a teacher and student may select items for inclusion on the basis of predetermined criteria, such as artifacts that reflect conceptual understanding, problem solving, mathematical skills acquired, etc. The portfolio could include items such as work samples, tests, CBM probes, quizzes and assignments, checklists, math journal entries, observations of the student doing math, teacher conference notes, and so on. A rubric may be used to assess specific levels of performance along criteria such as comprehension, strategy use, and problem solving (Spinelli, 2006).

STUDENT ATTITUDES TOWARD MATH

There are many variables that affect student attitudes toward math. In fact, some adults, even teachers, shy away from teaching and learning new math concepts because of their anxiety and negative attitudes about math. Math learning is influenced by early opportunities to learn math, effective instruction, student motivation, and parental and cultural attitudes toward mathematics. For instance, Cocking and Chipman (1988) found variances in cultural perceptions toward mathematics; Native American and Hispanic women perceived mathematics as "calculating" in the sense of being scheming, and consequently they wanted to avoid math.

Researchers have investigated factors such as achievement goals, competence beliefs, and utility value of math, each of which contributes to the motivation to expend effort and do well in the subject. For instance, Chouinard, Karsenti, and Roy (2007) found that secondary-school students who believe themselves to be competent in math and who set high goals for themselves tended to demonstrate greater effort. In addition, they found that parental support and encouragement influenced how much students valued math, whereas teacher support influenced their sense of math competence. High school students often demonstrate a decline in their level of motivation from the start to the end of the school year (Chouinard & Roy, 2008).

Teachers can determine students' attitudes toward mathematics using interviews and personal observations. Math attitude measures like the two measures that follow are commercially available as well:

Attitudes Toward Mathematics Inventory (Tapia & Marsh, 2004)—This measure includes 49 items that assess four factors: self-confidence, value of mathematics, enjoyment of mathematics, and motivation. The inventory uses a 5-point Likert scale and takes 10–20 minutes to administer. This scale appears to have strong reliability and validity data.

Fennema-Sherman Mathematics Attitude Scales (Fennema & Sherman, 1976)— This popular measure includes 108 items across nine instruments that assess students' attitudes toward mathematics: 1) Attitude Toward Success in Mathematics Scale, 2) Mathematics as a Male Domain Scale, 3) Mother Scale, and 4) Father Scale, 5) Teacher Scale, 6) Confidence in Learning Mathematics Scale, 7) Mathematics Anxiety Scale, 8) Effectance Motivation Scale in Mathematics, and 9) Mathematics Usefulness Scale. The scale takes about 45 minutes to administer. This tool has been widely used for research purposes, but recent researchers have questioned its reliability and validity.

MATHEMATICS ASSESSMENTS IN STUDENTS WITH LANGUAGE DIFFICULTIES

Mathematical and verbal abilities are positively correlated. Students usually acquire content-area knowledge and skills, including mathematical knowledge and skills, through language learning. It is likely that the same processing difficulties that affect language skills also affect math skills. As described earlier in this chapter, students who exhibit language difficulties either due to a disability or due to being English learners often tend to have difficulties learning math.

Past practice assumed that math was a "universal language" and that math learning generally was nonverbal, therefore that it was easier for English learners to acquire mathematics than literacy skills. Increasingly, researchers have found that language is a key foundational skill for math learning and that, as in other content areas, the specific language (or register) of the discipline must be explicitly taught and learned (Ron, 1999). English learners are particularly disadvantaged when they encounter linguistically complex math concepts (Martiniello, 2008). Word problems pose unique challenges for English learners because reading fluency and comprehension problems overlay the already challenging math vocabulary and comprehension that are required to solve word problems.

One way to reduce the language demand on these students and thereby level the playing field is to reduce the linguistic complexity by using simple rather than complex sentences, shorter sentences with fewer words, active rather than passive voice, simple vocabulary, few multimeaning words, and no irrelevant statements in the math word problems. According to principles of universal design for assessment, math word problems should be at a level that is comprehensible to students and that does not use language which limits the students' comprehension of the math concept and application. Math tests that use simplified wording have been found to increase the test performance of both English learners and other students (Abedi & Lord, 2001).

The Northwest Regional Educational Laboratory (2005) published some suggestions for teaching math to English learners:

1. Use visuals and manipulative learning strategies.
2. Introduce new academic vocabulary at the start of the lesson, thereby increasing familiarity with the concepts.
3. Use direct instruction, including demonstration and modeling and guided practice prior to having the students engage in independent practice.
4. Use group-based learning strategies to facilitate active learning, motivation, and more opportunities to hear, see, and learn the information.
5. Simplify both oral and written instructions.
6. Make learning personal and put it in context for students, using details from their lives to make learning more meaningful.
7. Supplement instruction with bilingual materials as applicable.

NORM-REFERENCED MATH TESTS AND THEIR ROLE IN AN RTI MODEL

In an RTI model, norm-referenced tests may be used for screening students, diagnosing their learning strengths and difficulties, and determining their eligibility for special education. Typically, such tests are not used for progress-monitoring purposes because they are not sensitive to small changes in performance and cannot be readministered weekly or biweekly, the frequency that is recommended for students who are receiving intensive interventions. Some of the commonly used norm-referenced tests in mathematics that have sound technical qualities are described here.

Test of Early Mathematical Ability, Third Edition (TEMA-3; Ginsburg & Baroody, 2003)—Developed for use with children aged 3 years to 8 years 11 months, the TEMA is an untimed test that is intended for early identification of learning difficulties in math. The test has 72 items that tap into both school and nonschool learning of math. Two alternate forms are available. The TEMA-3 includes additional Assessment Probes to follow up on students' thinking and Instructional Activities. The test is grounded in theory and demonstrates strong reliability and fair content validity (Crehan, 2004). The TEMA-3 has been criticized for not having sufficient technical documentation of its validity and norm sample.

Test of Mathematical Ability, Second Edition (TOMA-2; Brown, Cronin, & McEntire, 1994)—Developed for use in children and youth aged 8 years to 18 years

11 months, this individually administered test measures math abilities and can be useful as a screening measure. It takes 45 to 90 minutes to administer the test. The TOMA-2 includes scores in the areas of Vocabulary, Computation, General Information, Story Problems, and Attitude Toward Math, as well as the total score. The test is criticized on the basis of the wide range of abilities and ages it assesses. For instance, there is a high correlation between subtests and the overall test is correlated with IQ tests, raising the question of whether the test measures aptitude, math ability, or overall academic ability. Reliability coeffients are adequate and the norm sample is clearly described (Harnisch, 2004).

Key Math Revised/Normative Update: A Diagnostic Inventory of Essential Mathematics (Key Math-R/NU; Connolly, 1998)—This individually administered test of mathematics is developed for children from kindergarten to grade 9. The test measures math concepts, skills, operations, and applications and takes 35 to 50 minutes to administer. The reliability is low for the subtests and adequate for the overall test. It is recommended that users of this test evaluate its match with the local curriculum in order to ascertain its content validity.

Comprehensive Mathematical Ability Test (CMAT; Hresko, Schlieve, Herron, Swain, & Sherbenou, 2003—Individually administered and appropriate for students aged 7 years to 18 years 11 months, this test assesses mathematical abilities in the areas of comprehension, calculation, and application. The standard test battery takes between 45–60 minutes to administer. The test has solid reliability and validity data and is a useful tool in determining students' strengths and weaknesses in math.

End-of-Chapter Questions

1. What mathematical content does the NCTM recommend be incorporated into all school curricula?
2. Discuss some key guidelines to follow when applying the RTI model to preventing mathematical difficulties in children and youth.
3. Explain how CBM can be used to monitor student progress in math. What types of probes are used at different grade levels?
4. How is error analysis used to determine mathematical difficulties? What common error patterns do children display?
5. Describe what data can be obtained about a student's math performance using observation, interviews, and portfolios.
6. Explain the factors that affect students' attitudes toward math. How can math attitudes be assessed?
7. What role does language play in mathematical learning?
8. Describe some ways to assist English learners to learn math and perform well on math assessments.
9. What are some commonly used norm-referenced tests of mathematics?

References

Abedi, J., & Lord, C. (2001). The language factor in mathematics tests. *Applied Measurement in Education, 14*, 219–234.

Brown, V. L., Cronin, M. E., & McEntire, E. (1994). *Test of mathematical abilities* (2nd ed.). Austin, TX: Pro-Ed.

Bryant, D. P., Bryant, B. R., Gersten, R. M., Scammacca, N. N., Funk, C., Winter, A., et al. (2008). The effects of tier 2 interventions on the mathematics performance of first-grade students who are at risk for mathematics difficulties. *Learning Disability Quarterly, 31*(2), 47–63.

Carpenter, T., Fennema, E., & Franke, M. (1996). Cognitively guided instruction: A knowledge base for reform in primary mathematics instruction. *The Elementary School Journal, 97,* 3–20.

Chouinard, R., Karsenti, T., & Roy, N. (2007). Relations among competence beliefs, utility value, achievement goals, and effort in mathematics. *British Journal of Educational Psychology, 77,* 501–517.

Chouinard, R., & Roy, N. (2008). Changes in high school students' competence beliefs, utility value and achievement goals in mathematics. *British Journal of Educational Psychology, 78,* 31–50.

Cocking, R. R., & Chipman, S. (1988). Conceptual issues related to mathematics achievement of language minority children. In R. R. Cocking & J. P. Mestre (Eds.), *Linguistic and cultural influences on learning mathematics* (pp. 17–46). Hillsdale: Erlbaum.

Connolly, A. J. (1998). *Key Math Revised/NU.* Circle Pines, MN: American Guidance Service.

Crehan, K. D. (2004). Review of the test of early mathematics ability, third edition. *Mental Measurement Yearbook.* Lincoln, NE: Buros Institute of Mental Measurements and University of Nebraska.

Fennema, E., & Sherman, J. A. (1976). Fennema-Sherman Mathematics Attitudes Scales: Instruments designed to measure attitudes toward the learning of mathematics by females and males. *Journal for Research in Mathematics Education, 7*(5),324–326.

Foegen, A. (2000). Technical adequacy of general outcome measures for middle school mathematics. *Diagnostique, 25,* 175–203.

Foegen, A., & Deno, S. L. (2001). Identifying growth indicators for low-achieving students in middle school mathematics. *Journal of Special Education, 35,* 4–16.

Fuchs, L. S., Fuchs, D., & Hollenbeck, K. N. (2007). Extending responsiveness to intervention to mathematics at first and third grades. *Learning Disabilities Research & Practice, 22*(1), 13–24.

Fuchs, L. S., Fuchs, D., Karns, K., Hamlett, C. L., & Katzaroff, M. (1999). Mathematics performance assessment in the classroom: Effects on teacher planning and student learning. *American Educational Research Journal, 36,* 609–646.

Fuchs, L. S., Hamlett, C. L., & Fuchs, D. (1999). *Monitoring basic skills progress: Basic math concepts and applications.* Austin, TX: Pro-Ed.

Gersten, R., Beckmann, S., Clarke, B., Foegen, A., Marsh, L., Star, J. R., et al. (2009). *Assisting students struggling with mathematics: Response to Intervention (RTI) for elementary and middle schools* (NCEE 2009-4060). Washington, D.C.: National Center for Education Evaluation and Regional Assistance, Institute of Education Sciences, U. S. Department of Education. Retrieved June 27, 2009, from http://ies.ed.gov/ncee/wwc/pdf/practiceguides/rti_math_pg_042109.pdf

Ginsburg, H. P., & Baroody, A. J. (2003). *Test of early mathematics ability* (2nd ed.).Austin, TX: Pro-Ed.

Harnisch, D. (2004). Review of the Test of Mathematical Abilities, Second Edition. *Mental Measurement Yearbook.* Lincoln, NE: Buros Institute of Mental Measurements and University of Nebraska.

Hosp, M. K., Hosp, J. L., & Howell, K. W. (2007). *The ABCs of CBM: A practical guide to curriculum-based measurement.* New York: Guilford Press.

Hresko, W., Schlieve, P., Herron, S., Swain, C., & Sherbenou, R. (2003). *Comprehensive Mathematical Ability Test.* Austin, TX: Pro-Ed.

Kelley, B., Hosp, J. L., & Howell, K. W. (2009). Curriculum-based evaluation in math: An overview. *Assessment for Effective Instruction, 33*(4), 250–256.

Lembke, E., Foegen, A., Whittaker, T. A., & Hampton, D. (2008). Establishing technically adequate measures of progress in early literacy. *Assessment for Effective Instruction, 33*(4), 206–214.

Martiniello, M. (2008). Language and performance of English language learners in math word problems. *Harvard Education Review, 78,* 333–368.

National Center on Response to Intervention. (2010). *Using CBM for progress monitoring in math.* Retrieved October 5, 2010, from http://www.rti4success.org/index.php?option=com_content&task=blogcategory& id=10&Itemid=56

National Council of Teachers of Mathematics. (2000). *Principles and standards for school mathematics.* Reston, VA: NCTM.

National Council of Teachers of Mathematics. (2009). *Guiding principles for math curriculum and assessment.* Retrieved June 21, 2009, from http://www.nctm.org/standards/content.aspx?id=23273

National Mathematics Advisory Panel. (2008). *Foundations for Success: The final report of the national mathematics advisory panel.* Washington, DC: U.S. Department of Education.

Northwest Regional Educational Laboratory. (2005). Teaching Math to English Language Learners. *Northwest Education, 25, 11*(2). Retrieved July 2, 2009, from http://educationnorthwest.org/webfm_send/ 761

Ron, P. (1999). Spanish–English language issues in the mathematics classroom. In W. Secada, L. Ortiz-Franco, N. G. Hernandez, & Y. de la Cruz (Eds.), *Changing the faces of mathematics: Perspectives on Latinos* (pp. 22–33). Reston, VA: National Council of Teachers of Mathematics.

Spinelli, C. (2005). *Classroom assessment for students in special and general education.* (2nd ed). Upper Saddle River, NJ :Prentice- Hall.

Tapia, M., & Marsh, G. E., II. (2004). An instrument to measure mathematics attitudes. *Academic Exchange Quarterly, 8 (2).* Retrieved June 30, 2009, from http://www.rapidintellect.com/AEQweb/cho25344l.htm

VanDerHayden, A. (2009). *Using RTI to improve learning in mathematics.* Retrieved June 25, 2009 from http://www.rtinetwork.org/learn/why/rtiandmath

CHAPTER 14

Assessment Issues in an RTI Approach

Al Schuster is the principal at Jefferson Middle School, which is situated in a low-income neighborhood in a large urban metropolis. Over 80% of Jefferson students are from poverty backgrounds, 45% are English learners, and 17% of the students are labeled as having a disability. Al has worked very closely with the community social worker and the school PTA to involve parents and the community in all school activities. The school is a thriving social hub that hosts several community events, parent education programs, and a daily health and nutrition program. Parents regularly volunteer at the school; those who lack literacy skills often help with nonacademic tasks. Four years ago, the school worked closely with professors from the nearby state university to establish a Response to Intervention (RTI) model. The school psychologist coordinated implementation of the RTI model, and all teachers participated in professional development activities over a 2-year period. Since RTI was established, Jefferson Middle School has managed to reduce referrals to special education and to meet its Adequate Yearly Progress targets. Each year, however, it has become more difficult to attain progress across all subgroups. Al would like a consultant to evaluate the effectiveness of the school's RTI model and to suggest some recommendations for modifying this model to better meet the needs of all students at the school.

Reflections on the Scenario

1. What are some of the strengths of Jefferson Middle School?
2. What were some challenges faced by this school?
3. What questions do you have regarding how this school implemented the RTI model?
4. What information might the school seek from a consultant to enhance RTI effectiveness?

ASSESSMENT ISSUES IN AN RTI FRAMEWORK

The U.S. Department of Education has identified RTI as a scientifically validated educational practice (What Works Clearinghouse, 2010). RTI techniques have been widely used and empirically proven to enhance instruction and student outcomes in reading and math (Case, Speece, & Molloy, 2003; Marston, Muyskens, Lau, & Canter, 2003; VanDerHeyden, Witt, & Gilbertson, 2007). Founded on sound theoretical principles, the tiered levels of intervention have been proven to be effective with struggling students. As has been described in earlier chapters, Tier 1 interventions are high-quality empirically based interventions that are provided to all students. Tier 2 supplemental instruction is

To learn more about how to implement the different components of an RTI model, including assessing students who are at risk for learning and behavioral difficulties, go to the IRIS Center website at http://iris.peabody.vanderbilt.edu/resources.html
   This website includes several very informative, self-paced learning modules on the topic of RTI.

provided only to small groups of students who are struggling academically and/or have behavioral challenges according to screening and progress-monitoring measures. Tier 3 interventions are intensive and systematic interactions that often supplement regular classroom instruction for students who continue to struggle even after receiving high-quality small-group interventions for a reasonable period. Students who continue to struggle after receiving Tier 3 assistance are referred for special education services. The ongoing monitoring of student progress and the analysis of student performance data are critical to the effective working of this tiered approach to intervention.

Assessment in an RTI model serves four primary functions: 1) screening to identify students who are at risk for learning or behavior difficulties and assigning them to tiered instruction groups, 2) monitoring students' progress toward instructional objectives, 3) diagnosing learning problems, and 4) determining the eligibility for special education of students who are nonresponsive to increasingly intensive and prolonged interventions. Although an RTI model allows the use of a range of assessment tools, curriculum-based evaluations and measurement are used most frequently for screening and progress-monitoring purposes. Assessment tools that are selected for use in an RTI model must be reliable and valid, must be sensitive to student growth, and must yield accurate and precise data on the behavior being monitored (Danielson, Doolittle, & Bradley, 2007). The use of norm-referenced tests is usually limited to supplementing curriculum-based measures in determining eligibility for special education services.

DECISION MAKING IN AN RTI MODEL

It is recommended that a school identify an RTI team that includes administrators, the school psychologist, one or two veteran teachers, possibly a special educator and speech/language pathologists, and others who would help develop RTI policy and practices, consult with teachers, and regularly review data on students receiving interventions to help plan for next steps. It is advisable to consult with the parents or primary caregivers of a target student prior to developing an intervention plan for that student to ensure that the plan has support from both school and home. RTI teams need to address the following questions:

1. How will the intervention be selected? It must be scientifically validated and should address the identified learning needs of the student.
2. What materials, resources, and ongoing professional development and support are needed to assist the student's teachers to implement the RTI model?

3. How will the student's responsiveness to intervention be assessed? The team should select technically adequate measures that are sensitive to student progress, easy to use, and cost effective. The frequency of progress monitoring (e.g., weekly or monthly) must also be decided ahead of time.

4. What is the appropriate "strength" of intervention? This factor affects the duration and intensity of the intervention, both of which vary among the three tiers in the RTI model. For instance, a 20–30 minute intervention three or four times a week may be sufficient for Tier 2, but the time may need to be increased to 45–60 minutes, five times a week in Tier 3. The frequency and duration of intervention has implications for scheduling and the need for additional support personnel to assist the classroom teacher in implementing the intervention.

5. What data are needed to evaluate the effectiveness of the interventions? Data for evaluation include feedback from teachers, students, and parents that can help determine the feasibility and effectiveness of the selected interventions so that necessary modifications may be made to the model.

QUESTIONS RELATED TO THE IMPLEMENTATION OF RTI

Problem-solving teams and prereferral interventions have been used widely in schools across the country over the past several decades. Established RTI models, however, originated fairly recently—primarily since the passage of the Individuals with Disabilities Education Act (IDEA) in 2004. Consequently, there are still many unanswered questions regarding effective RTI techniques and the wide-scale implementation of RTI across schools, districts, and states. Some of these unanswered questions are discussed here.

Empirically Based RTI Practices

Although RTI was declared as an evidence-based practice by the U.S. Department of Education's What Works Clearinghouse, the efficacy of the associated assessment and intervention practices for a variety of learners are still in the process of being validated. Much of the RTI research has been identified as "emerging" and "contemporary" (Hollenbeck, 2007, p. 138). The majority of what is known relates to the content domains of reading and mathematics. Most of these validated techniques are applicable for elementary and middle-school levels.

Questions still remain about all levels of the RTI implementation process, starting with the efficacy of instructional materials and strategies used by teachers to instruct students in the core, general education curriculum (Brown-Chidsey & Steege, 2005). Similarly, although there are several reliable and validated screening tools (as described in the preceding chapters of this book), questions remain about the technical qualities of other screening measures such as district benchmark tests that continue to be widely used. We also need to build our knowledge base regarding the small-group intensive instruction strategies that are effective in yielding strong and continued positive outcomes for students with a range of learning needs.

Fidelity of Treatment Intervention

An intervention or program only meets its desired outcomes when it is implemented both correctly and consistently. As an example, let us say that Jefferson Middle School decides to adopt the Language! Program for students who demonstrate below-grade proficiency in Language Arts. After 2 years of program implementation the school finds that students did not make any progress in Language Arts, so it decides to adopt a new curriculum. Such a decision would be a large oversight. Before abandoning a program, school administrators should investigate several factors in order to conclude that the program was ineffective. They need to determine whether the teachers have been trained to use the program correctly, whether they received ongoing support to be proficient and comfortable teaching the curriculum, whether the scheduling of the school day permitted adequate time to implement the program, and whether teachers indeed implemented the program consistently as it was designed to be implemented. If any of these factors was lacking, the district should reexamine them before looking for a replacement curriculum.

Fidelity, also known as *treatment integrity*, refers to the implementation of an assessment or intervention in the manner in which it was designed and validated. In an RTI model, data on treatment integrity are critical in isolating whether student responsiveness, or lack thereof, was a function of the intervention that was implemented. One cannot conclude that an intervention was not effective if it was implemented haphazardly or not at all. As Duhon, Mesmer, Gregerson and Witt (2009) point out, having incomplete or inaccurate data on treatment integrity breaches a student's right to due process just as administering an incomplete cognitive assessment battery on a student and using the resulting data to make a special education referral does.

An evaluator should keep several considerations in mind when reviewing the fidelity of RTI approaches:

1. Generally, RTI research is conducted in fairly controlled settings by research associates who are paid to provide the intervention. Even though the approaches are empirically validated in the controlled settings, they may not be feasible nor effective when they are implemented by teachers and other school professionals who are on the frontlines in schools, dealing with multiple competing demands on their time and expertise. To what extent can practitioners implement these strategies with fidelity to bring about positive learning outcomes for students?
2. Teachers need ongoing professional development to build their proficiency with RTI approaches. For instance, professional development should cover how to collect data accurately and efficiently and how to interpret student data so that it is meaningful in driving instruction. This professional development assists teachers to adhere to established RTI procedures and fosters ongoing reflection and improved practice.
3. Schools need resources to implement interventions with fidelity. Schools may not always have optimal class sizes, readily available instructional materials, a school day schedule that can accommodate all critical teaching and learning activities, realistic curriculum-pacing expectations that allow for coverage of key concepts without rushing, additional adult support that can ensure small group instruction, and so on.

Determining Decision Rules

Decision rules are used to identify appropriate groupings and place students in tiered groups on the basis of their initial screening, to determine progress and move students to more or less intensive intervention groups on the basis of their skill levels, and to make the decision to remove a student from tiered interventions or refer a student for special education eligibility determination (Noell & Gansle, 2006). Grouping in tiers is considered to be flexible and dynamic; a student should be moved into a particular tiered group, out of a group, or retained in a group depending on his or her level of progress. Progress monitoring data must be reviewed every 6–8 weeks to ensure that the student is not "stuck" at a particular tier of intervention.

School personnel often worry about overidentifying students as needing interventions (false positives), which can place a strain on fiscal and temporal resources that are already tight. *Cut scores* are used as benchmark data and inform teachers and RTI teams what target score indicates adequate performance. Decision rules need to be established and clarified for all stakeholders in an RTI model. The next section describes two important decision rules in the RTI process:

1. What level of discrepancy needs to exist between the performance of a target student and that of his or her typical peers, in order for the student to qualify for Tier 2 and Tier 3 interventions? Alternately, what is the cut score on the selected benchmark screening and/or progress-monitoring tool, below which all students are classified as needing intervention? If a large percentage of students in a particular grade receive scores below the predetermined cut score, the school should re-examine and enrich its core curriculum and instruction.

2. What is the basis for determining student responsiveness to intervention? What level of student growth indicates adequate responsiveness? What amount of growth indicates that a student has made some progress and needs to sustain it by continuing with the same intervention? What amount of growth suggests the need for more intensive intervention? A basic rule of thumb is to look for a trend in the last (most recent) four data points plotted on the progress-monitoring graph to see whether they are at, above, or below the goal line. Growth can be measured in three ways: i) the student's attainment of a predetermined level or criterion score that has been established as a goal by published norms (e.g., 35 words correct per minute), ii) the slope score that indicates the rate of growth (described in the box that follows), or iii) a dual discrepancy analysis, which involves both the student's attained level of performance and the trend or rate of growth.

Limited Curriculum-Based Measurement (CBM) Techniques for Secondary Grades and Across Subject Areas

Assessment and evaluation procedures (e.g., CBM, curriculum-based evaluation) exist in the areas of reading, mathematics, and writing. These measures have been proven to have strong technical adequacy for students in elementary and middle school. Some measures offer extended norms for high school students, but they have not been studied extensively. Far less is known about the validity and reliability of measures for use in other content domains such as social studies and science (Fuchs & Deshler, 2007; D. Fuchs & L. Fuchs, 2006). Similarly, there is only preliminary empirical support for an RTI model in the social-emotional-behavioral domain (Fairbanks, Sugai, Guardino, & Lathrop, 2007), and additional research is required to scientifically validate progress monitoring tools for tracking behavioral progress in students.

Calculating and Using Slope Scores

The slope or rate of improvement is an analysis of the trends in a student's graphed scores and is used to determine progress over several weeks of an intervention.

Here are the steps to calculate a slope:

Step 1. Collect the student's progress-monitoring data for the previous 6–8 weeks (e.g., words correct per minute for reading, digits correct per minute for math)

Step 2. Collect the following:
  - The score on the first probe, y_1 (e.g., 3)
  - The score on the last probe, y_2 (e.g., 21)
  - The first administration period, x_1 (e.g., 1)
  - The last administration period, x_2 (e.g., 8)

Step 3. Apply the following formula:

$$\text{Slope} = \frac{y_2 - y_1}{x_2 - x_1} = \frac{21 - 3}{8 - 1} = \frac{18}{7} = 2.57$$

Step 4. Compare the target student's slope with the expected slope according to published norms.

Interpreting Slope Scores

Student's slope score equals expected slope → adequate response to interventions; no changes needed.

Student's slope score above expected slope → student is responding to the intervention; increase expectations.

Student's slope score below expected slope → student needs more intensive intervention.

RTI has been described as an early intervention model: one that prevents further academic and behavioral difficulties in students. Consequently, its applicability and relevance to the middle- and high-school levels have been questioned (Fuchs & Deshler, 2007). Hughes and Deshler (2007) point out that the RTI approach in secondary schools differs in significant ways from elementary school models because the focus of instruction at the secondary level is on content rather than basic skill development. Fewer validated programs are used to teach content and it becomes more challenging to provide interventions to assist the student to catch up with age and grade peers at this level. Furthermore, students at the secondary school level interact with five to seven different teachers, all of whom have their own instructional styles and preferences. Much of the large and small group interventions involve strategy instruction, in which students who demonstrate intensive needs receive basic skills instruction from a support teacher in a small group (Hughes & Deshler).

Clearly, there is a greater sense of urgency to remediate academic or behavioral difficulties in middle- and high-school students and the tiers of intervention may need to be implemented at such levels with greater flexibility (Duffy, 2007). At the high-school level, RTI is used to monitor ongoing progress in students who already receive supplemental interventions and tutoring and to identify new students whose learning and behavioral difficulties were not identified in elementary or middle school.

Facilitating the Collection and Use of Data for Instructional Decision Making

Data collection and interpretation are key components of the RTI process, and often the components that are most difficult to implement consistently in schools. Adequate teacher training in using these techniques, including modeling and demonstration of how these data can be used in instructional planning, helps facilitate data use. It also is important to consider feasibility issues in data collection and interpretation. Time is one of the resources that is in shortest supply for teachers. Consequently, in order for teachers to use progress-monitoring measures such as CBM consistently, it is important for them to use efficient and timesaving ways to assess ongoing progress. Jenkins (2009) offers some suggestions:

1. *Consolidated rather than distributed progress monitoring*—Rather than monitoring a student's progress weekly, teachers may be able to consolidate assessment in a single day in a month (Johnson, Jenkins, Petscher, & Catts, 2009). Teachers can administer two or three probes in a single sitting, thereby simplifying the scheduling, transitions, and set-up time. Initial research indicates that growth estimates that are obtained by administering multiple probes on a single day are almost exactly the same as growth estimates that are obtained from administering CBM over 2–3 separate days.

2. *Progress-monitoring data collected every 3 weeks rather than weekly*—Recent research suggests that CBM growth slopes that are obtained from probes administered every 3 weeks were almost identical to slopes that were obtained using weekly progress monitoring. It was important, however, to collect data using multiple probes at the 3-week intervals rather than relying on data collected from a single CBM probe. These findings suggest that teachers may be able to schedule progress monitoring for a third of their students each week, thereby assessing each of their students over a 3-week timeframe. It is important for teachers to make instructional changes that are based on these data in order to improve student performance.

3. *Analyzing growth trajectories*—Teachers must modify instruction in a timely manner using reviews of students' growth trajectories as indicated on their CBM growth charts. Generally speaking, having data that are based on 6–8 weeks of instruction is sufficient for determining whether the student has an accelerating, decelerating, or flat trajectory, and teachers can make instructional changes accordingly.

Involving Families in the RTI Process

Parental input in decision making is not only mandated under IDEA, it is a critical component of any intervention and support plan. Partnering with parents in an RTI model is very desirable and requires outreach to the family and community at multiple levels. It starts with increasing parents' awareness of and education about RTI and the types of supports that are available to students. Communication with parents and involvement of parents in educational decisions strengthens the interventions that are implemented

(Duffy, 2007). There is a need for additional research on effective parent participation models in an RTI approach and for parental education and training programs.

Role of the Multidisciplinary Team in Eligibility Determination

The field is fairly divided on the issue of whether formal assessment by a multidisciplinary team is a required component of the RTI model. Some practitioners argue that the increasingly intensive levels of intervention and ongoing progress monitoring and documentation of student progress already provide systematic and rich data on student progress that is sufficient to make eligibility determinations for special education (Batsche, Kavale, & Kovaleski, 2006; Reschly, 2005). Many elements that are assessed in a multidisciplinary team evaluation (e.g., IQ, processing speed, memory) have only limited instructional applicability and do not guide instructional decisions and planning. Other experts (Olfiesh, 2006; Wodrich, Spencer, & Daley, 2006) argue in favor of the need to collect multidisciplinary data to rule out exclusionary factors that may cause learning difficulties (e.g., cognitive delays, language disorders, sensory difficulties, social-emotional problems) in order to make eligibility decisions and to arrive at an accurate diagnosis of the student's disability.

RTI and Students with Moderate or Severe Disabilities and Gifts and Talents

Another debate in the field relates to the applicability and inclusiveness of the RTI model for all diverse learners at a school. RTI was developed to address the needs of struggling readers and students with potential learning disabilities. It is readily applicable to populations of students considered to be at risk for learning and behavioral difficulties. Far less is known about how RTI approaches can be applied to help students who have more significant disabilities or gifted students who require academic enrichment beyond what is offered by the standard curriculum.

It has been argued that there is no need to go through the increasingly intensive stages of intervention and assessment in order to determine a student's eligibility for moderate or severe disability diagnoses, as students with severe cognitive, physical, and sensory disabilities usually are identified at a very young age. If one sees RTI as a way to determine eligibility determination for special education, this argument appears to be valid. However, RTI also may be used as a systematic data-based decision-making model that allows for flexible groupings of students according to their instructional needs and that enables instruction to be guided by ongoing data and driven by student performance outcomes. Used for this purpose, RTI has a lot of potential for all students, including those with the most exceptional learning needs.

SCALING UP FOR WIDESPREAD IMPLEMENTATION

In order to make RTI approaches sustainable and entrenched as a way of doing business in schools, it is critical to consider issues that are related to *scalability* or widespread implementation in schools. Early RTI models were initiated at individual schools, often on a voluntary basis, by an eager teacher or group of teachers at a particular grade level. In some cases, district-level administrators mandated an RTI approach across the district. There has been a lot of variability in the implementation of RTI, but state departments of education increasingly are targeting more systematic and purposeful implementation of RTI across school districts.

Although many questions remain with regard to implementing a robust large-scale RTI model that is effective for all learners, we do know some of the ingredients that must be in place for its success. Danielson, Doolittle, and Bradley (2007) and Fuchs and Deshler (2007) summarize some of the components that help build capacity for successful RTI implementation:

1. *Sustained professional development to build teacher skills*—Such professional development includes professional learning communities and sustained teacher support networks.
2. *Committed administrators*—Administrators can play an important role by setting clear expectations for the implementation of RTI, ensuring that adequate resources are available, and supporting the use of empirically based practices. It is important for practices to be sustainable and implemented with fidelity.
3. *District-level support in recruiting and hiring qualified teachers*—Teachers should be knowledgeable and committed to early intervention and empirically based practices.
4. *Flexible staff and teachers who are willing to redefine their roles to better serve students*—Teachers must be able to share their turf with special-education colleagues in order for an RTI approach to succeed. For instance, with RTI special educators may serve students who do not have disability diagnoses, general educators may conduct ongoing assessment and progress-monitoring functions of students who do have disabilities, and there may be greater collaboration across grade-level teams to group students during the reading and/or math block.
5. *Support for staff and teachers to adopt RTI*—Educators need to have time to include RTI in their school day and ongoing support and opportunities for consultation to have their questions and concerns addressed.
6. *Grassroots-level decisions about how RTI is implemented at a school*—Decisions that are made at the local level are far more effective than decisions that are mandated from administrators at the district level.

Clearly there are many competing demands on the limited time and resources that are available in schools. However, there are compelling reasons to initiate systemic changes in how students are served that will achieve positive outcomes for diverse learners.

End-of-Chapter Questions

1. Briefly describe an RTI model. Explain the reasons for assessing students in such a model.
2. Discuss some operational considerations that should be kept in mind as schools consider implementation of an RTI model.
3. What is known about the empirical basis of RTI?
4. Explain what treatment integrity is and why this concept is of utmost importance in an RTI model.

5. Why are decision rules required? Explain the two broad decision rules that guide RTI decision making.
6. What is a slope? What information does it provide?
7. How can RTI be applied to the secondary-school level? What are some unique challenges that are encountered at this level?

8. What are some ways to increase the frequency of administration and use of CBM in an RTI model?
9. Why should parents be involved in an RTI approach?
10. What role does the multidisciplinary team play in an RTI approach?
11. In what ways does RTI apply to all the diverse students served in a public school setting? Discuss its relevance and applicability to the following populations:
    i) English learners
    ii) Struggling readers
    iii) Students with moderate mental retardation
    iv) Gifted and talented students
12. Why is it important to consider issues of scalability with RTI? At what levels can RTI be scaled up?
13. What considerations guide the scaling up of RTI across schools, districts, and states?

References

Batsche, G., Kavale, K., & Kovaleski, J. (2006). Competing views: A dialogue on response to intervention. *Assessment for Effective Intervention, 32,* 6–19.

Brown-Chidsey, R., & Steege, M. (2005). *Response to intervention: Principles and strategies for effective practice.* New York: Guilford Press.

Case, L. P., Speece, D., L., & Molloy, D. E. (2003). The validity of response to instruction paradigm to identify reading disabilities: A longitudinal analysis of individual differences and contextual factors. *School Psychology Review, 32,* 557–582.

Danielson, L., Doolittle, J., & Bradley, R. (2007). Professional development, capacity building, and research needs: Critical issues for response to intervention implementation. *School Psychology Review, 36*(4), 632–637.

Duffy, H. (2007). *Meeting the needs of significantly struggling learners in high school: A look at approaches to tiered intervention.* National High School Center, American Institutes of Research.

Duhon, G. J., Mesmer, E. M., Gregerson, L., & Witt, J. C. (2009). Effects of public feedback during RTI team meetings on teacher implementation integrity and student academic performance. *Journal of School Psychology, 47,* 19–37.

Fairbanks, S., Sugai, G., Guardino, D., & Lathrop, M. (2007). Response to intervention: Examining classroom behavior support in second grade. *Exceptional Children, 73,* 288–310.

Fuchs, D., & Deshler, D. (2007). What we need to know about responsiveness to intervention (and shouldn't be afraid to ask). *Learning Disabilities Research and Practice, 22,* 129–136.

Fuchs, D., & Fuchs, L. (2006). Introduction to response to intervention: What is it, why and how valid is it? *Reading Research Quarterly, 41,* 93–98.

Hughes, C., & Deshler, D. (2007, April). *RTI in middle and high school: How will the game play out?* Paper presented at the Council for Exceptional Children Conference, Louisville, KY.

Hollenbeck, A. F. (2007). From IDEA to implementation: A discussion of foundational and future responsiveness to intervention research. *Learning Disabilities Research and Practice, 22,* 137–146.

Jenkins, J. (2009). Measuring reading growth: New findings on progress monitoring. *New Times for DLD, 27*(1), 1–2.

Johnson, E., Jenkins, J., Petscher, Y., & Catts, H. (2009). How can we improve the accuracy of screening instruments? *Learning Disabilities Research & Practice, 24*(4), 174–185.

Marston, D., Muyskens, P., Lau, M., & Canter, A. (2003). Problem-solving model for decision making with high-incidence disabilities: The Minneapolis experience. *Learning Disabilities Research & Practice, 18,* 187–200.

Noell, G. H., & Gansle, K. A. (2006). Assuring the form has substance: Treatment plan implementation as the foundation of assessing response to intervention. *Learning Disabilities Research & Practice, 32,* 32–39.

Olfiesh, N. (2006). Response to Intervention and the identification of specific learning disabilities: Why we need comprehensive evaluations as part of the process. *Psychology in the Schools,* *43*(8), 883–888.

Reschly, D. J. (2005). LD identification: Primary intervention, secondary intervention, then what? *Journal of Learning Disabilities, 38,* 510–515.

VanDerHeyden, A., Witt, J., & Gilbertson, D. (2007). A multi-year evaluation of the effects of a Response to Intervention (RTI) model on the identification of children for special education. *Journal of School Psychology, 45,* 225–256.

What Works Clearinghouse (2010). *Practice Guides.* Retrieved October 7, 2010, from http://ies.ed. gov/ncee/wwc/

Wodrich, D. L., Spencer, M., & Daley, K. B. (2006). Combining RTI and psychoeducational assessment: What we must assume to do otherwise. *Psychology in the Schools, 43*(7), 797–806.

NAME INDEX

SUBJECT INDEX